BLADE
RUNNER
2019

TITAN®
COMICS

ALCON
PUBLISHING®

Also Available:
Blade Runner 2019
Volume 1 – *Los Angeles*

Blade Runner 2019
Volume 2 – *Off-World*
Coming soon:
Blade Runner Artist's Edition (March 2021)

BLADE RUNNER 2019: HOME AGAIN, HOME AGAIN

SENIOR CREATIVE EDITOR | David Leach

TITAN COMICS

Managing Editor | MARTIN EDEN
Assistant Editor | PHOEBE HEDGES
Production Controller | CATERINA FALQUI
Senior Production Controller | JACKIE FLOOK
Senior Designer | ANDREW LEUNG
Art Director | OZ BROWNE
Sales & Circulation Manager | STEVE TOTHILL
Marketing & Advertisement Assistant | LAUREN NODING

Direct Marketing Assistant | GEORGE WICKENDEN
Publicist | IMOGEN HARRIS
Marketing Manager | RICKY CLAYDON
Head Of Rights | JENNY BOYCE
Editorial Director | DUNCAN BAIZLEY
Operations Director | LEIGH BAULCH
Co-Publisher | VIVIAN CHEUNG
Co-Publisher | NICK LANDAU

ALCON PUBLISHING
Director/Editor | JEFF CONNER
COO/CFO | SCOTT PARISH
Legal/Business Affairs | JEANNETTE HILL
Publishers | ANDREW KOSOVE & BRODERICK JOHNSON

BLADE RUNNER 2019: HOME AGAIN, HOME AGAIN

FEBRUARY 2021. Published by Titan Comics, a division of Titan Publishing Group, Ltd. 144 Southwark Street, London SE1
0UP. Titan Comics is a registered trademark of Titan Publishing Group, Ltd. All rights reserved. ©2021 – Blade Runner 2019
and all related marks and characters are trademarks and copyrights of Alcon Publishing ®. All rights reserved. Licensed
by Alcon Publishing ®. All Rights Reserved.

Published by Titan Comics, a division of Titan Publishing Group, Ltd. Titan Comics is a registered trademark of Titan
Publishing Group, Ltd. 144 Southwark Street, London SE1 0UP

STANDARD EDITION ISBN 9781787731936

FORBIDDEN PLANET EXCLUSIVE ISBN 9781787737266

A CIP catalogue for this title is available from the British Library.

First Edition FEBRUARY 2021
10 9 8 7 6 5 4 3 2 1
Printed in China

www.titan-comics.com
Follow us on twitter@ComicsTitan | Visit us at facebook.com/comicstitan
For rights information contact: jenny.boyce@titanemail.com

BLADE RUNNER 2019

HOME AGAIN, HOME AGAIN

WRITTEN BY
MIKE JOHNSON

CREATIVE CONSULTANT
MICHAEL GREEN

ART BY
ANDRES GUINALDO

COLORS BY
MARCO LESKO

LETTERING BY
JIM CAMPBELL

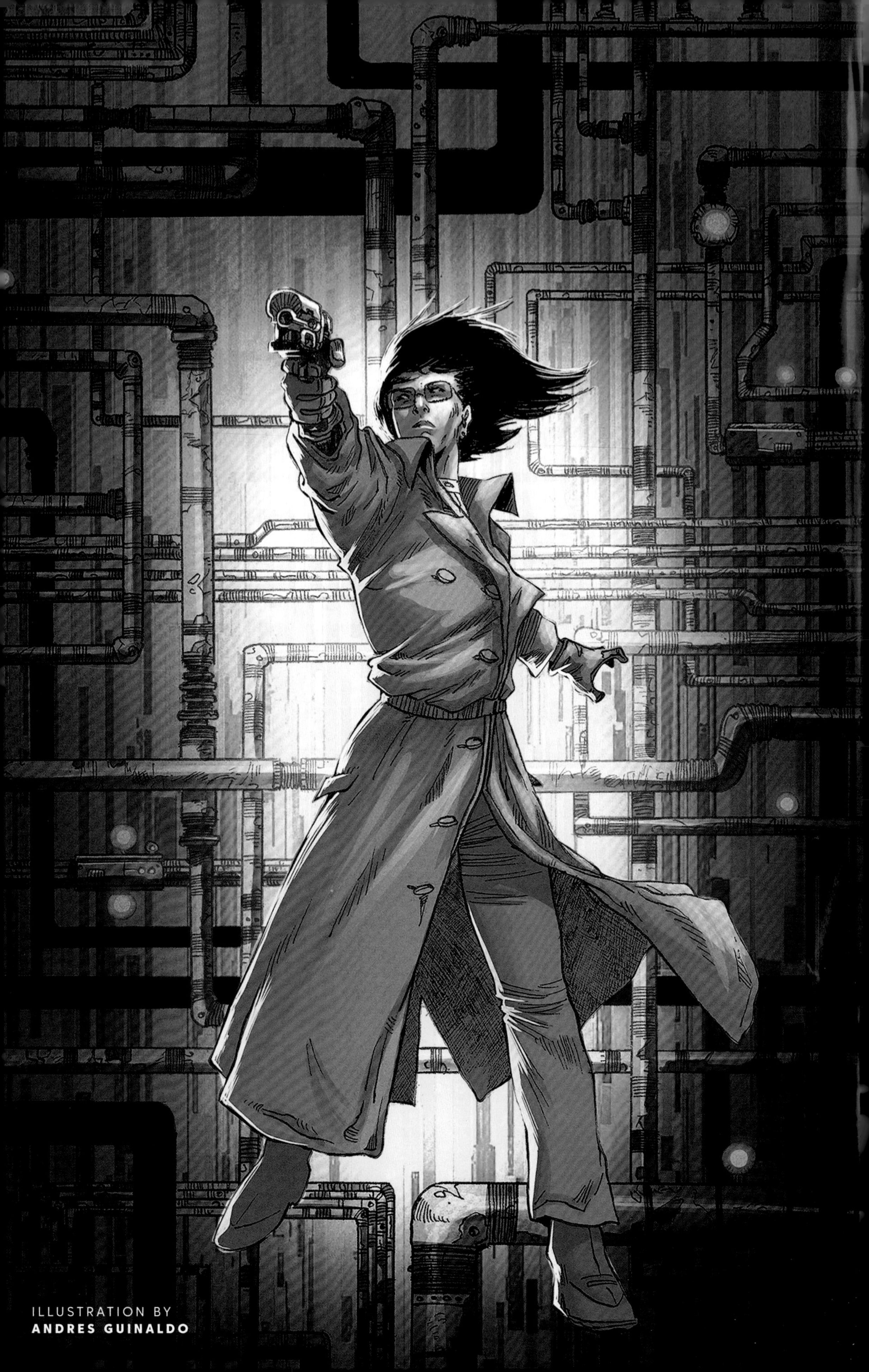

ILLUSTRATION BY
ANDRES GUINALDO

IN 2019, THE BLADE RUNNER **AAHINA** 'ASH' ASHINA RESCUED CLEO SELWYN, DAUGHTER OF THE AGRIBUSINESS TYCOON ALEXANDER SELWYN, FROM A PLOT TO GIVE THE GIRL TO THE TYRELL CORPORATION FOR GENETIC EXPERIMENTATION.

ASH AND CLEO ESCAPED TO THE OFF-WORLD COLONIES AND ASSUMED NEW IDENTITIES. CLEO'S FATHER NEVER STOPPED LOOKING FOR THEM.

SIX YEARS LATER, FOLLOWING A REPLICANT MUTINY, ASH AND CLEO WERE SEPARATED. CLEO FLED WITH THE RENEGADE REPLICANTS, WHILE ASH, BELIEVED DEAD, WAS TAKEN INTO CUSTODY BY HYTHE, A CORPORATE BLADE RUNNER, AND FORCIBLY RECRUITED TO TRACK DOWN HER SURROGATE DAUGHTER.

HYTHE AND ASH TRACKED THE REPLICANTS TO THE WAY STATION OF RAMANUJA. THERE THEY ENCOUNTERED THE REPLICANT ISOBEL, WHOM ASH BELIEVED TO HAVE DIED BACK ON EARTH WHEN SHE AND CLEO FIRST ESCAPED. THE THREE WOMEN SEARCHED FOR CLEO AMONG PASSENGERS PREPARING TO EMBARK TO THE OFF-WORLD COLONY WORLD OF ARCADIA.

CLEO WAS SPOTTED BY ASH, BUT BEFORE SHE COULD ACT, HYTHE DOUBLE-CROSSED HER, TRIGGERING A FURIOUS GUN BATTLE THAT LEFT HYTHE DEAD. CLEO AND ISOBEL WERE AT LONG LAST REUNITED AND SET OFF FOR A NEW LIFE ON ARCADIA TOGETHER.

ASH RETURNED BACK TO EARTH...

LOS ANGELES,
2026

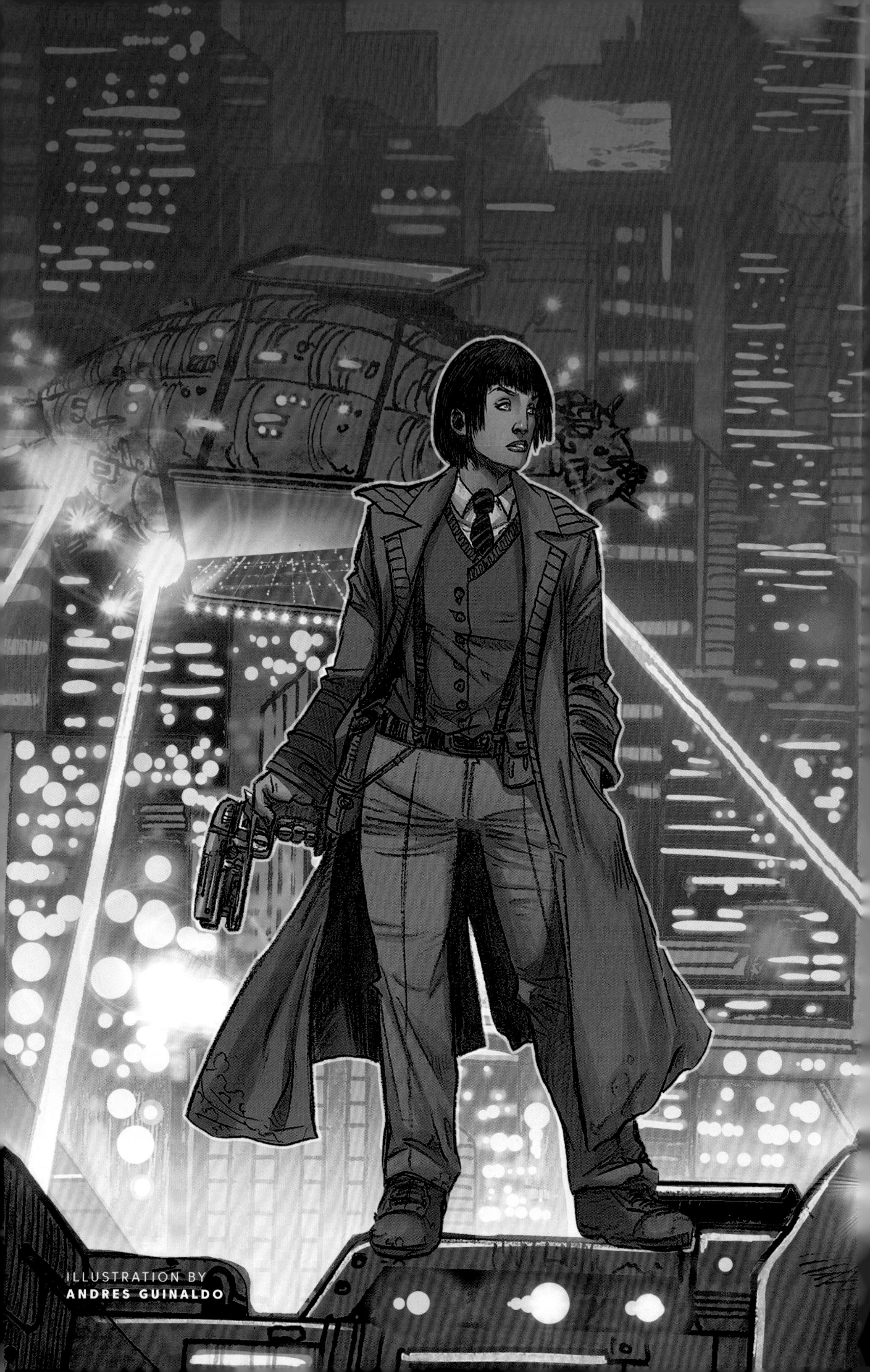

ILLUSTRATION BY
ANDRES GUINALDO

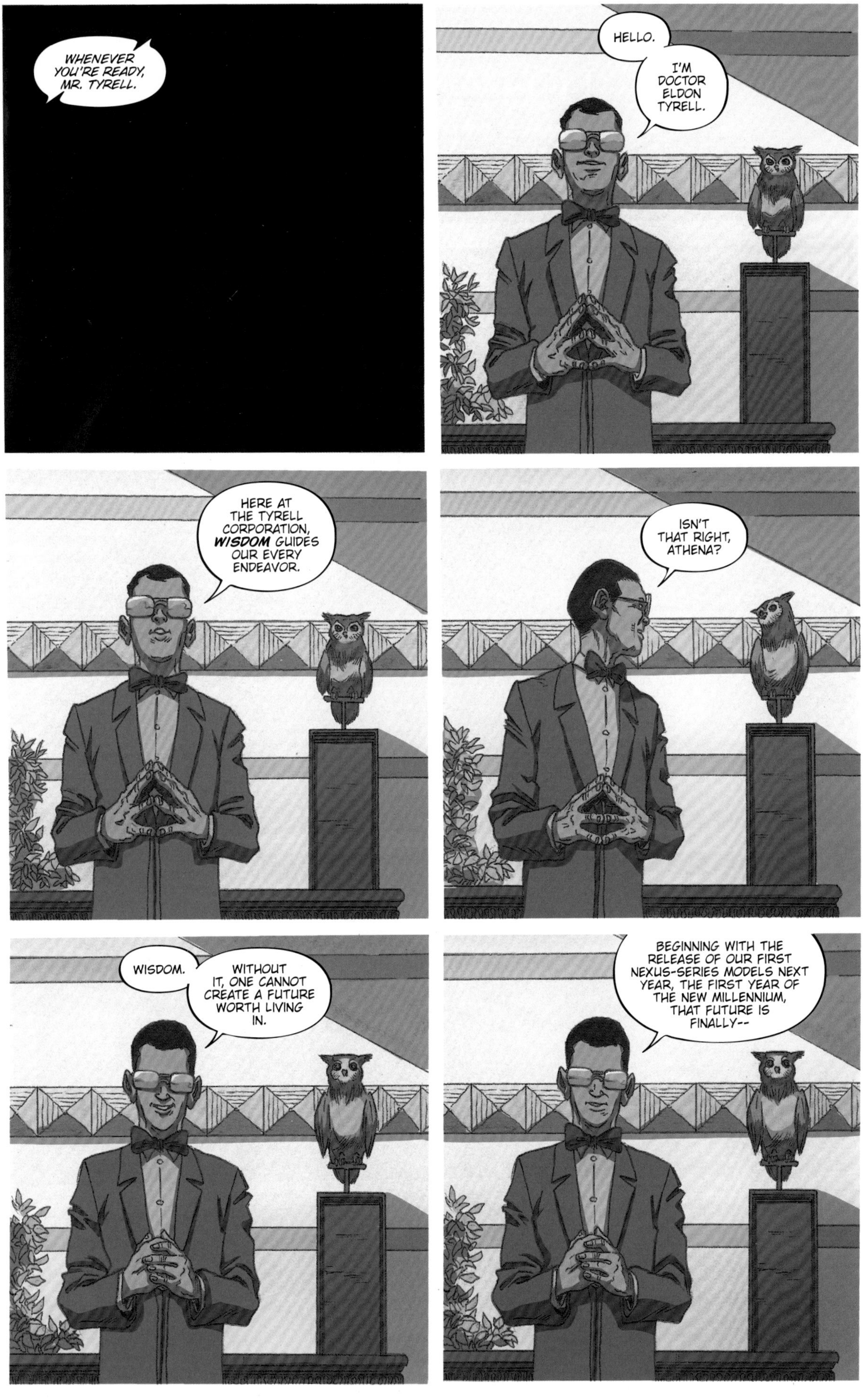
WHENEVER YOU'RE READY, MR. TYRELL.
HELLO.
I'M DOCTOR ELDON TYRELL.
HERE AT THE TYRELL CORPORATION, **WISDOM** GUIDES OUR EVERY ENDEAVOR.
ISN'T THAT RIGHT, ATHENA?
WISDOM.
WITHOUT IT, ONE CANNOT CREATE A FUTURE WORTH LIVING IN.
BEGINNING WITH THE RELEASE OF OUR FIRST NEXUS-SERIES MODELS NEXT YEAR, THE FIRST YEAR OF THE NEW MILLENNIUM, THAT FUTURE IS FINALLY--

LOS ANGELES
2000

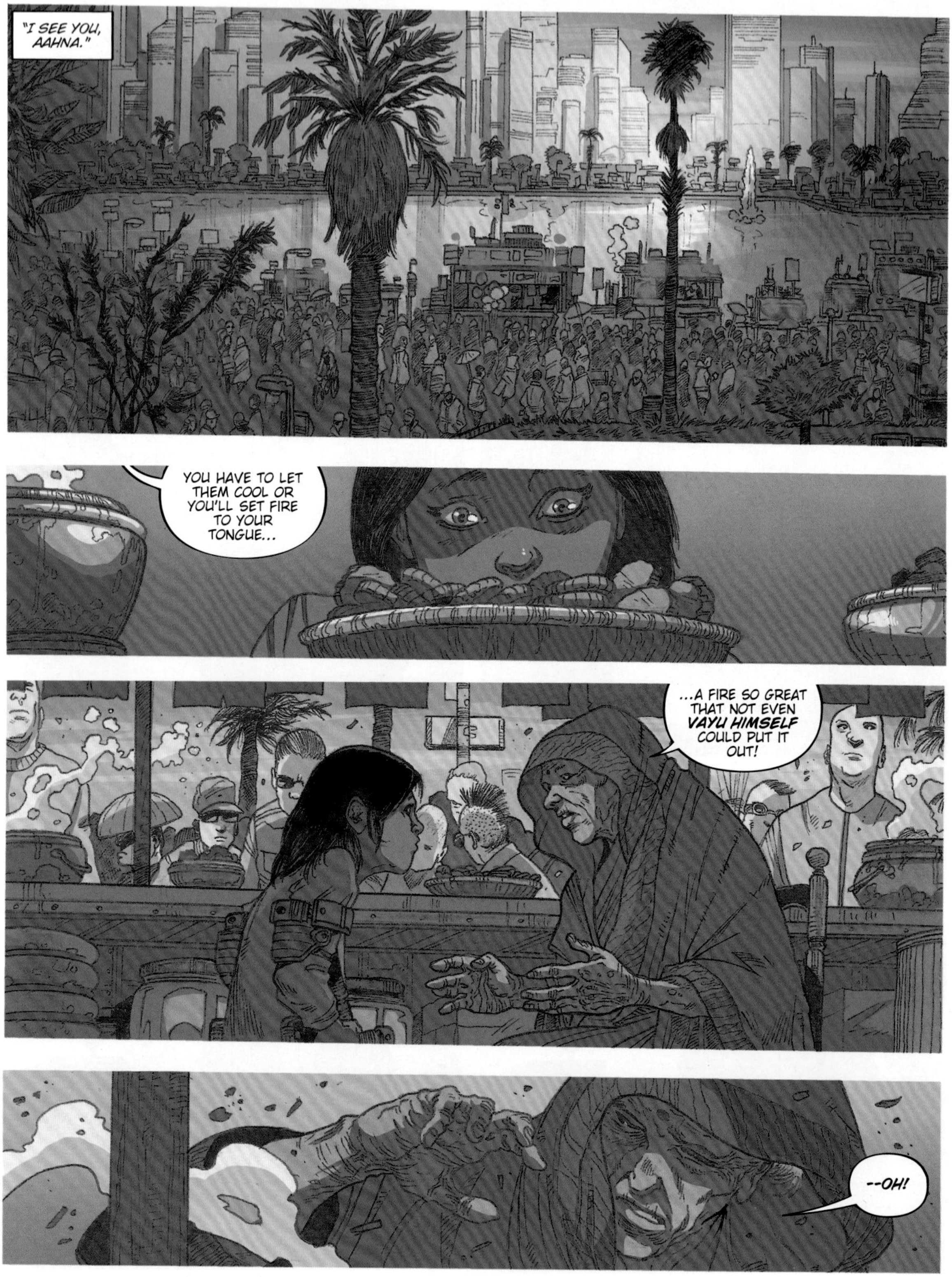
"I SEE YOU, AAHNA."
YOU HAVE TO LET THEM COOL OR YOU'LL SET FIRE TO YOUR TONGUE...
...A FIRE SO GREAT THAT NOT EVEN VAYU HIMSELF COULD PUT IT OUT!
--OH!

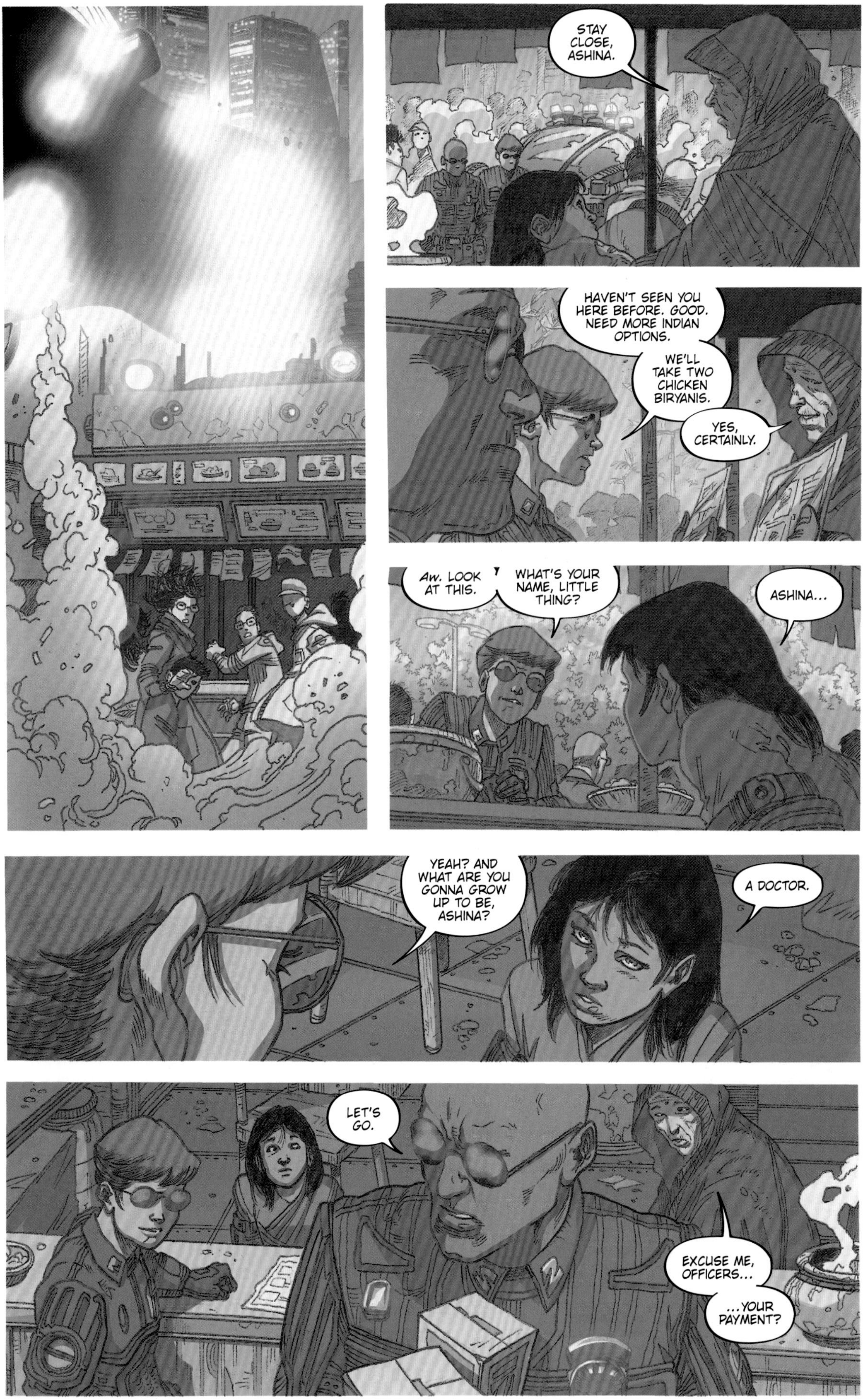
STAY CLOSE, ASHINA.
HAVEN'T SEEN YOU HERE BEFORE. GOOD. NEED MORE INDIAN OPTIONS.
WE'LL TAKE TWO CHICKEN BIRYANIS.
YES, CERTAINLY.
AW. LOOK AT THIS.
WHAT'S YOUR NAME, LITTLE THING?
ASHINA...
YEAH? AND WHAT ARE YOU GONNA GROW UP TO BE, ASHINA?
A DOCTOR.
LET'S GO.
EXCUSE ME, OFFICERS...
...YOUR PAYMENT?

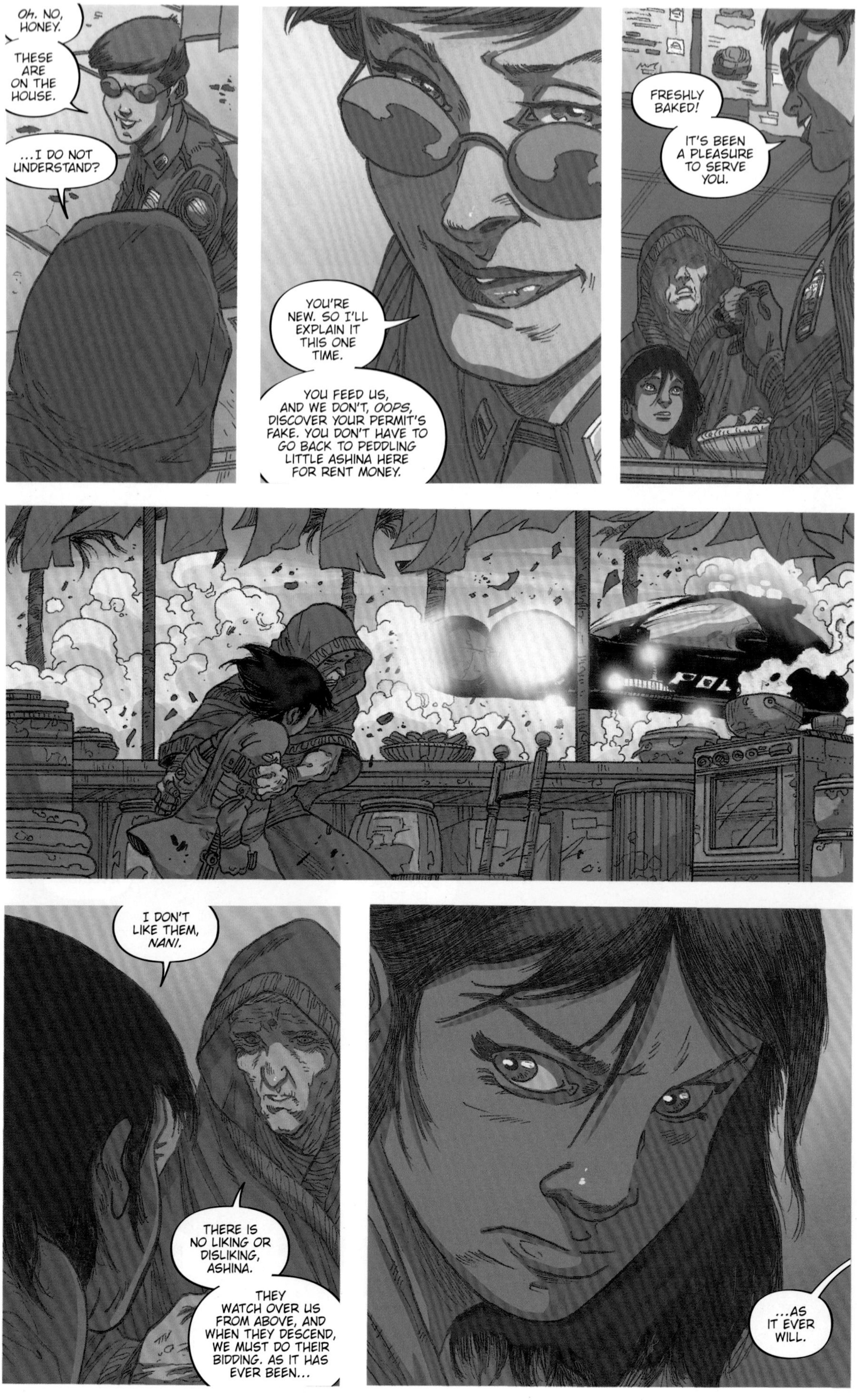

OH. NO, HONEY.
THESE ARE ON THE HOUSE.
...I DO NOT UNDERSTAND?
YOU'RE NEW. SO I'LL EXPLAIN IT THIS ONE TIME.
YOU FEED US, AND WE DON'T, *OOPS*, DISCOVER YOUR PERMIT'S FAKE. YOU DON'T HAVE TO GO BACK TO PEDDLING LITTLE ASHINA HERE FOR RENT MONEY.
FRESHLY BAKED!
IT'S BEEN A PLEASURE TO SERVE YOU.
I DON'T LIKE THEM, *NANI*.
THERE IS NO LIKING OR DISLIKING, ASHINA.
THEY WATCH OVER US FROM ABOVE, AND WHEN THEY DESCEND, WE MUST DO THEIR BIDDING. AS IT HAS EVER BEEN...
...AS IT EVER WILL.

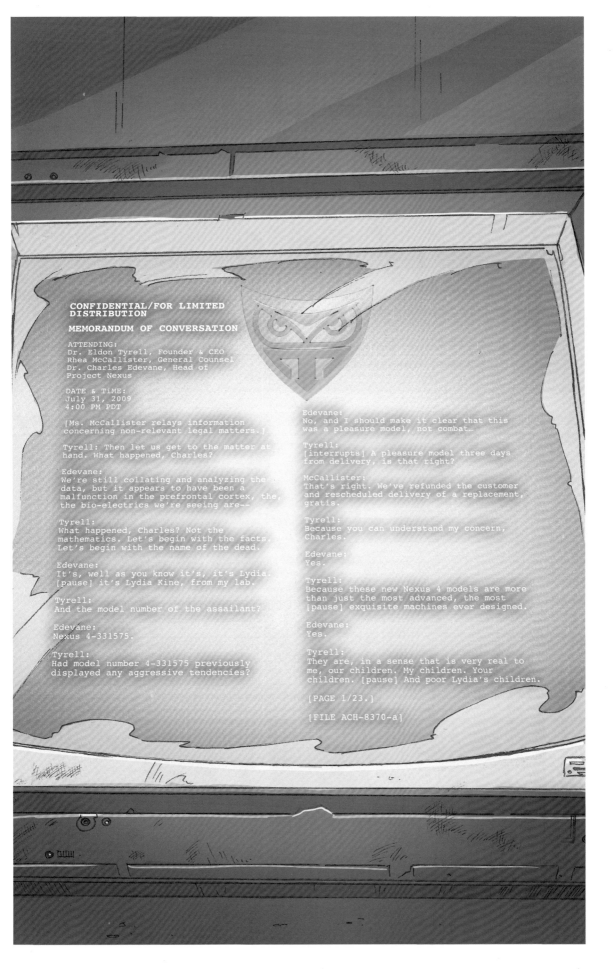

CONFIDENTIAL/FOR LIMITED DISTRIBUTION

MEMORANDUM OF CONVERSATION

ATTENDING:
Dr. Eldon Tyrell, Founder & CEO
Rhea McCallister, General Counsel
Dr. Charles Edevane, Head of Project Nexus

DATE & TiME:
July 31, 2009
4:00 PM PDT

[Ms. McCallister relays information concerning non-relevant legal matters.]

Tyrell: Then let us get to the matter at hand. What happened, Charles?

Edevane:
We're still collating and analyzing the data, but it appears to have been a malfunction in the prefrontal cortex, the the bio-electrics we're seeing are--

Tyrell:
What happened, Charles? Not the mathematics. Let's begin with the facts. Let's begin with the name of the dead.

Edevane:
It's, well as you know it's, it's Lydia. [pause] it's Lydia Kine, from my lab.

Tyrell:
And the model number of the assailant?

Edevane:
Nexus 4-331575.

Tyrell:
Had model number 4-331575 previously displayed any aggressive tendencies?

Edevane:
No, and I should make it clear that this was a pleasure model, not combat…

Tyrell:
[interrupts] A pleasure model three days from delivery, is that right?

McCallister:
That's right. We've refunded the customer and rescheduled delivery of a replacement, gratis.

Tyrell:
Because you can understand my concern, Charles.

Edevane:
Yes.

Tyrell:
Because these new Nexus 4 models are more than just the most advanced, the most [pause] exquisite machines ever designed.

Edevane:
Yes.

Tyrell:
They are, in a sense that is very real to me, our children. My children. Your children. [pause] And poor Lydia's children.

[PAGE 1/23.]

[FILE ACH-8370-a]

LOS ANGELES
2009

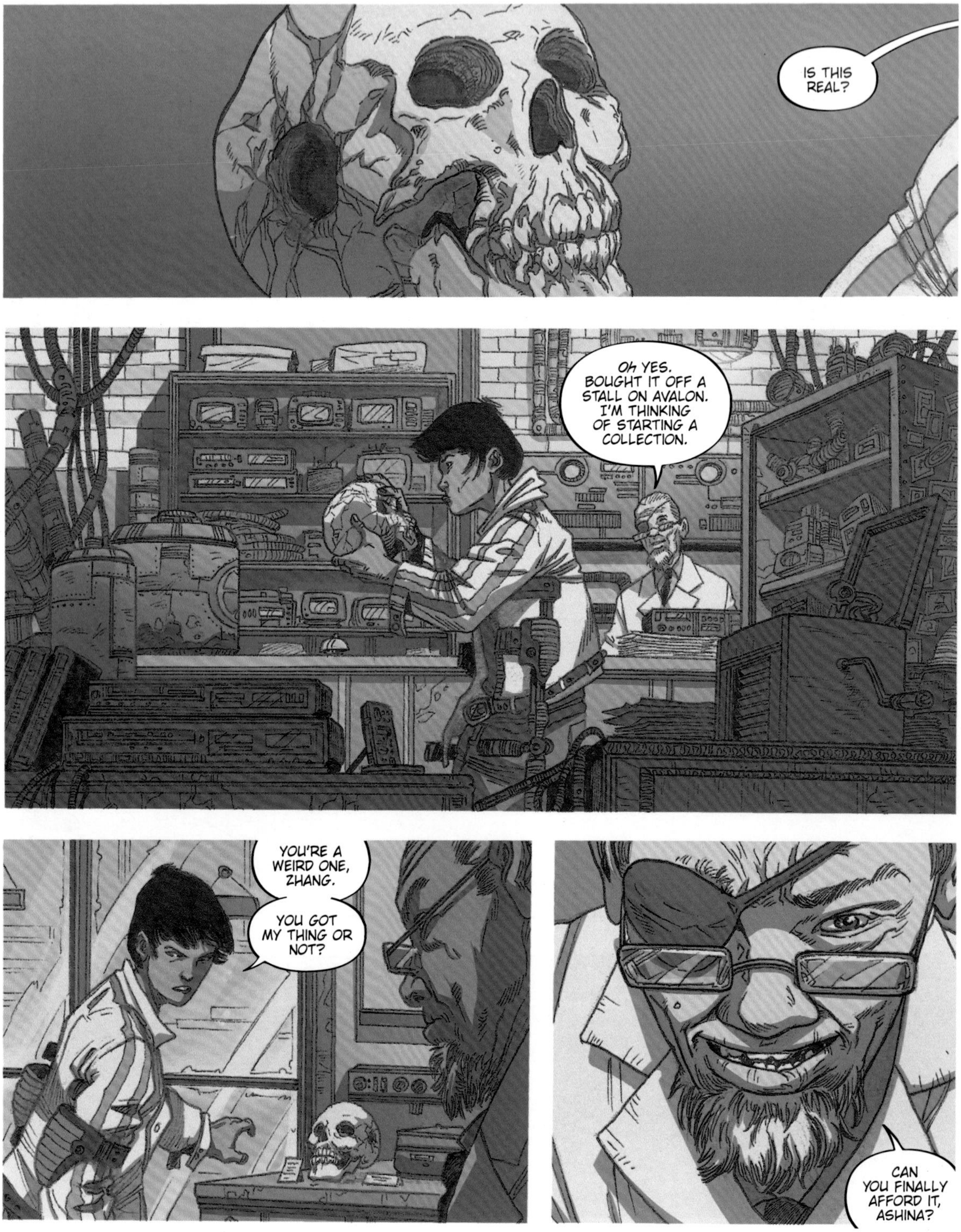
IS THIS REAL?
OH YES. BOUGHT IT OFF A STALL ON AVALON. I'M THINKING OF STARTING A COLLECTION.
YOU'RE A WEIRD ONE, ZHANG.
YOU GOT MY THING OR NOT?
CAN YOU FINALLY AFFORD IT, ASHINA?

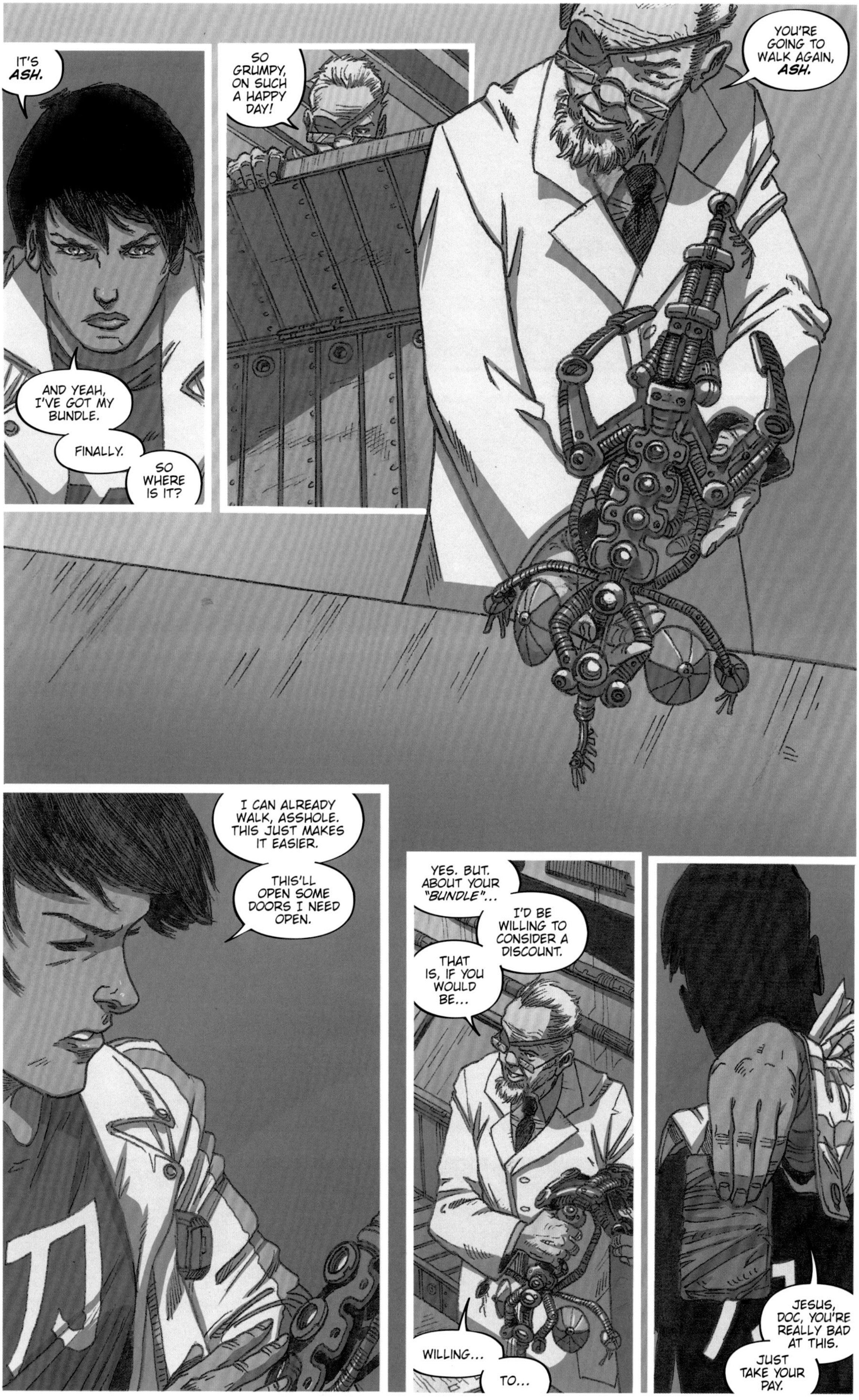
IT'S ASH.
AND YEAH, I'VE GOT MY BUNDLE.
FINALLY.
SO WHERE IS IT?
SO GRUMPY, ON SUCH A HAPPY DAY!
YOU'RE GOING TO WALK AGAIN, ASH.
I CAN ALREADY WALK, ASSHOLE. THIS JUST MAKES IT EASIER.
THIS'LL OPEN SOME DOORS I NEED OPEN.
YES. BUT. ABOUT YOUR "BUNDLE"...
I'D BE WILLING TO CONSIDER A DISCOUNT.
THAT IS, IF YOU WOULD BE...
WILLING...
TO...
JESUS, DOC, YOU'RE REALLY BAD AT THIS.
JUST TAKE YOUR PAY.

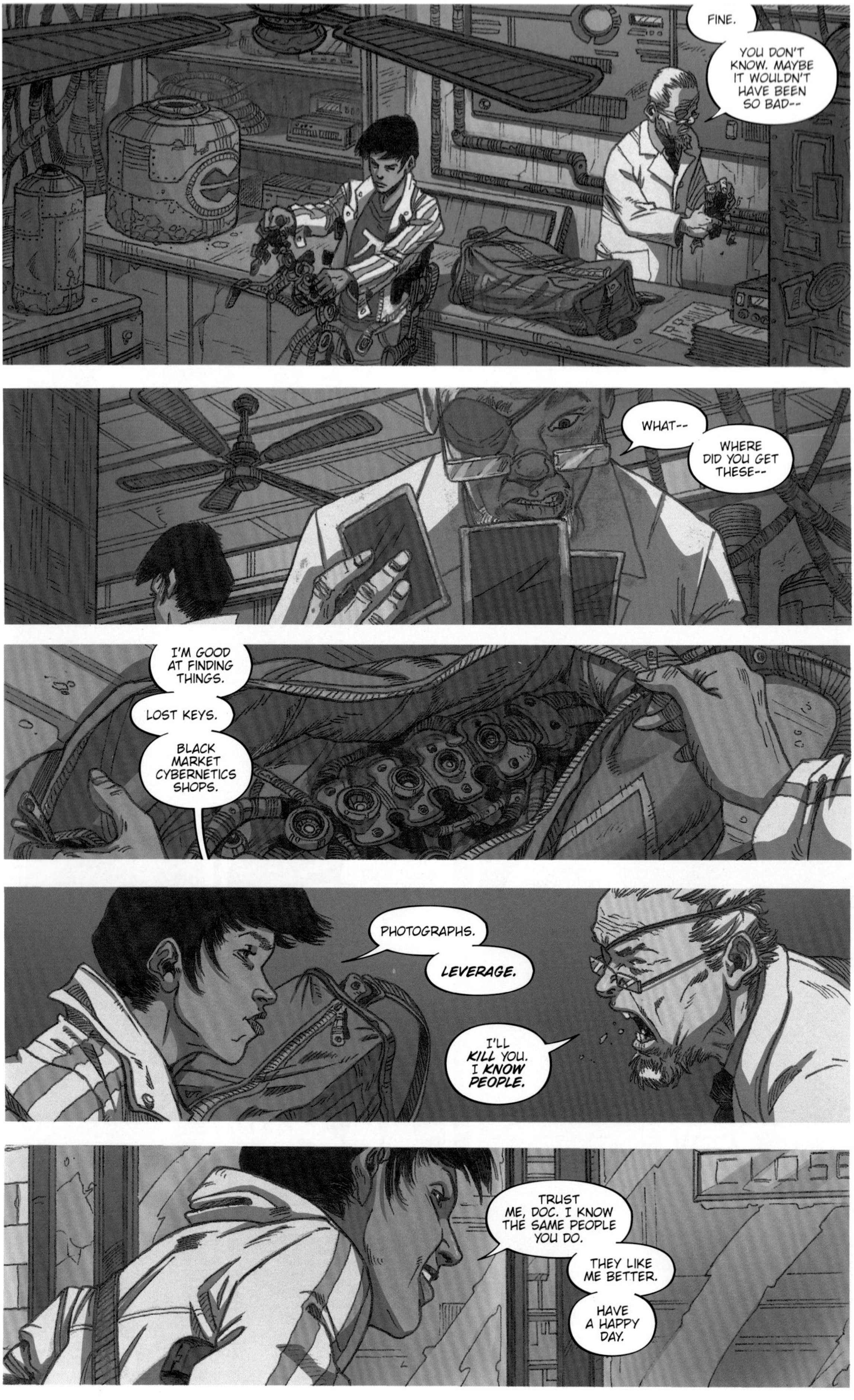
FINE.
YOU DON'T KNOW. MAYBE IT WOULDN'T HAVE BEEN SO BAD--
WHAT--
WHERE DID YOU GET THESE--
I'M GOOD AT FINDING THINGS.
LOST KEYS.
BLACK MARKET CYBERNETICS SHOPS.
PHOTOGRAPHS.
LEVERAGE.
I'LL *KILL* YOU. I *KNOW PEOPLE.*
CLOSE
TRUST ME, DOC. I KNOW THE SAME PEOPLE YOU DO.
THEY LIKE ME BETTER.
HAVE A HAPPY DAY.

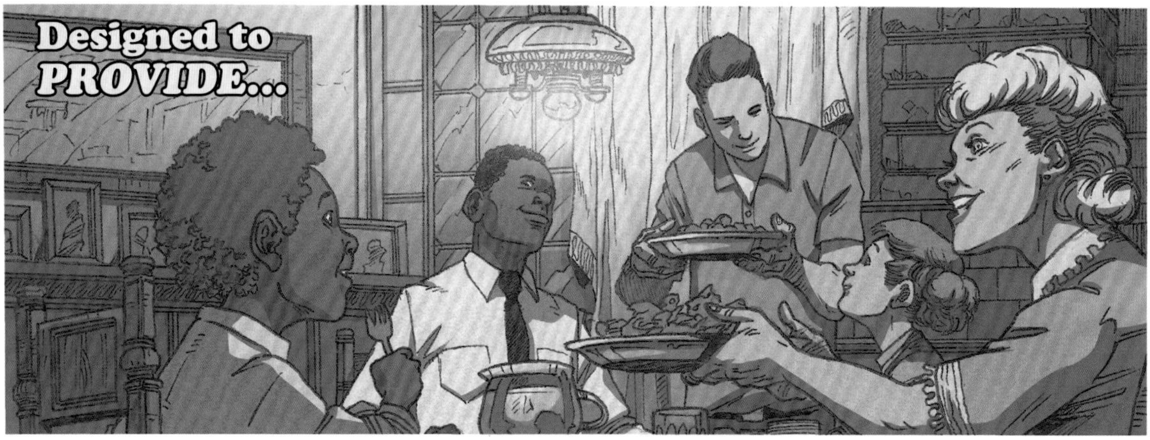
Designed to
PROVIDE...

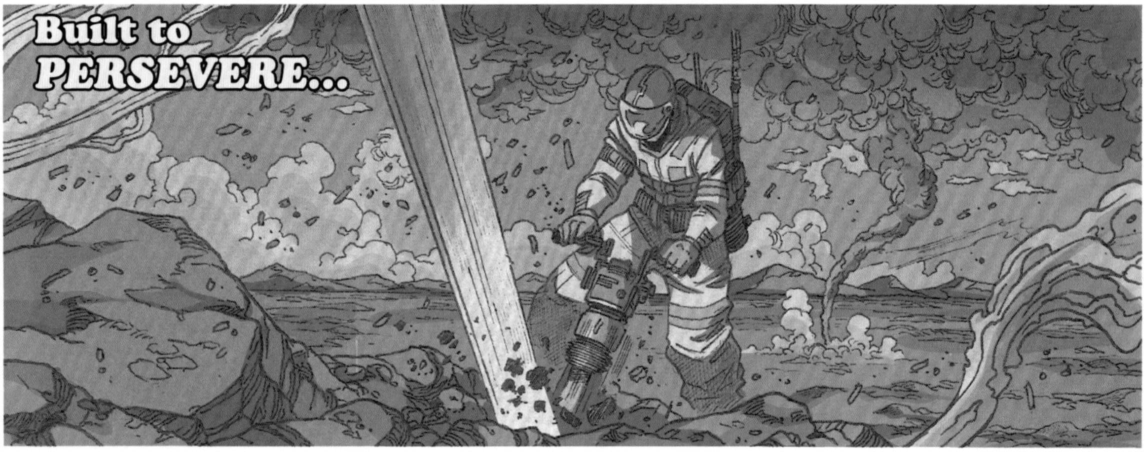
Built to
PERSEVERE...

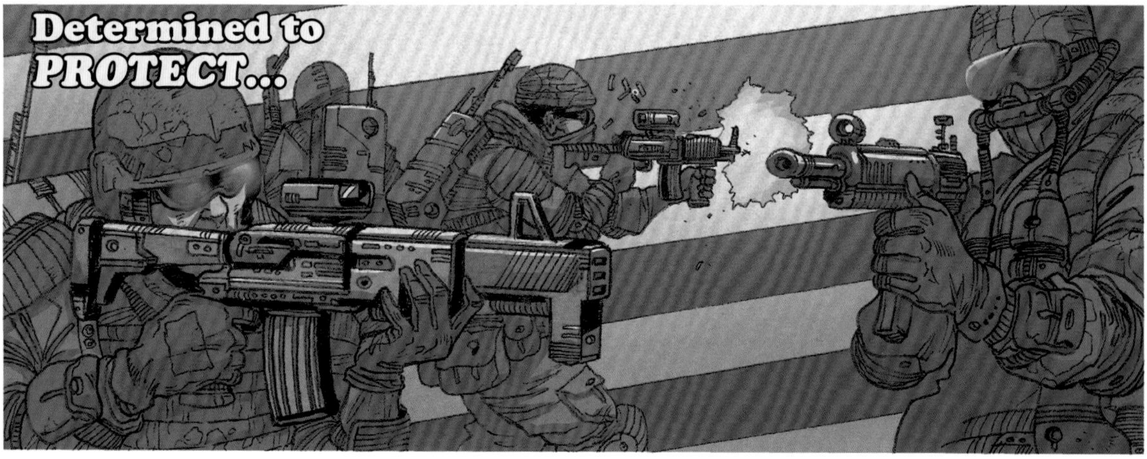
Determined to
PROTECT...

LOS ANGELES 2013

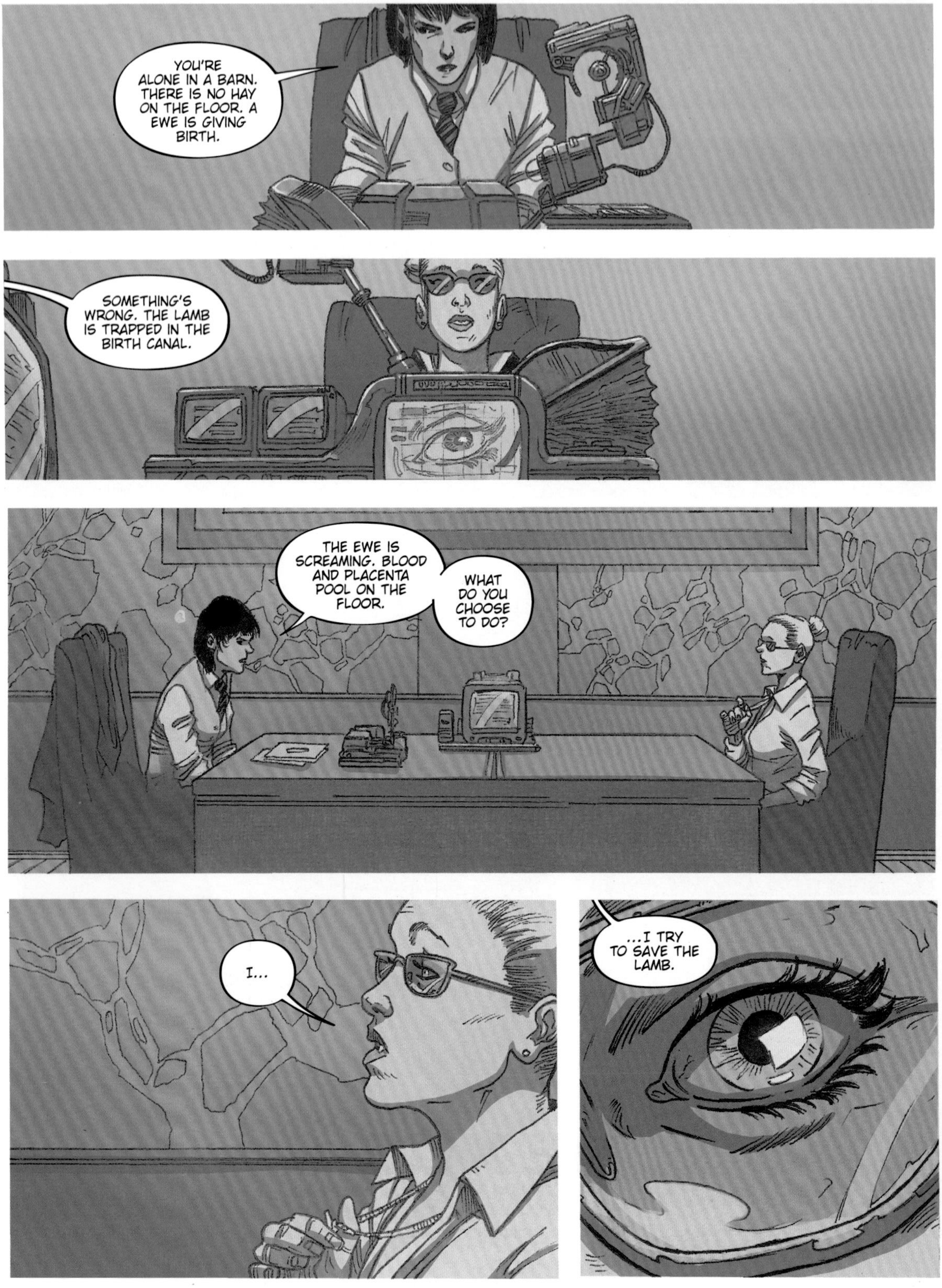
YOU'RE ALONE IN A BARN. THERE IS NO HAY ON THE FLOOR. A EWE IS GIVING BIRTH.
SOMETHING'S WRONG. THE LAMB IS TRAPPED IN THE BIRTH CANAL.
THE EWE IS SCREAMING. BLOOD AND PLACENTA POOL ON THE FLOOR.
WHAT DO YOU CHOOSE TO DO?
I...
...I TRY TO SAVE THE LAMB.

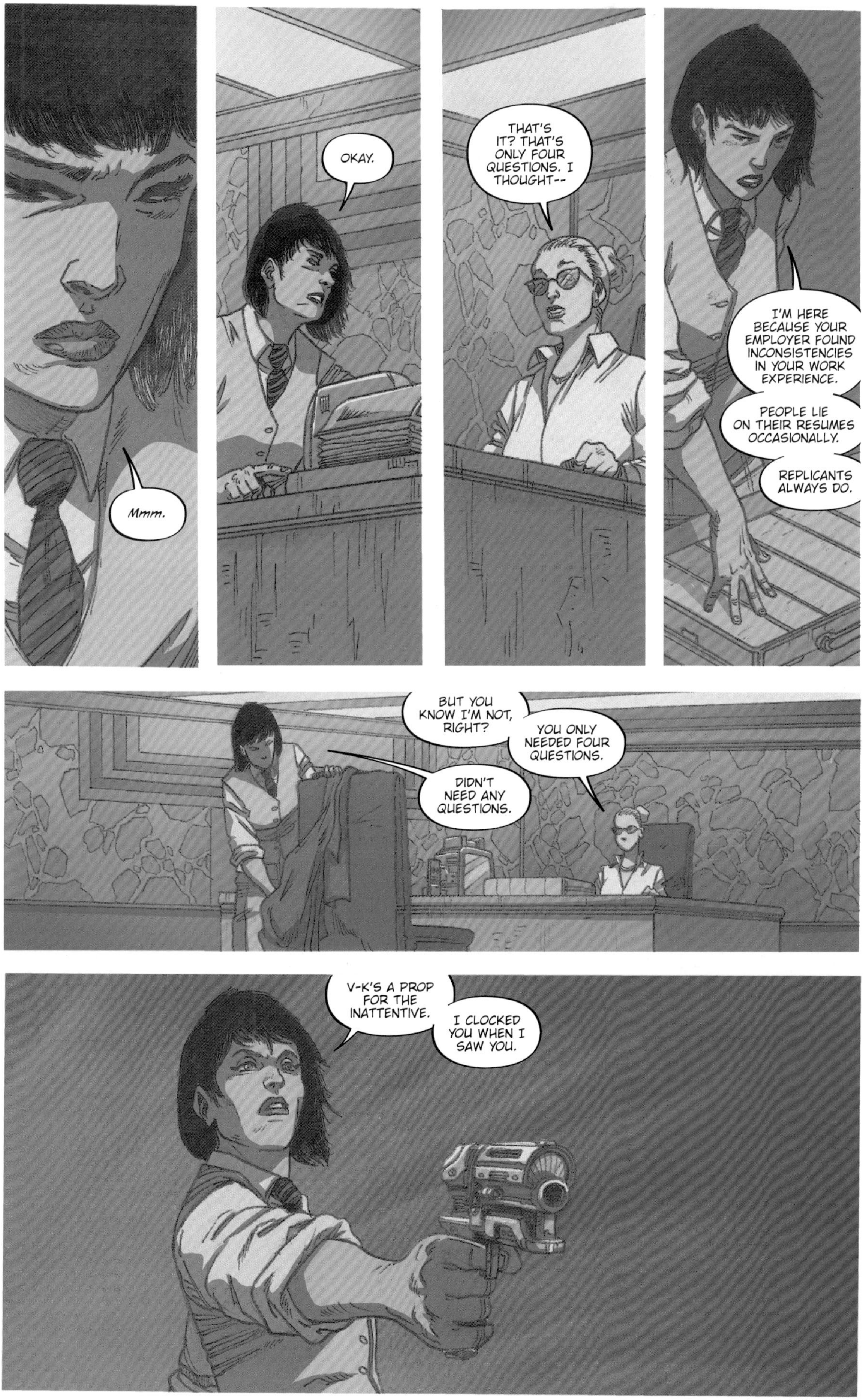
Mmm.
OKAY.
THAT'S IT? THAT'S ONLY FOUR QUESTIONS. I THOUGHT--
I'M HERE BECAUSE YOUR EMPLOYER FOUND INCONSISTENCIES IN YOUR WORK EXPERIENCE.
PEOPLE LIE ON THEIR RESUMES OCCASIONALLY.
REPLICANTS ALWAYS DO.
BUT YOU KNOW I'M NOT, RIGHT?
YOU ONLY NEEDED FOUR QUESTIONS.
DIDN'T NEED ANY QUESTIONS.
V-K'S A PROP FOR THE INATTENTIVE.
I CLOCKED YOU WHEN I SAW YOU.

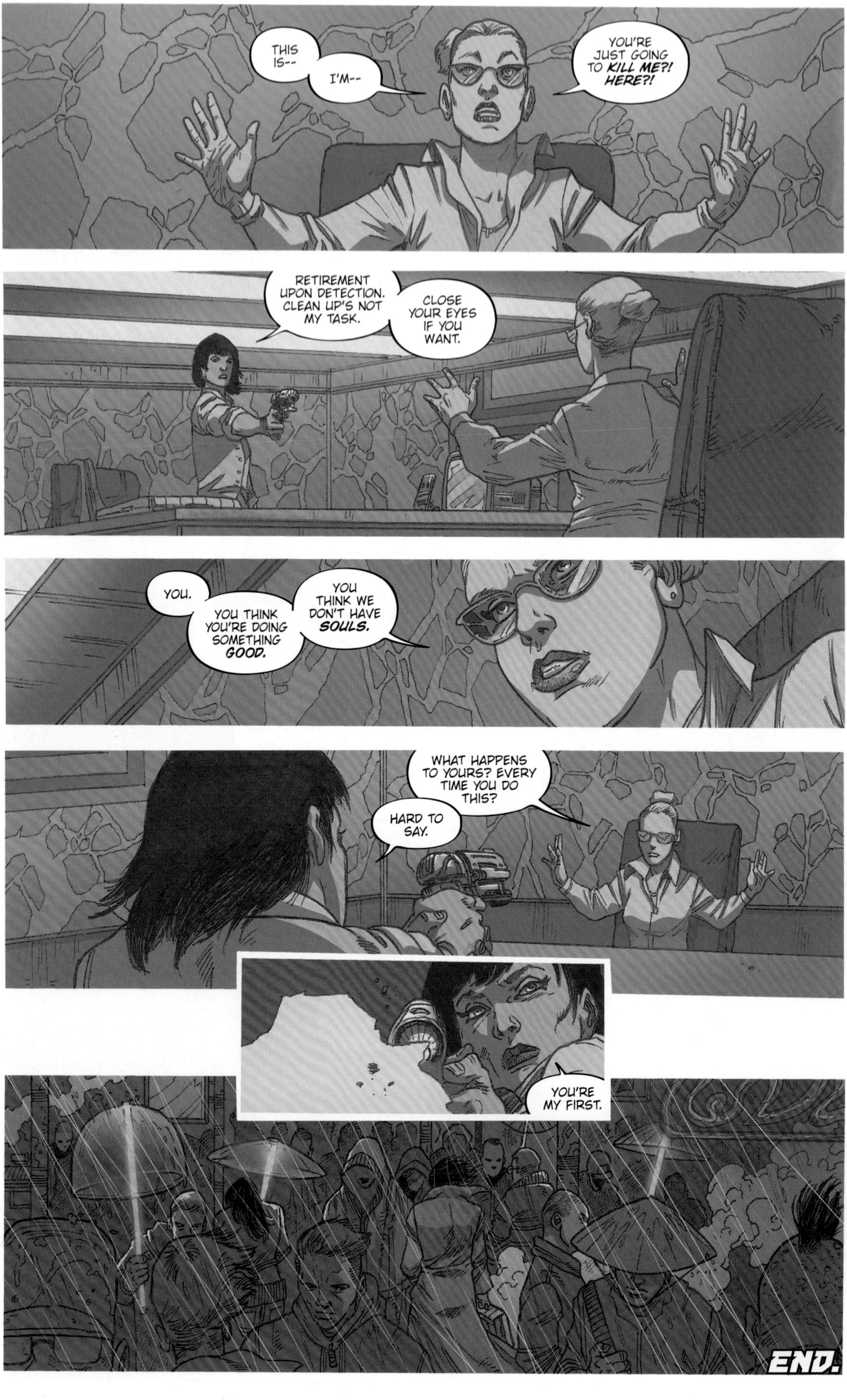
THIS IS--
I'M--
YOU'RE JUST GOING TO KILL ME?! HERE?!
RETIREMENT UPON DETECTION. CLEAN UP'S NOT MY TASK.
CLOSE YOUR EYES IF YOU WANT.
YOU.
YOU THINK YOU'RE DOING SOMETHING GOOD.
YOU THINK WE DON'T HAVE SOULS.
WHAT HAPPENS TO YOURS? EVERY TIME YOU DO THIS?
HARD TO SAY.
YOU'RE MY FIRST.
END.

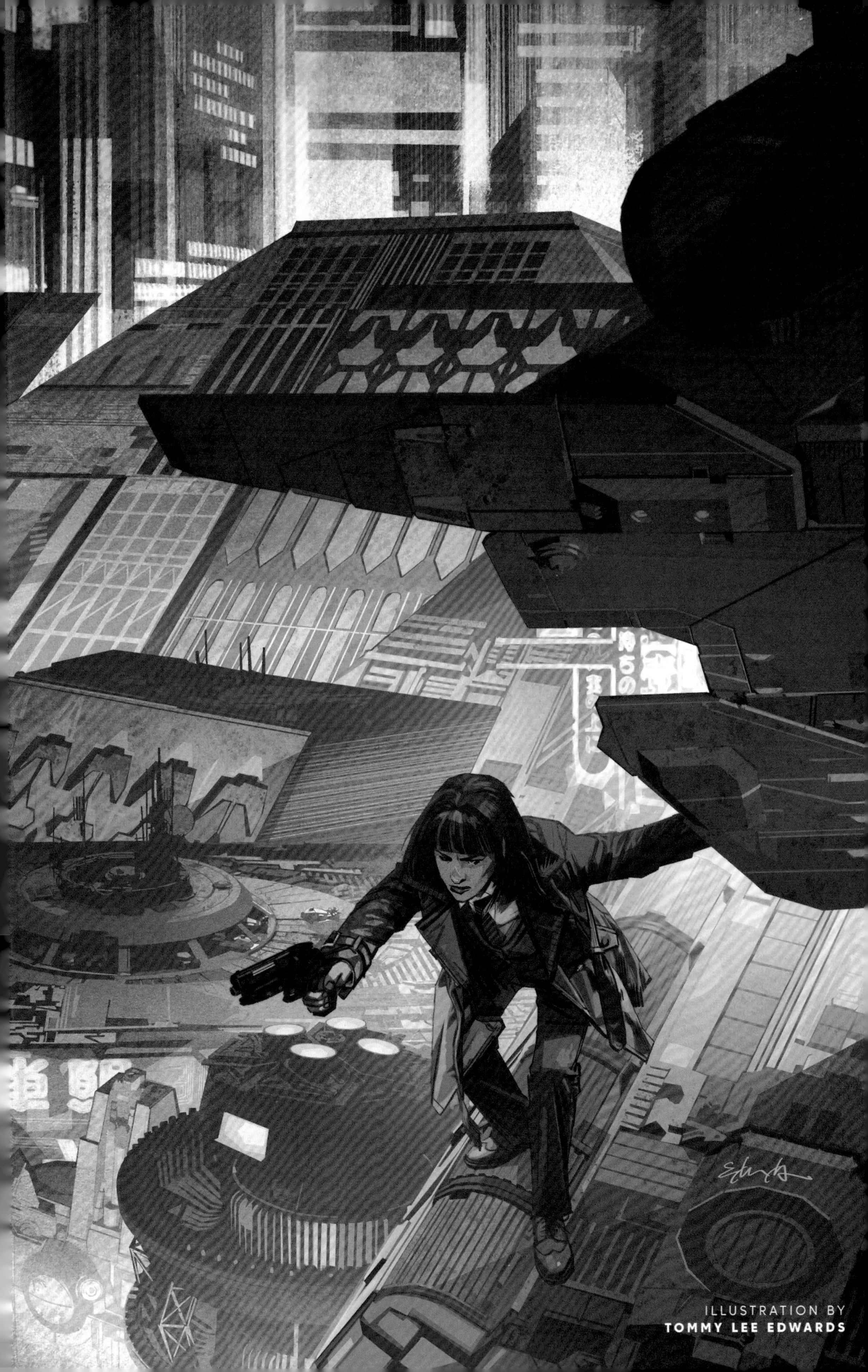

ILLUSTRATION BY
TOMMY LEE EDWARDS

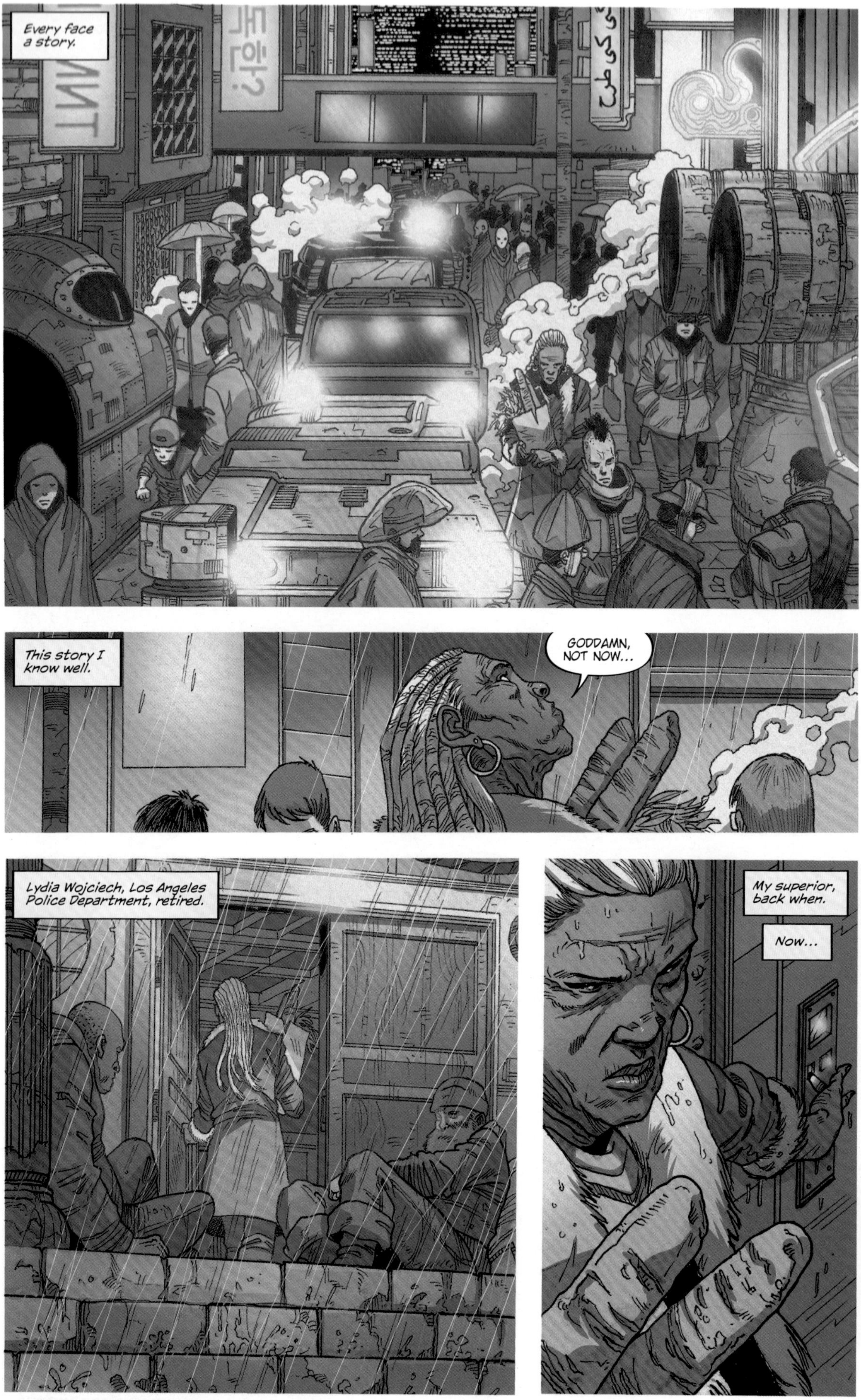

Every face a story.
This story I know well.
GODDAMN, NOT NOW...
Lydia Wojciech, Los Angeles Police Department, retired.
My superior, back when.
Now...

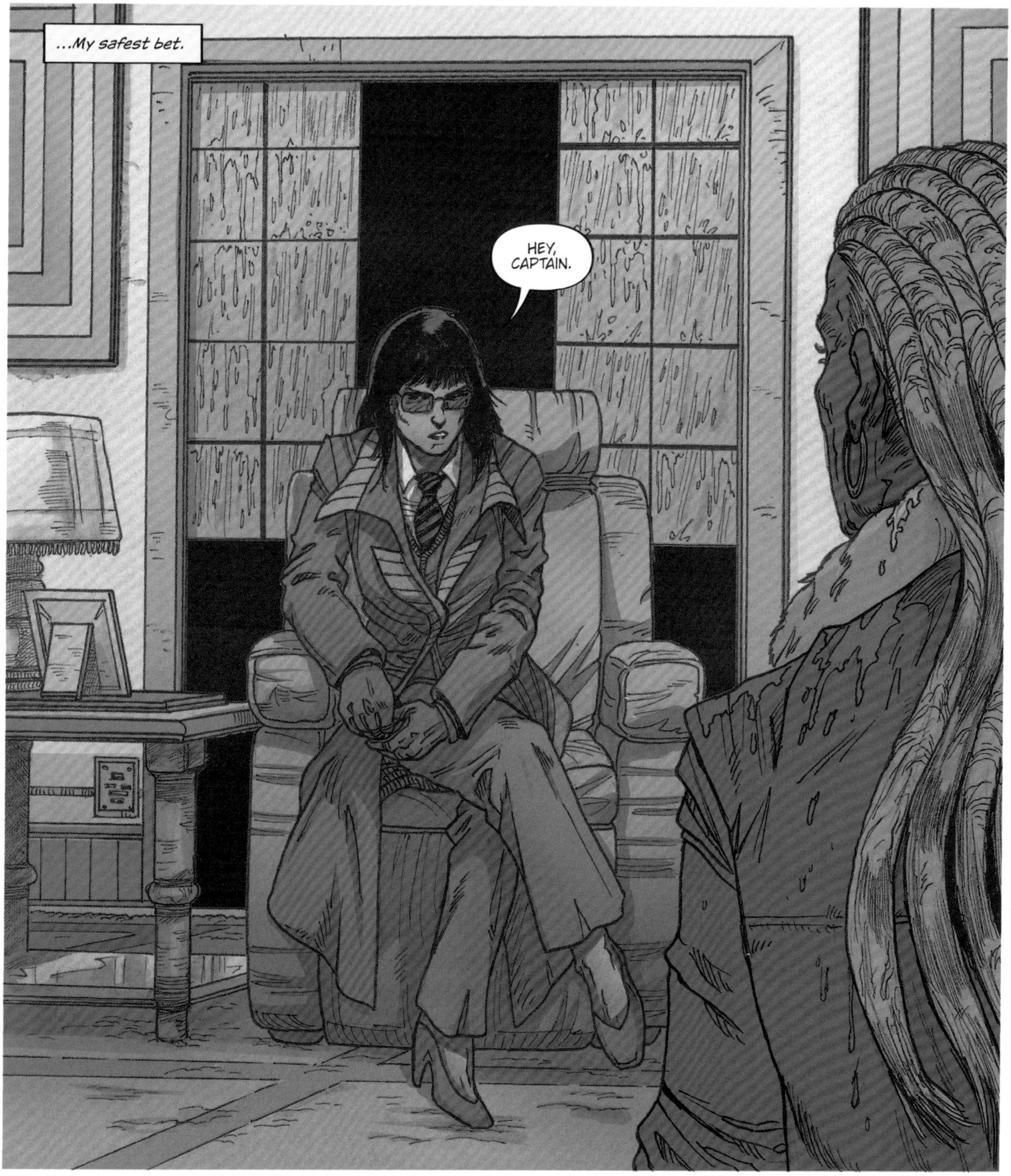
...My safest bet.
HEY, CAPTAIN.

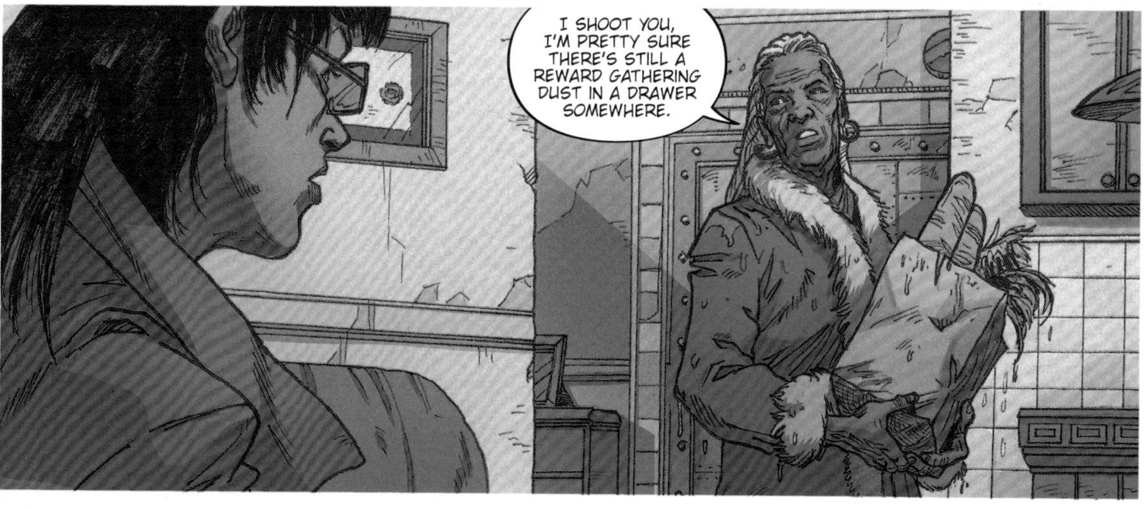
I SHOOT YOU, I'M PRETTY SURE THERE'S STILL A REWARD GATHERING DUST IN A DRAWER SOMEWHERE.

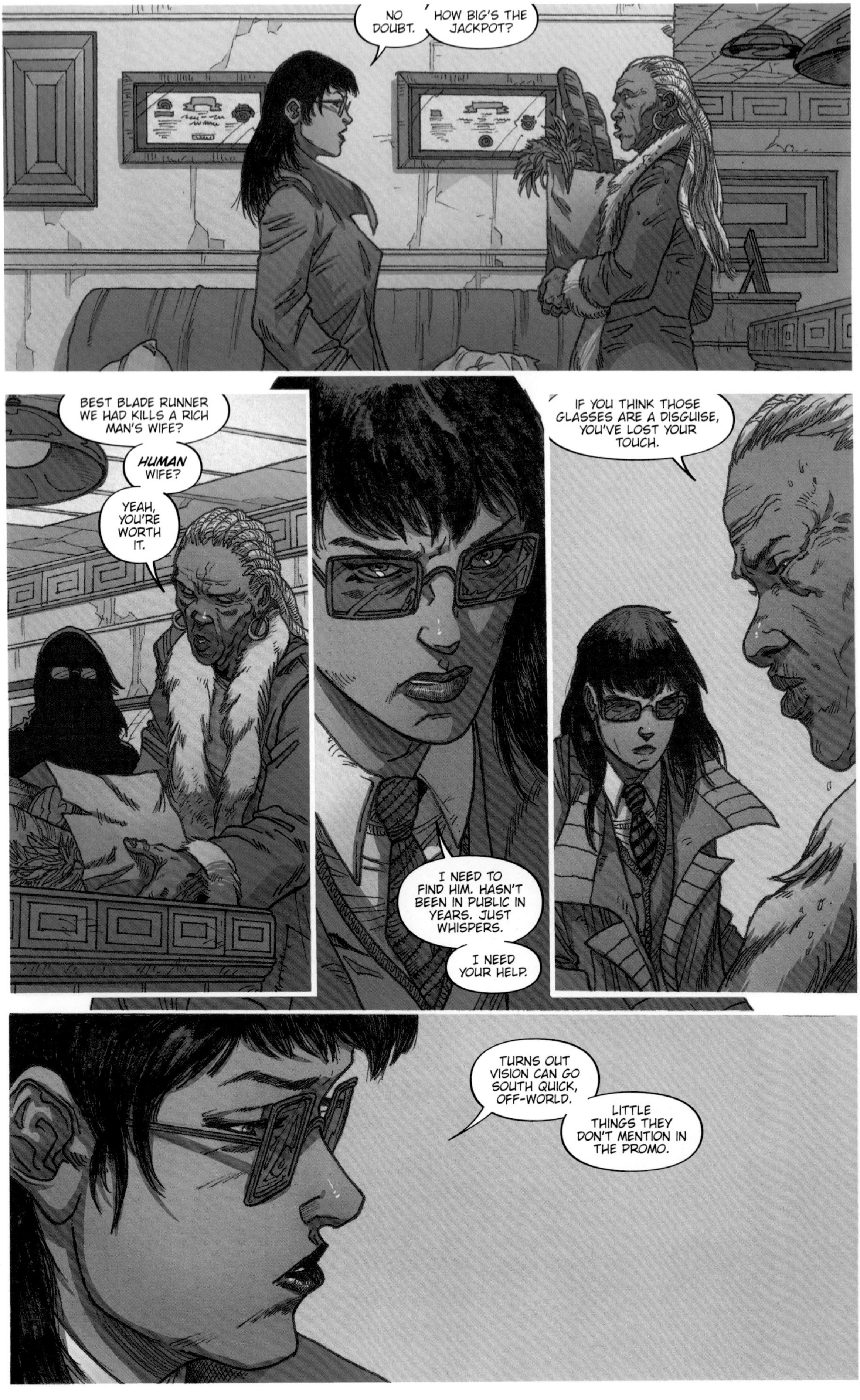
NO DOUBT.
HOW BIG'S THE JACKPOT?
BEST BLADE RUNNER WE HAD KILLS A RICH MAN'S WIFE?
HUMAN WIFE?
YEAH, YOU'RE WORTH IT.
I NEED TO FIND HIM. HASN'T BEEN IN PUBLIC IN YEARS. JUST WHISPERS.
I NEED YOUR HELP.
IF YOU THINK THOSE GLASSES ARE A DISGUISE, YOU'VE LOST YOUR TOUCH.
TURNS OUT VISION CAN GO SOUTH QUICK, OFF-WORLD.
LITTLE THINGS THEY DON'T MENTION IN THE PROMO.

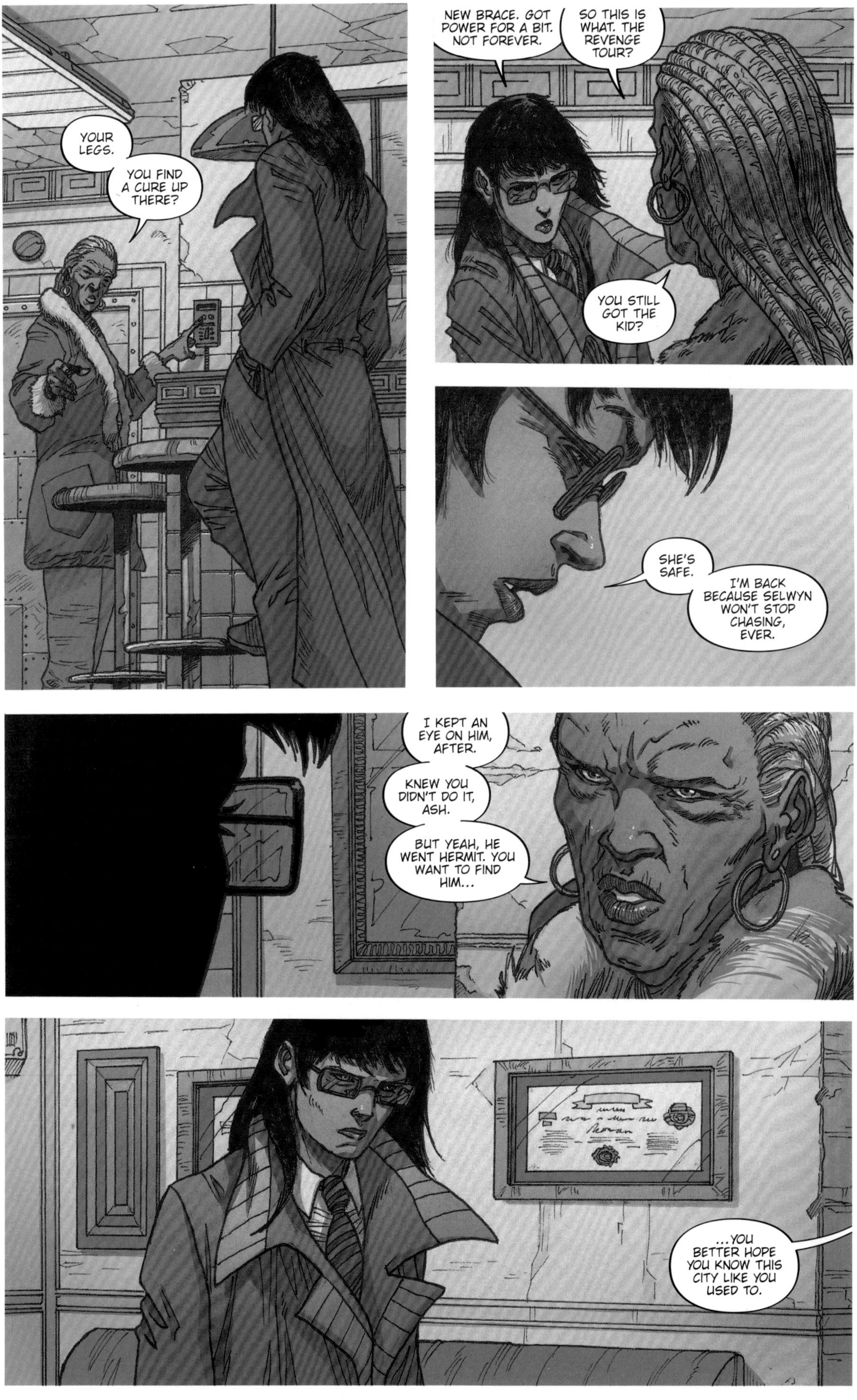
YOUR LEGS.
YOU FIND A CURE UP THERE?
NEW BRACE. GOT POWER FOR A BIT. NOT FOREVER.
SO THIS IS WHAT. THE REVENGE TOUR?
YOU STILL GOT THE KID?
SHE'S SAFE.
I'M BACK BECAUSE SELWYN WON'T STOP CHASING, EVER.
I KEPT AN EYE ON HIM, AFTER.
KNEW YOU DIDN'T DO IT, ASH.
BUT YEAH, HE WENT HERMIT. YOU WANT TO FIND HIM...
...YOU BETTER HOPE YOU KNOW THIS CITY LIKE YOU USED TO.

Wojciech says she'll drill down on Selwyn.

Says she'd never take the jackpot.

Saying so makes me wonder.

My old networks, the ones still around, aren't helping on Selwyn.

Their currency is ground-side, in the numbers, not up in the clouds with the few.

But there's still one place I need to look.

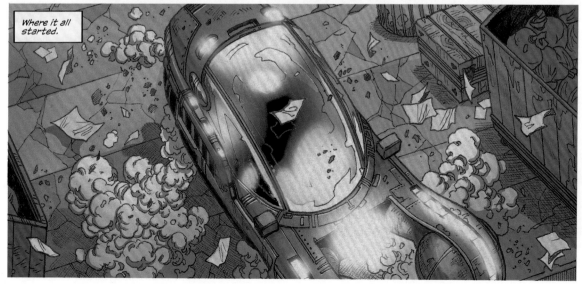

Where it all started.

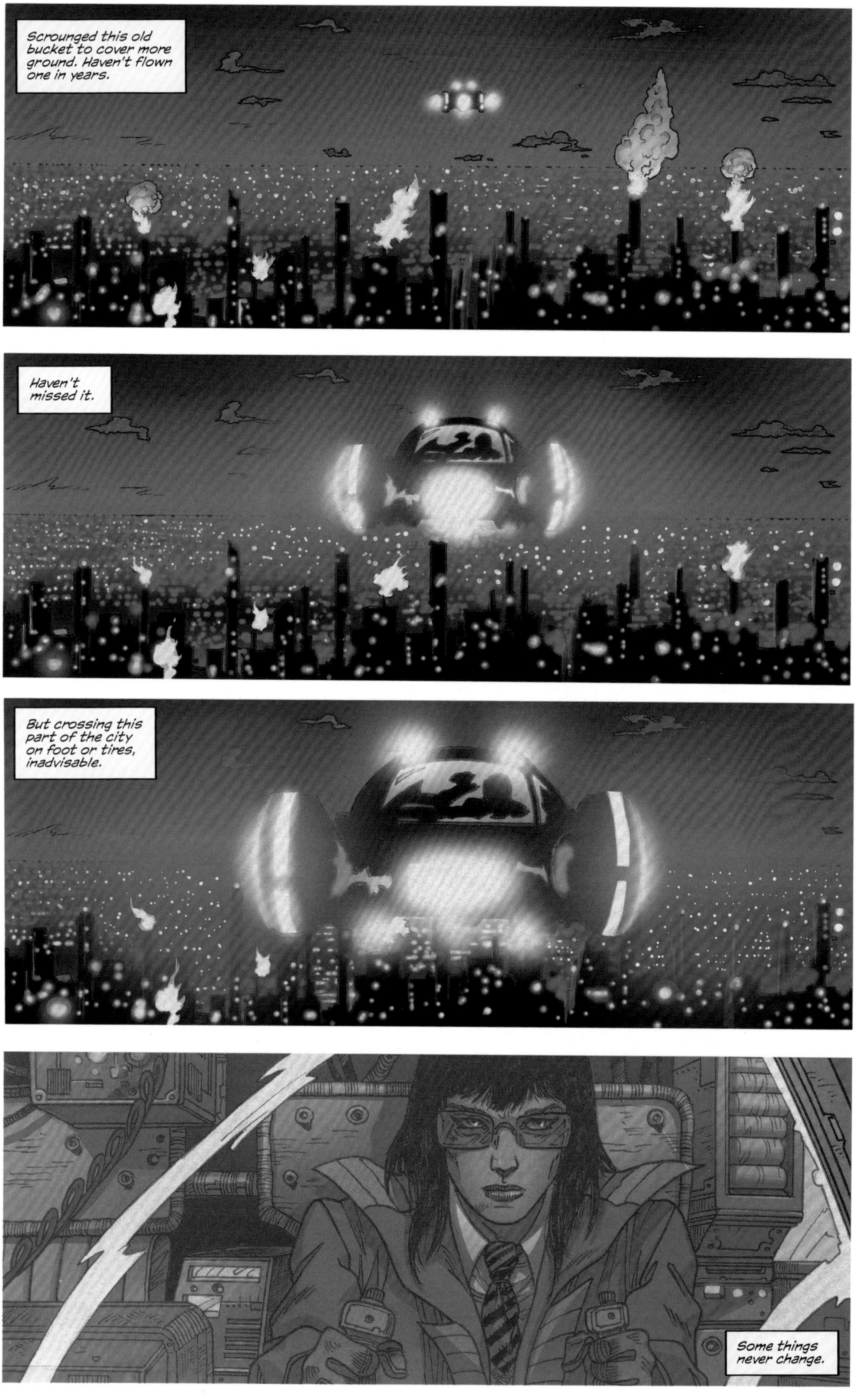
Scrounged this old bucket to cover more ground. Haven't flown one in years.
Haven't missed it.
But crossing this part of the city on foot or tires, inadvisable.
Some things never change.

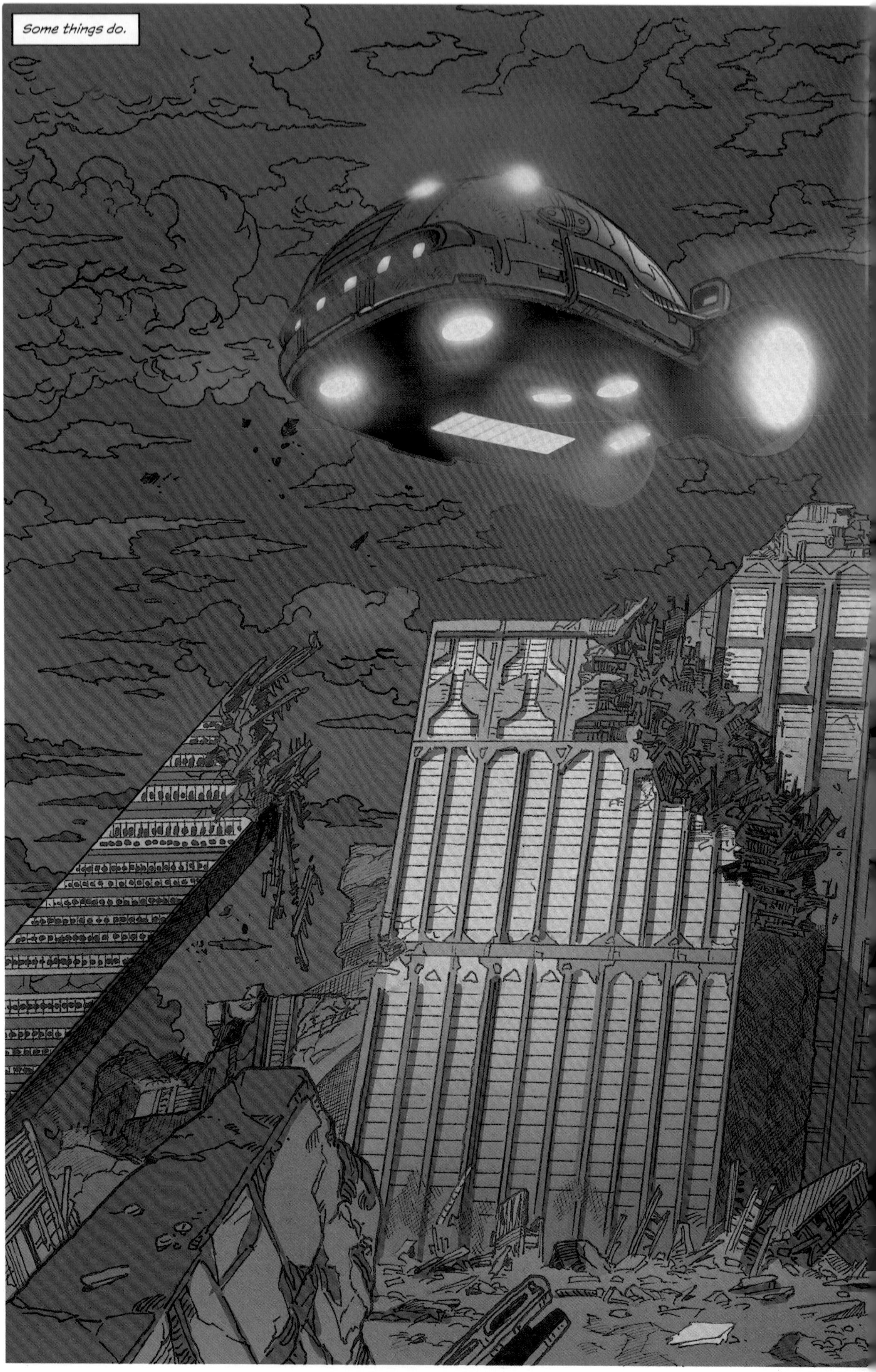
Some things do.

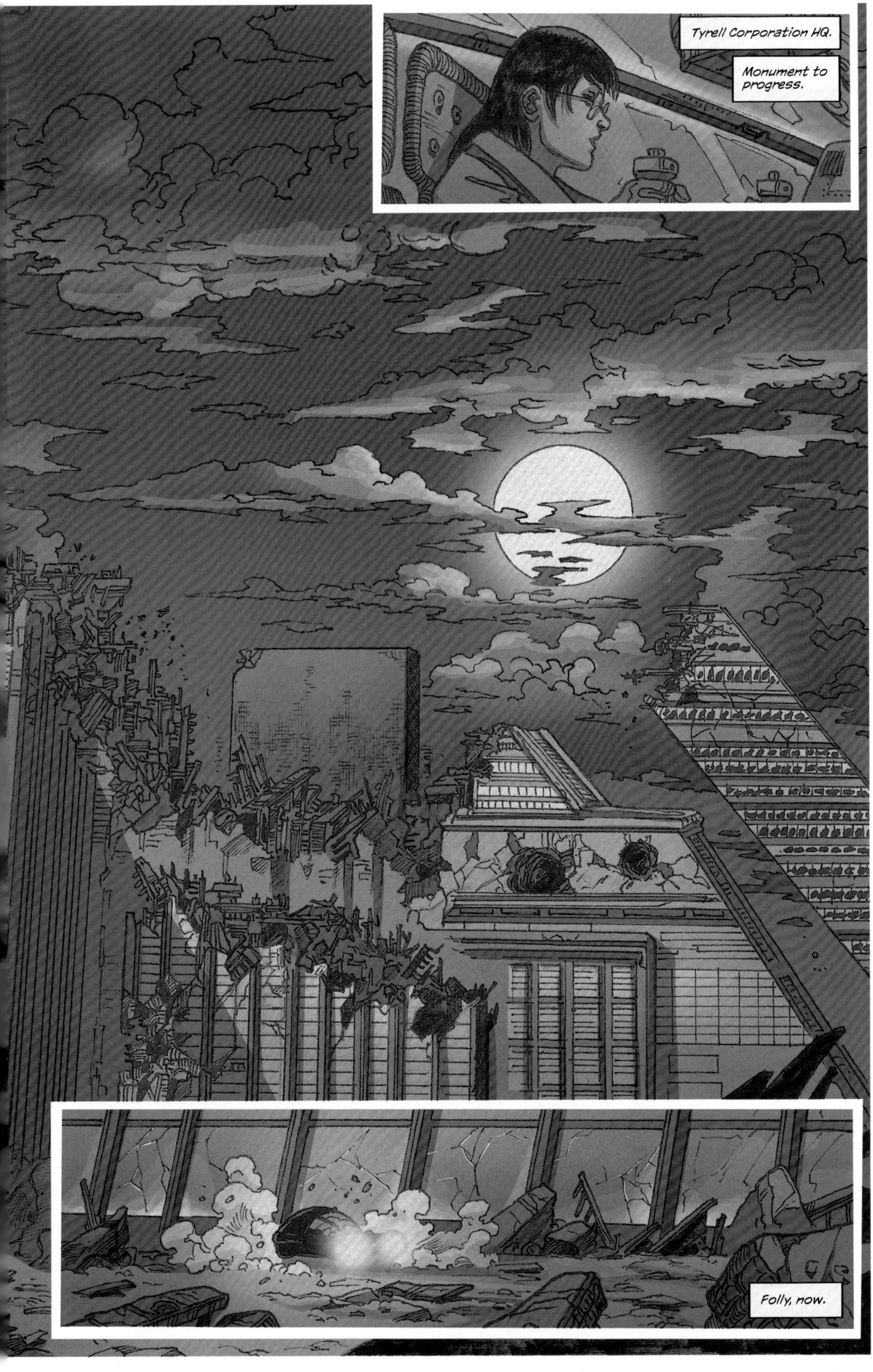
Tyrell Corporation HQ.
Monument to progress.
Folly, now.

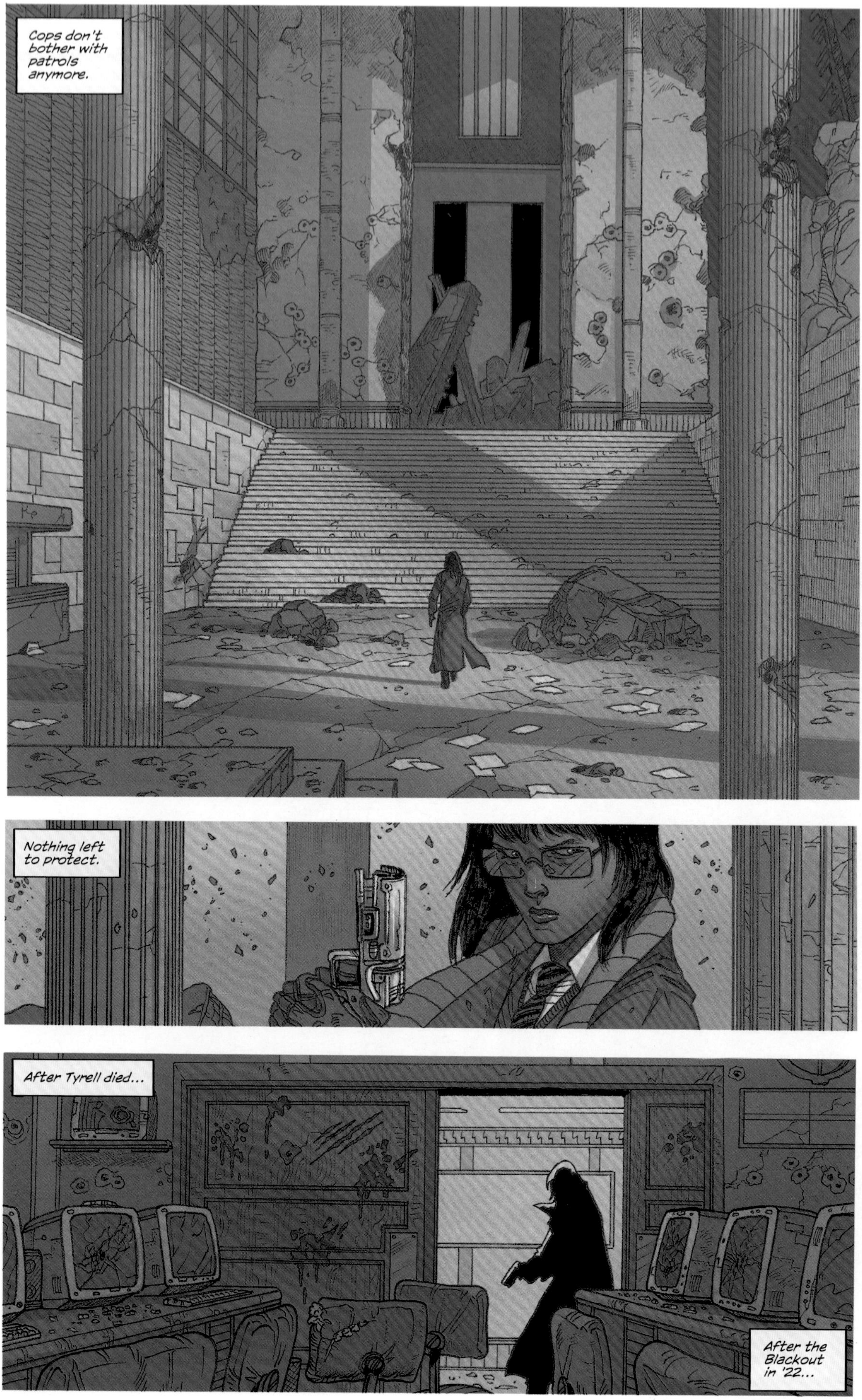
Cops don't bother with patrols anymore.
Nothing left to protect.
After Tyrell died...
After the Blackout in '22...

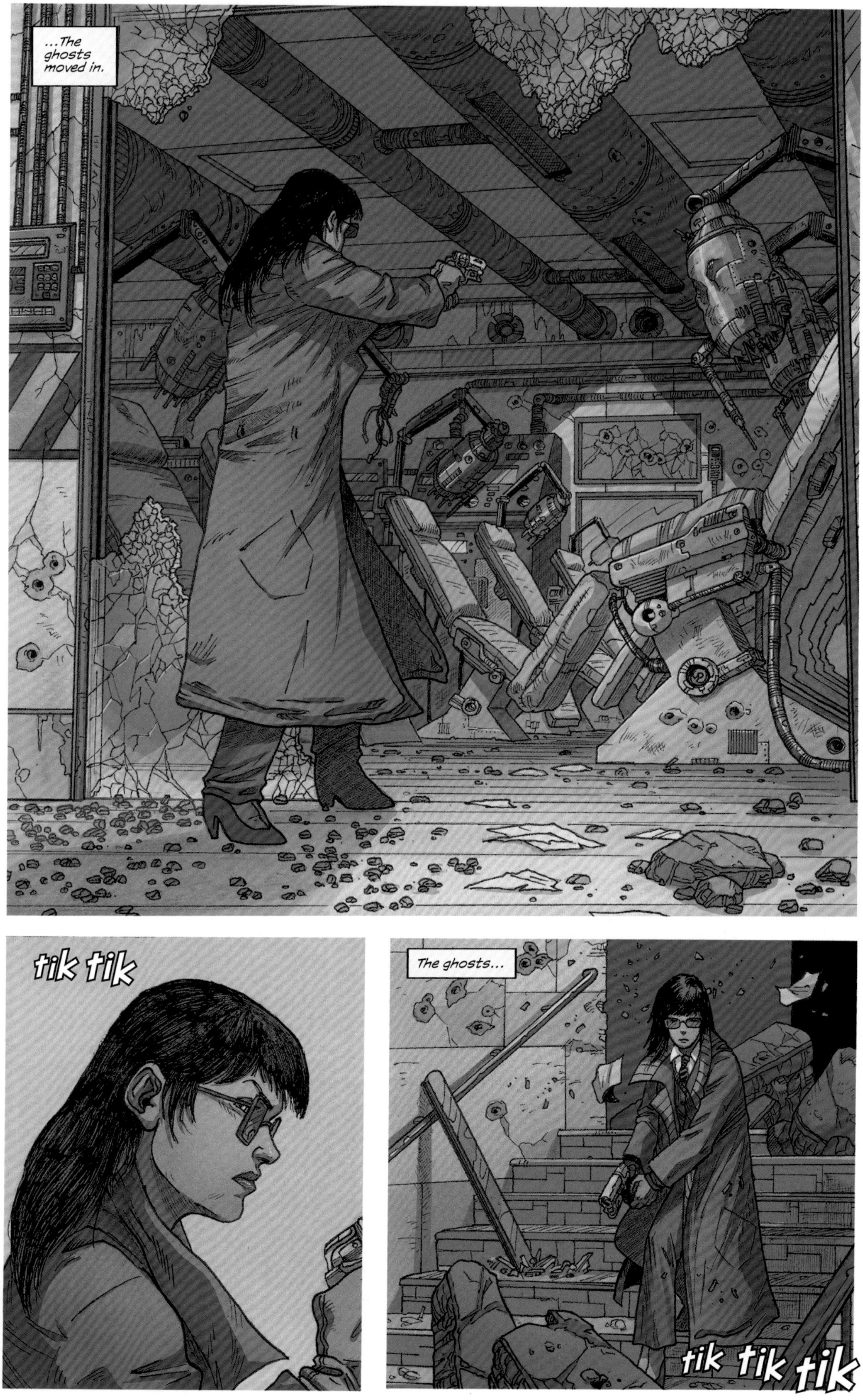
...The ghosts moved in.
tik tik
The ghosts...
tik tik tik

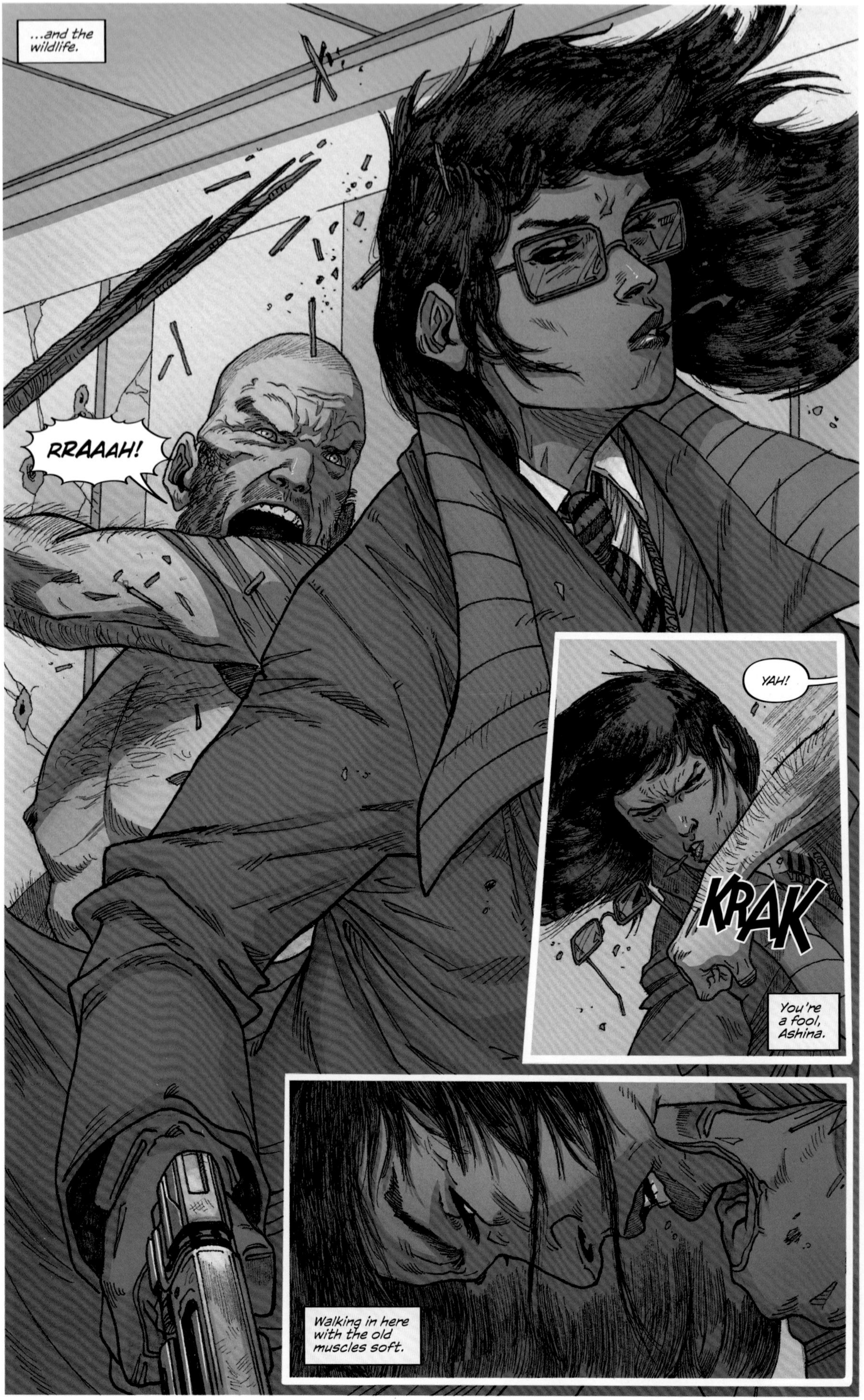
...and the wildlife.
RRAAAH!
YAH!
KRAK
You're a fool, Ashina.
Walking in here with the old muscles soft.

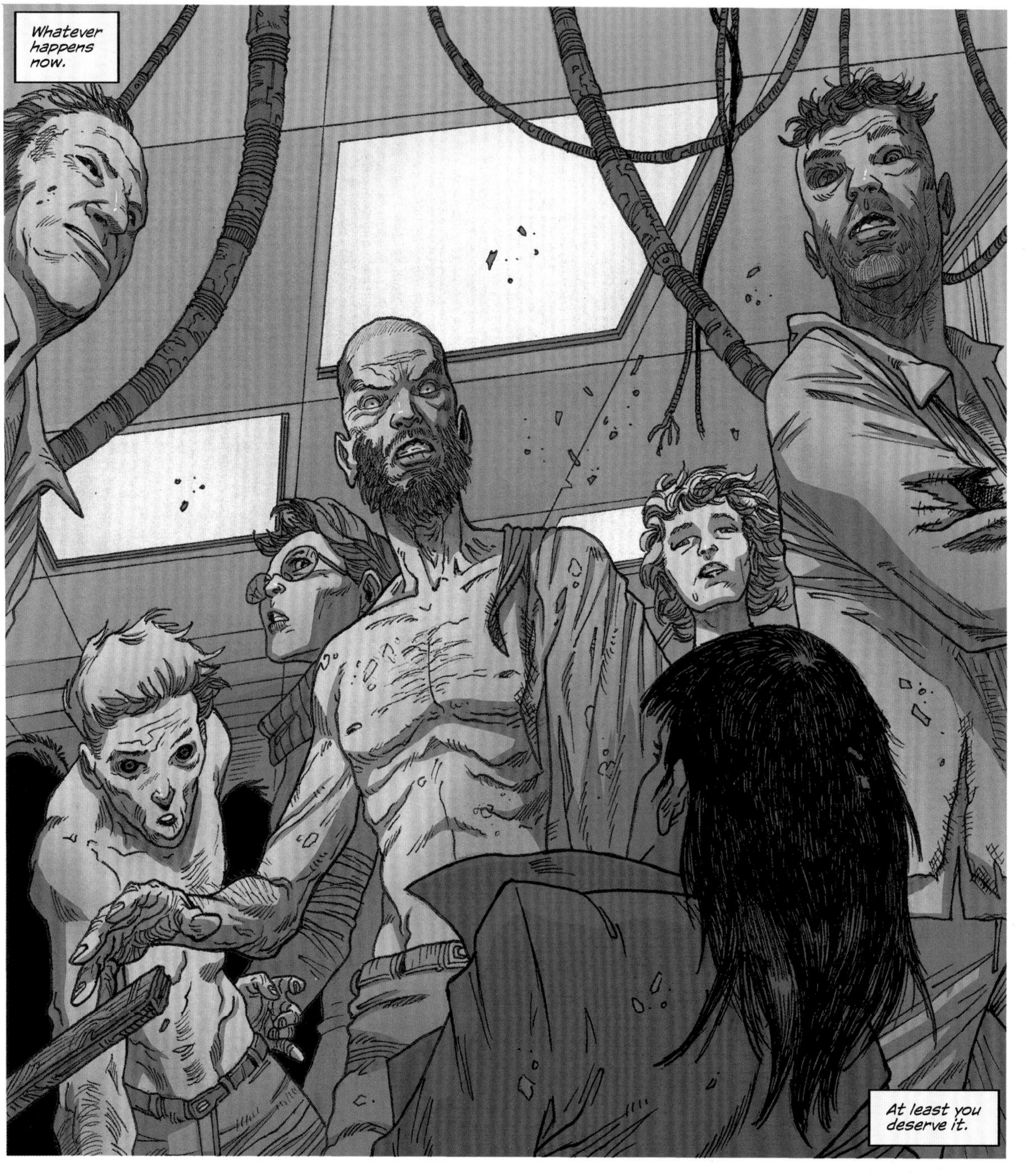
Whatever happens now.
At least you deserve it.

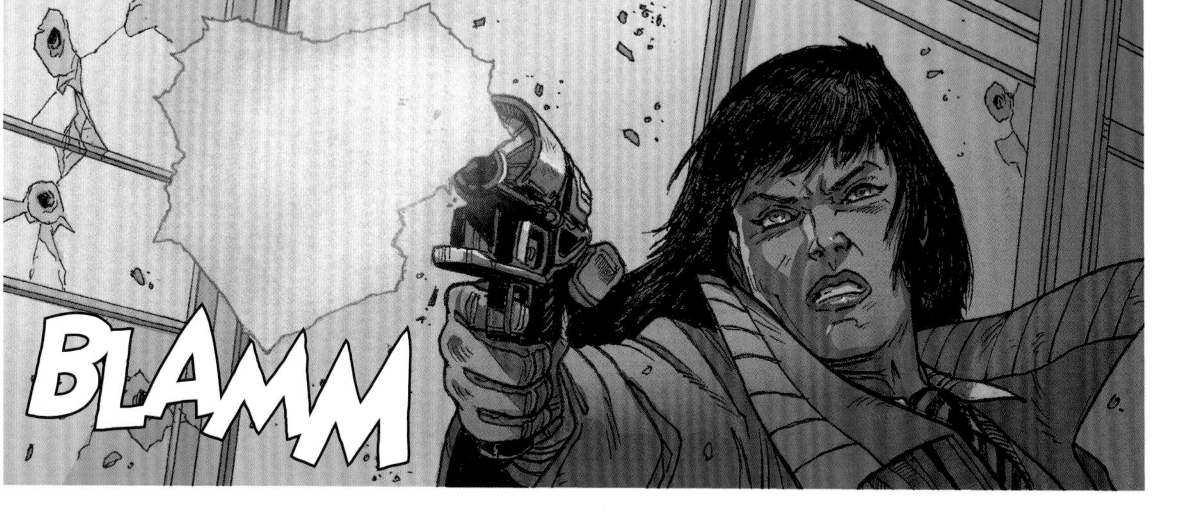
BLAMM

BLAMM
BLAMM
BLAMM

YOU SMELL DIFFERENT.

WRANGG

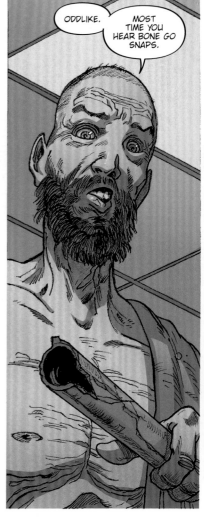

ODDLIKE. MOST TIME YOU HEAR BONE GO SNAPS.

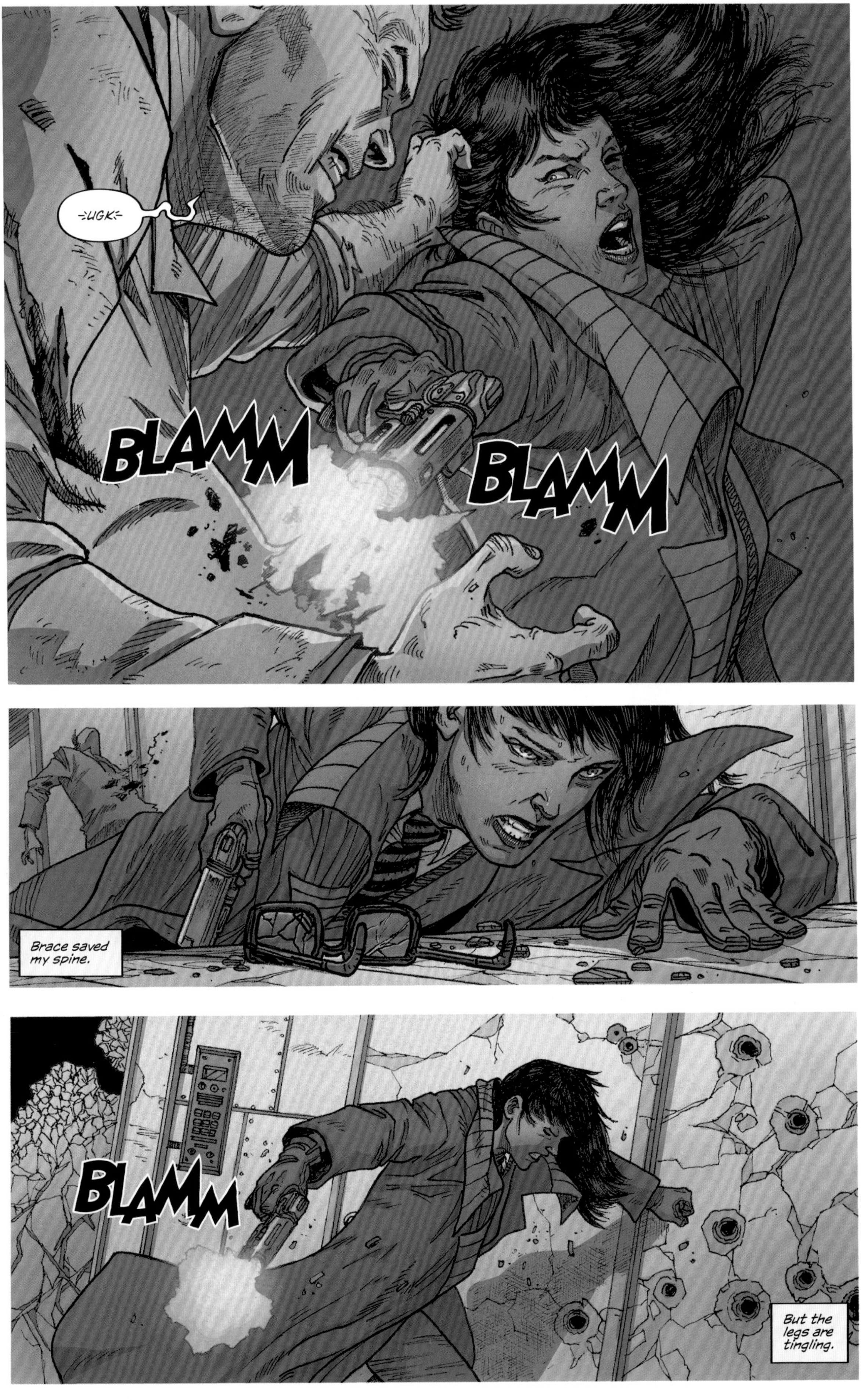
=UGK=
BLAMM
BLAMM
Brace saved my spine.
BLAMM
But the legs are tingling.

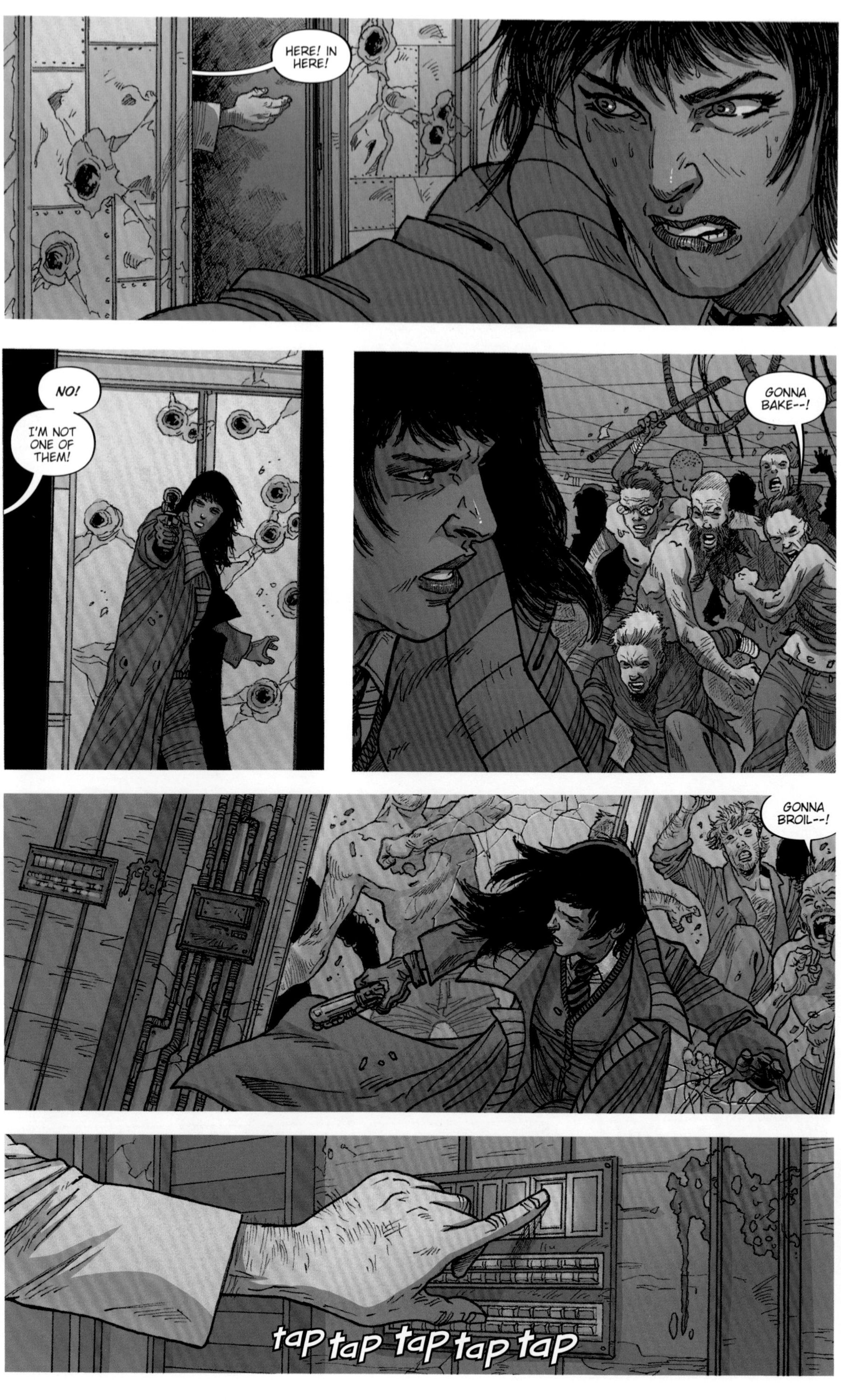
HERE! IN HERE!
NO!
I'M NOT ONE OF THEM!
GONNA BAKE--!
GONNA BROIL--!
tap tap tap tap tap

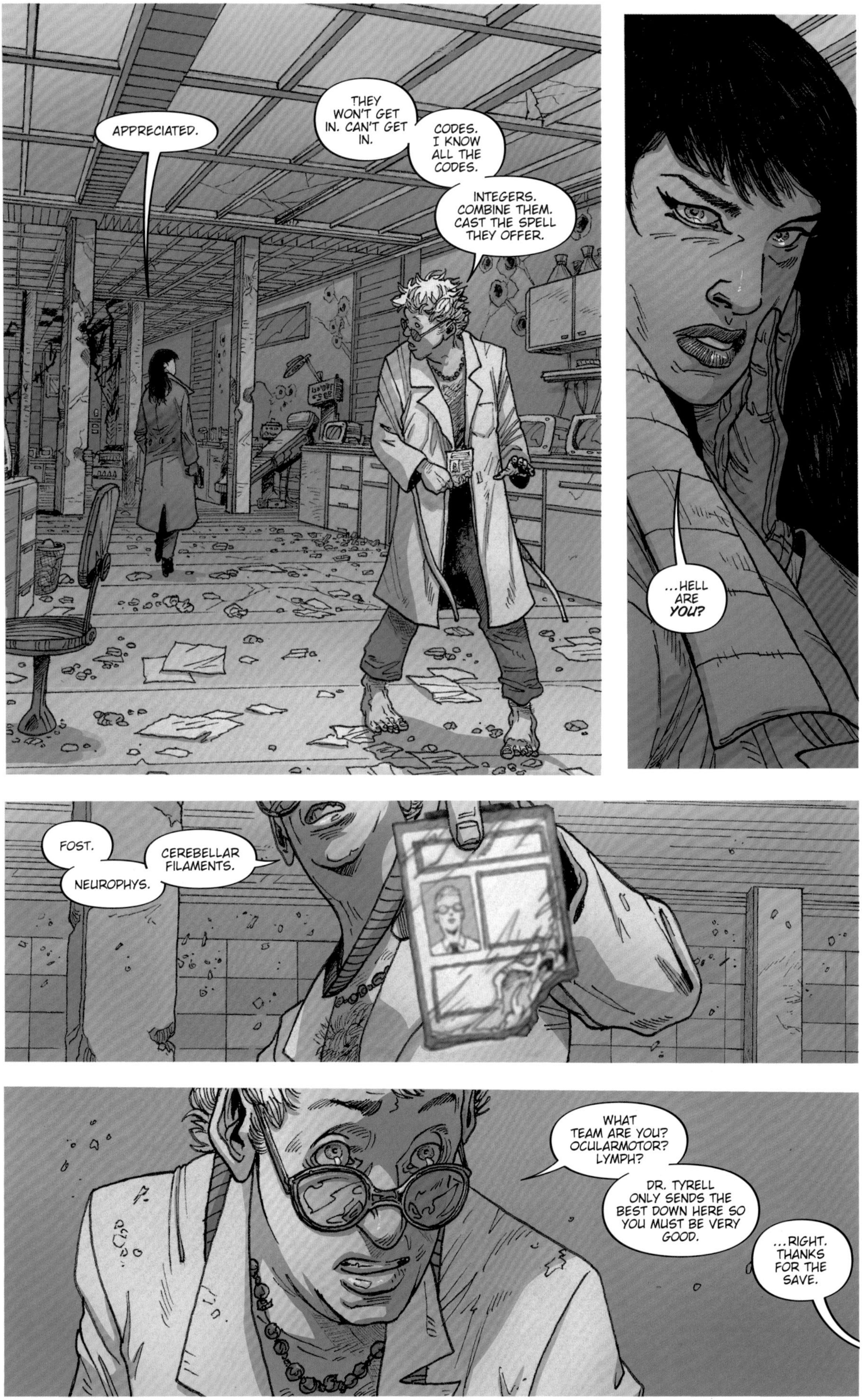
APPRECIATED.
THEY WON'T GET IN. CAN'T GET IN.
CODES. I KNOW ALL THE CODES.
INTEGERS. COMBINE THEM. CAST THE SPELL THEY OFFER.
...HELL ARE *YOU?*
FOST.
NEUROPHYS.
CEREBELLAR FILAMENTS.
WHAT TEAM ARE YOU? OCULARMOTOR? LYMPH?
DR. TYRELL ONLY SENDS THE BEST DOWN HERE SO YOU MUST BE VERY GOOD.
...RIGHT. THANKS FOR THE SAVE.

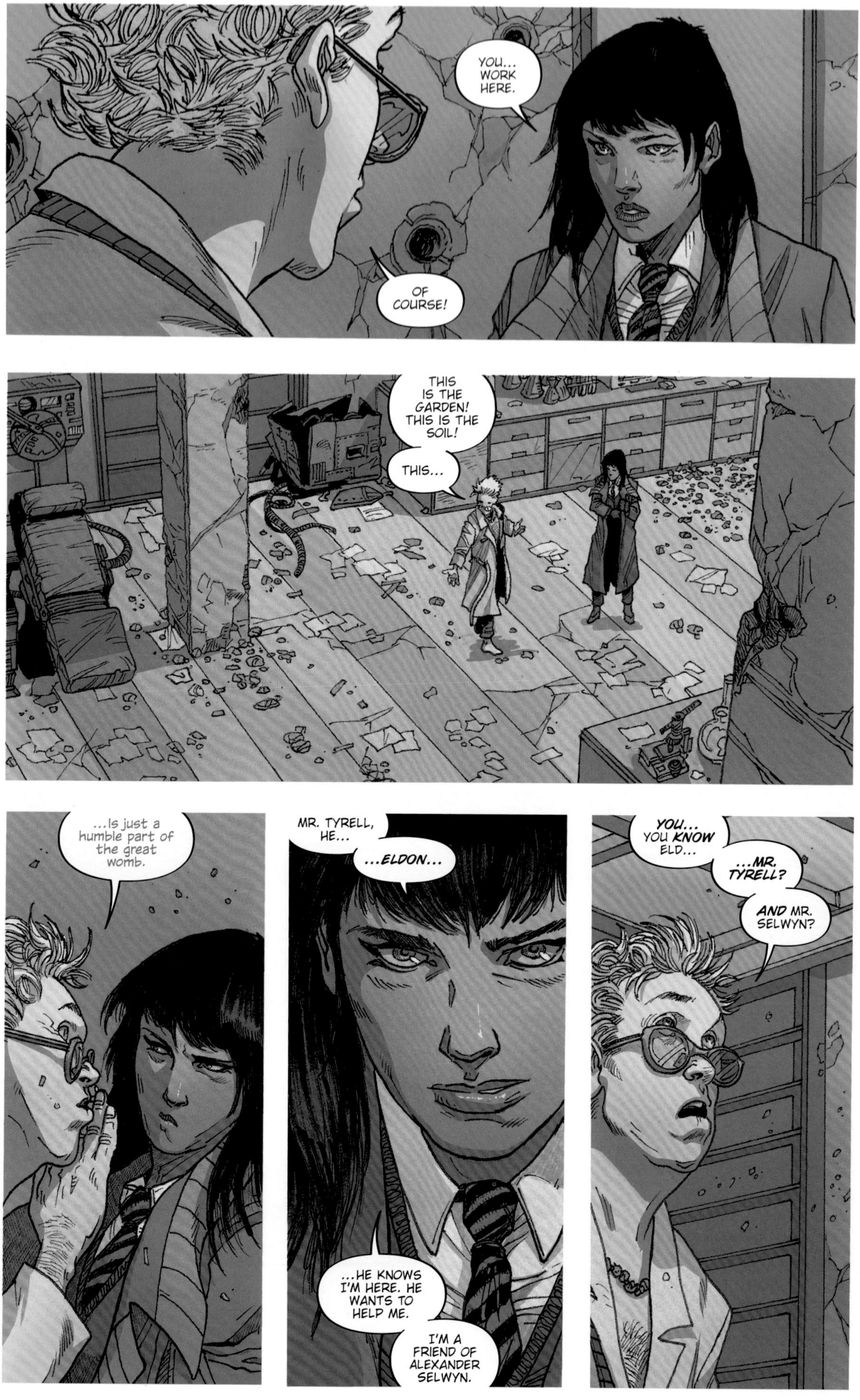
YOU... WORK HERE.
OF COURSE!
THIS IS THE GARDEN! THIS IS THE SOIL!
THIS...
...Is just a humble part of the great womb.
MR. TYRELL, HE...
...ELDON...
...HE KNOWS I'M HERE. HE WANTS TO HELP ME.
I'M A FRIEND OF ALEXANDER SELWYN.
YOU... YOU KNOW ELD...
...MR. TYRELL?
AND MR. SELWYN?

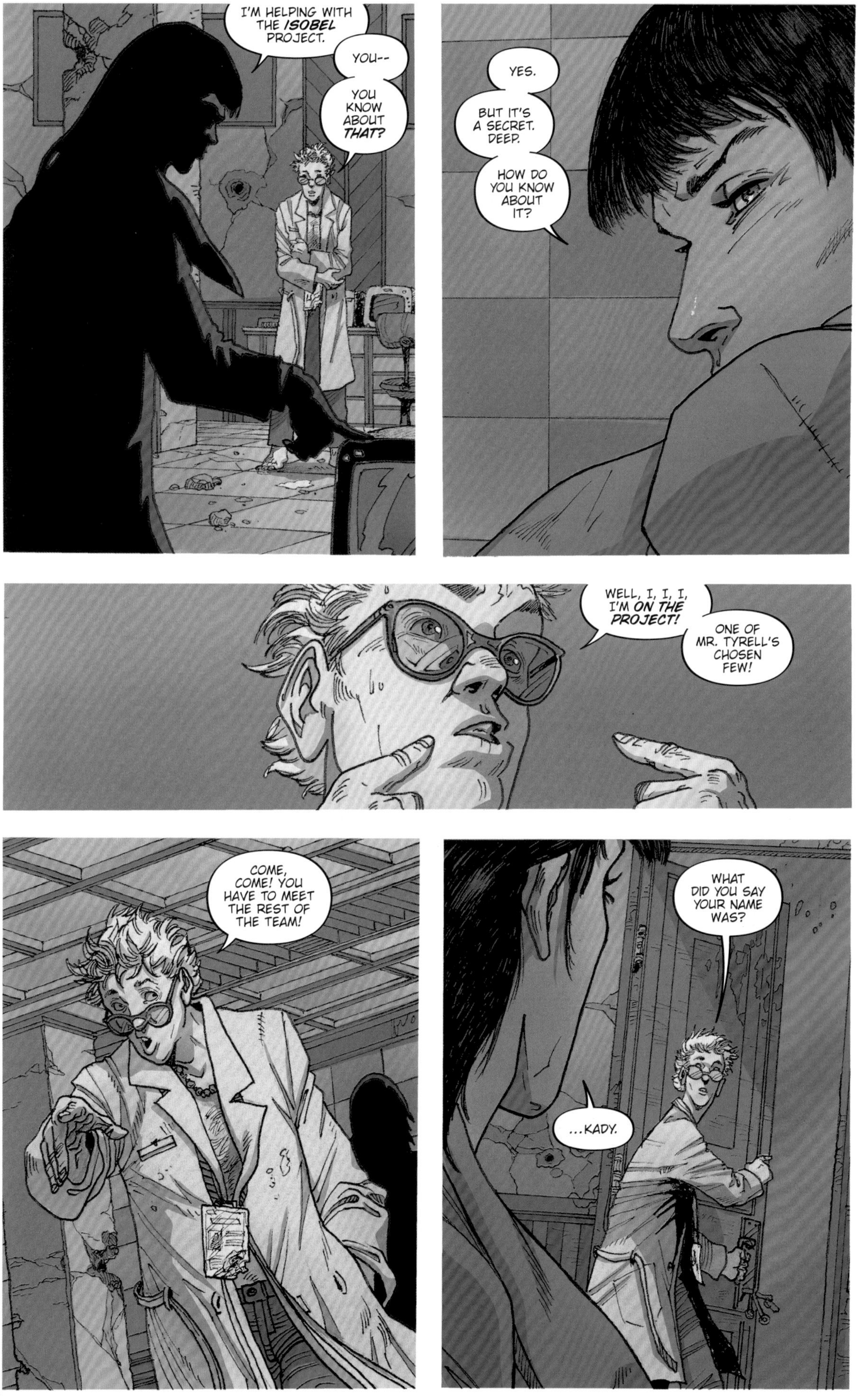
I'M HELPING WITH THE *ISOBEL* PROJECT.
YOU--
YOU KNOW ABOUT *THAT?*
YES.
BUT IT'S A SECRET. DEEP.
HOW DO YOU KNOW ABOUT IT?
WELL, I, I, I, I'M *ON THE PROJECT!*
ONE OF MR. TYRELL'S CHOSEN FEW!
COME, COME! YOU HAVE TO MEET THE REST OF THE TEAM!
WHAT DID YOU SAY YOUR NAME WAS?
...KADY.

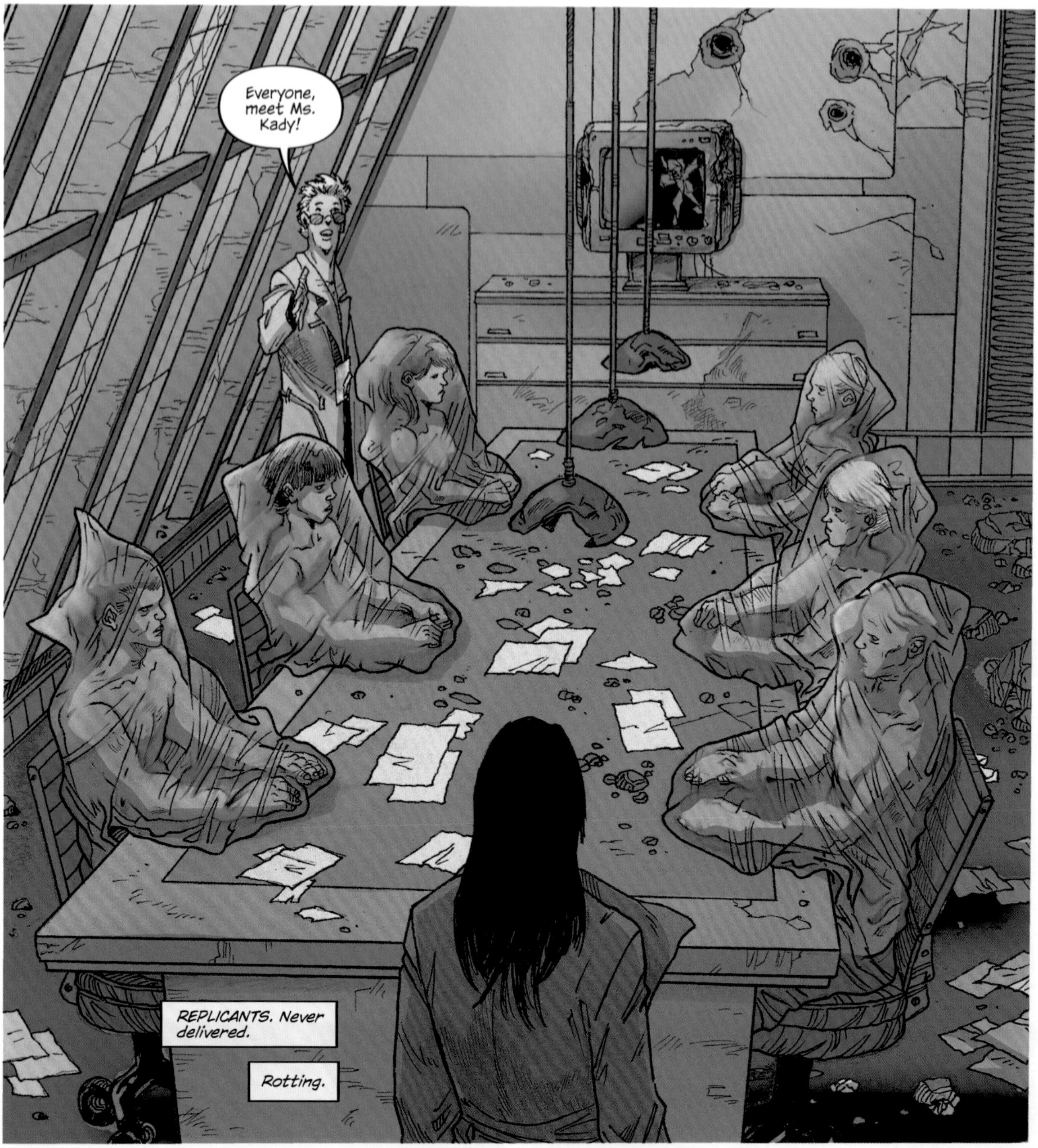

Everyone, meet Ms. Kady!
REPLICANTS. Never delivered.
Rotting.

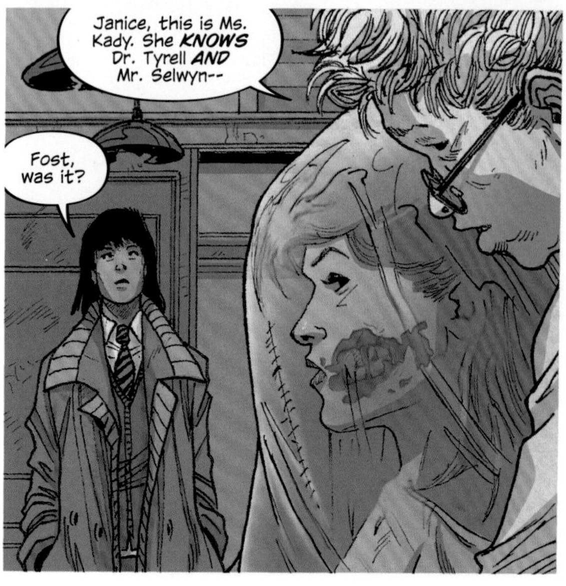

Janice, this is Ms. Kady. She KNOWS Dr. Tyrell AND Mr. Selwyn--
Fost, was it?

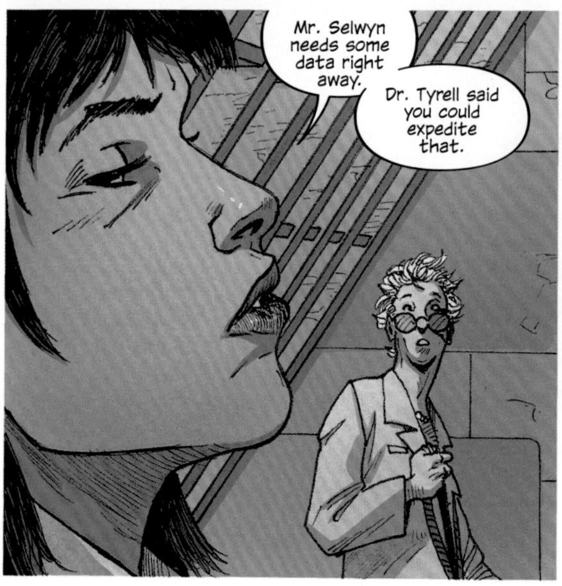

Mr. Selwyn needs some data right away.
Dr. Tyrell said you could expedite that.

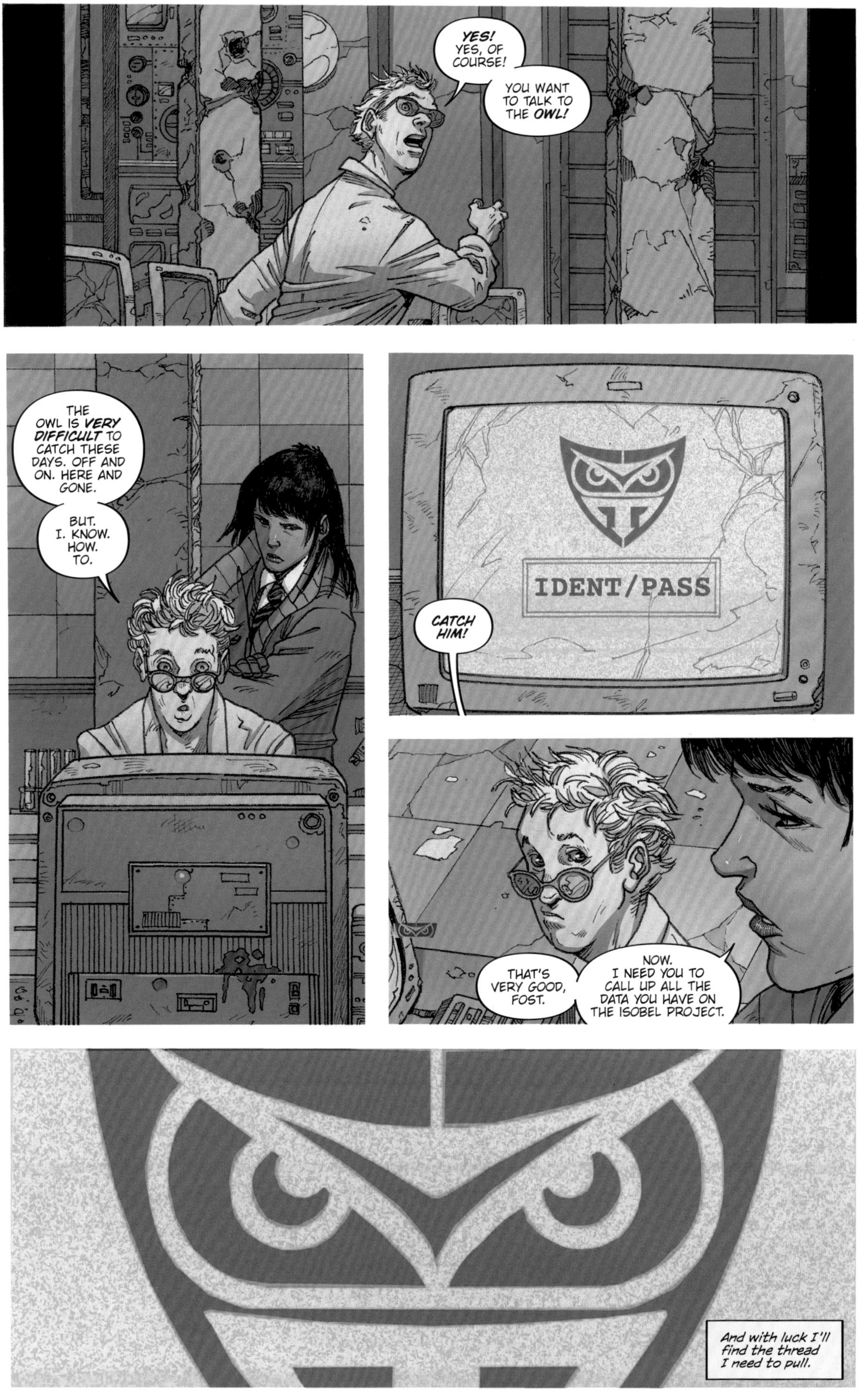
YES! YES, OF COURSE!
YOU WANT TO TALK TO THE OWL!
THE OWL IS VERY DIFFICULT TO CATCH THESE DAYS. OFF AND ON. HERE AND GONE.
BUT. I. KNOW. HOW. TO.
IDENT/PASS
CATCH HIM!
THAT'S VERY GOOD, FOST.
NOW. I NEED YOU TO CALL UP ALL THE DATA YOU HAVE ON THE ISOBEL PROJECT.
And with luck I'll find the thread I need to pull.

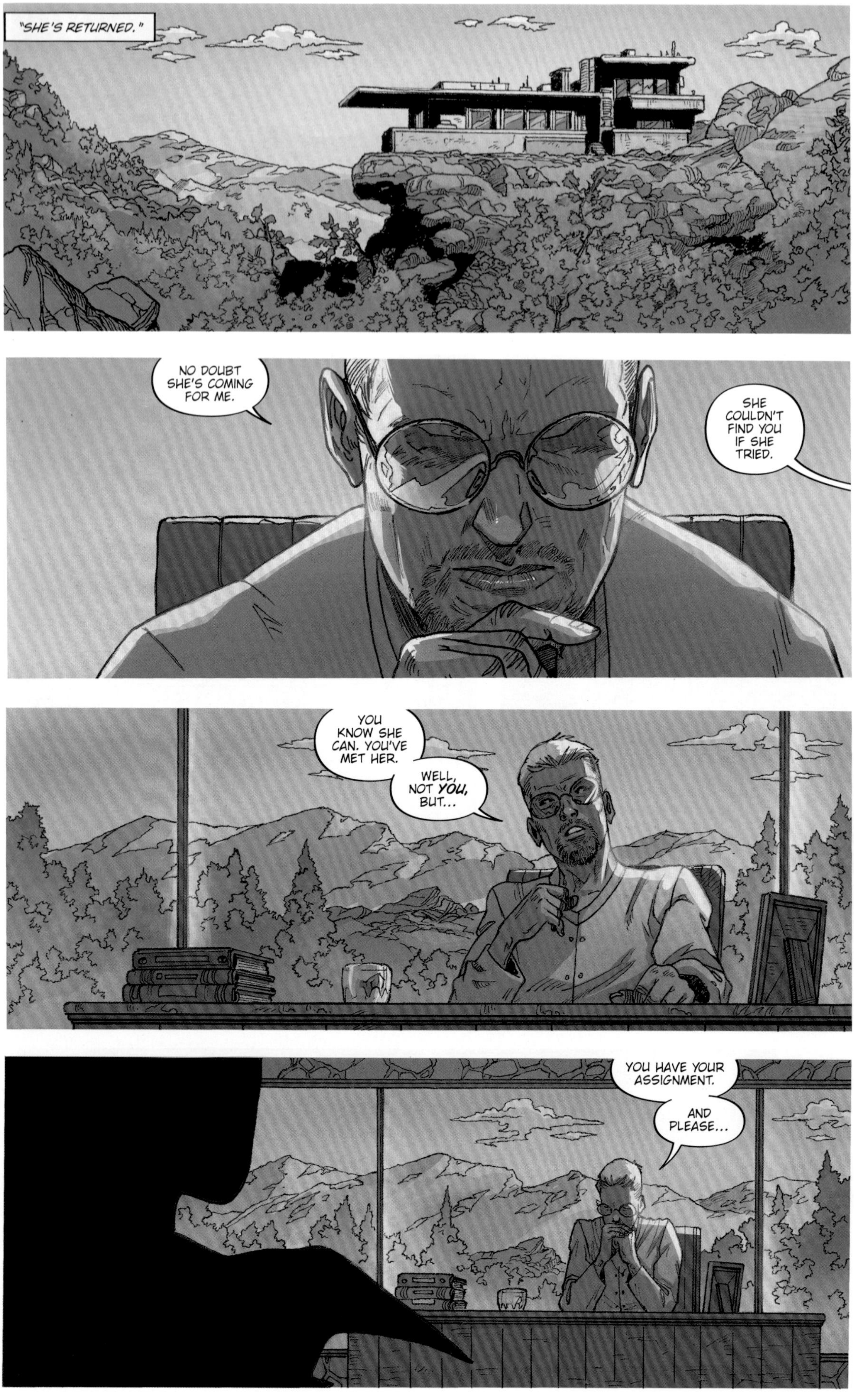
"SHE'S RETURNED."
NO DOUBT SHE'S COMING FOR ME.
SHE COULDN'T FIND YOU IF SHE TRIED.
YOU KNOW SHE CAN. YOU'VE MET HER.
WELL, NOT YOU, BUT...
YOU HAVE YOUR ASSIGNMENT.
AND PLEASE...

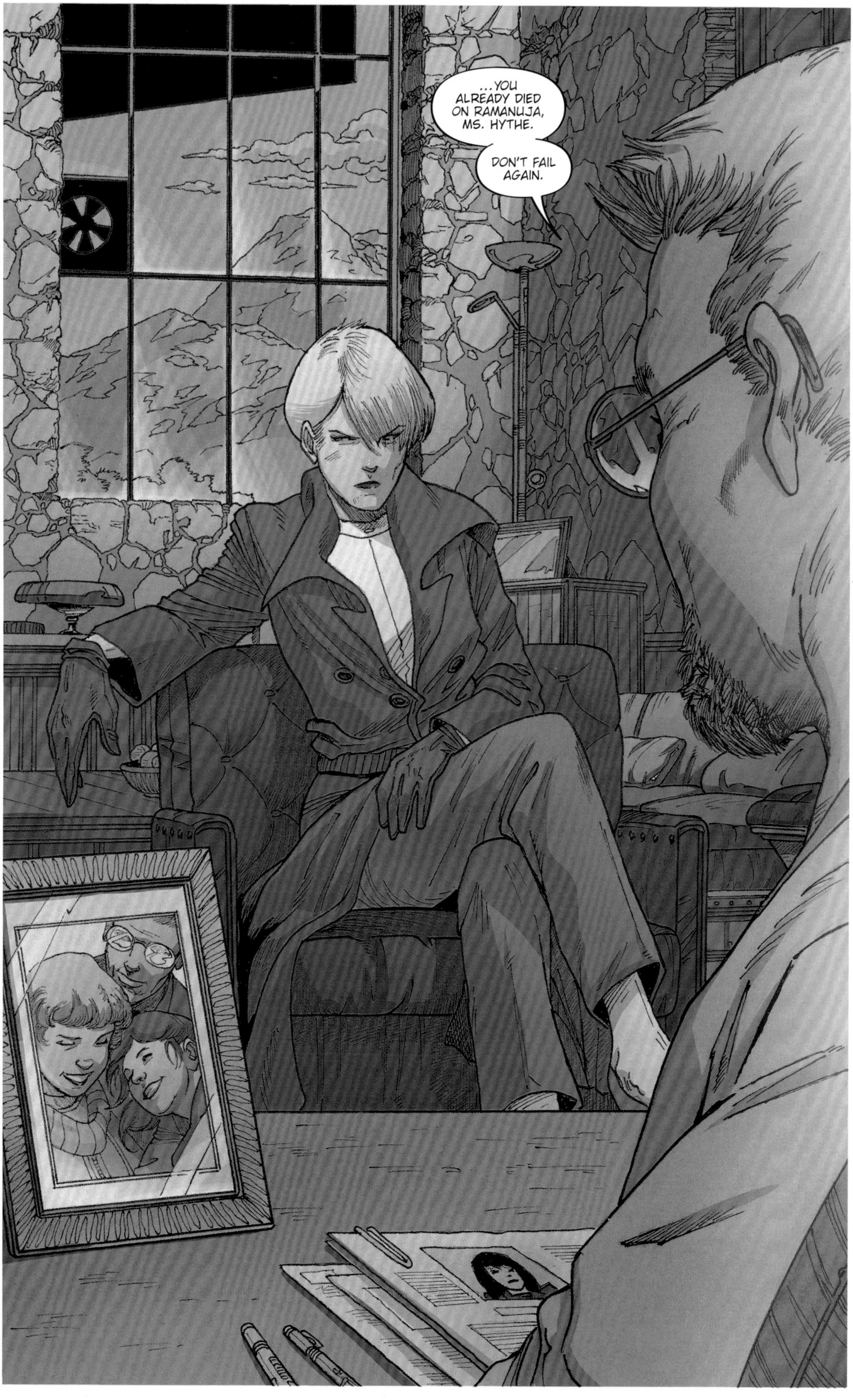
...YOU ALREADY DIED ON RAMANUJA, MS. HYTHE.
DON'T FAIL AGAIN.

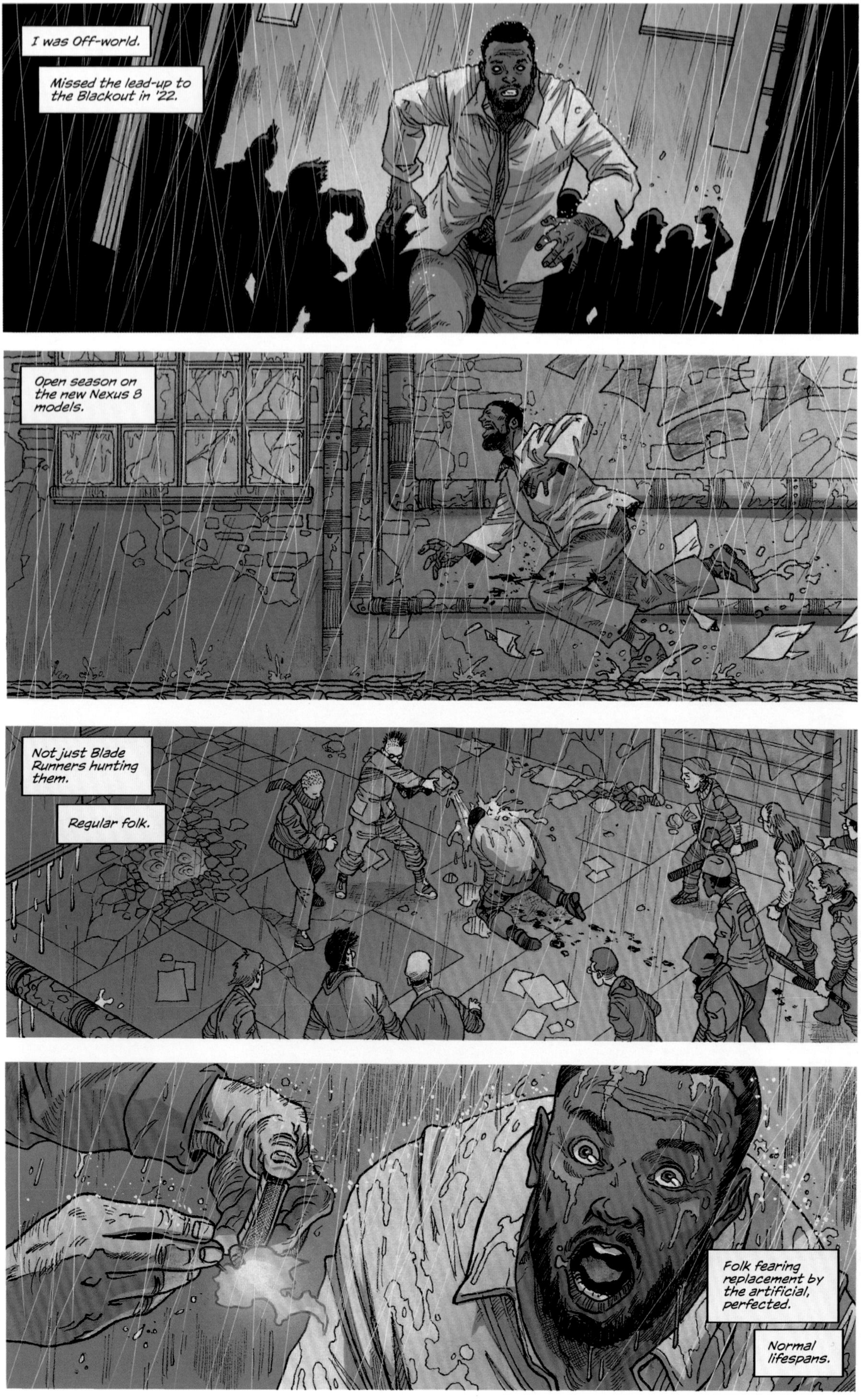
I was Off-world.
Missed the lead-up to the Blackout in '22.
Open season on the new Nexus 8 models.
Not just Blade Runners hunting them.
Regular folk.
Folk fearing replacement by the artificial, perfected.
Normal lifespans.

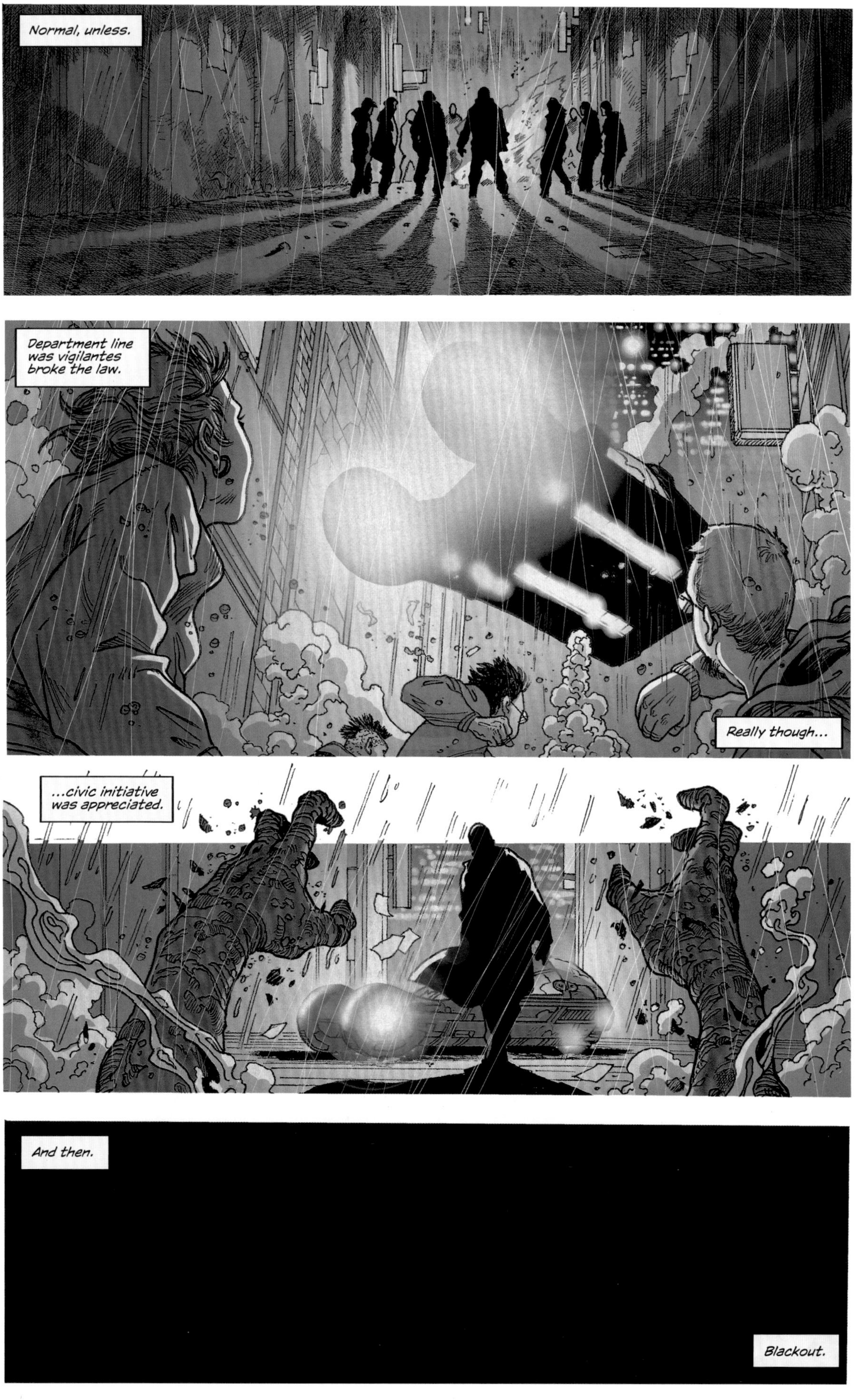
Normal, unless.
Department line was vigilantes broke the law.
Really though...
...civic initiative was appreciated.
And then.
Blackout.

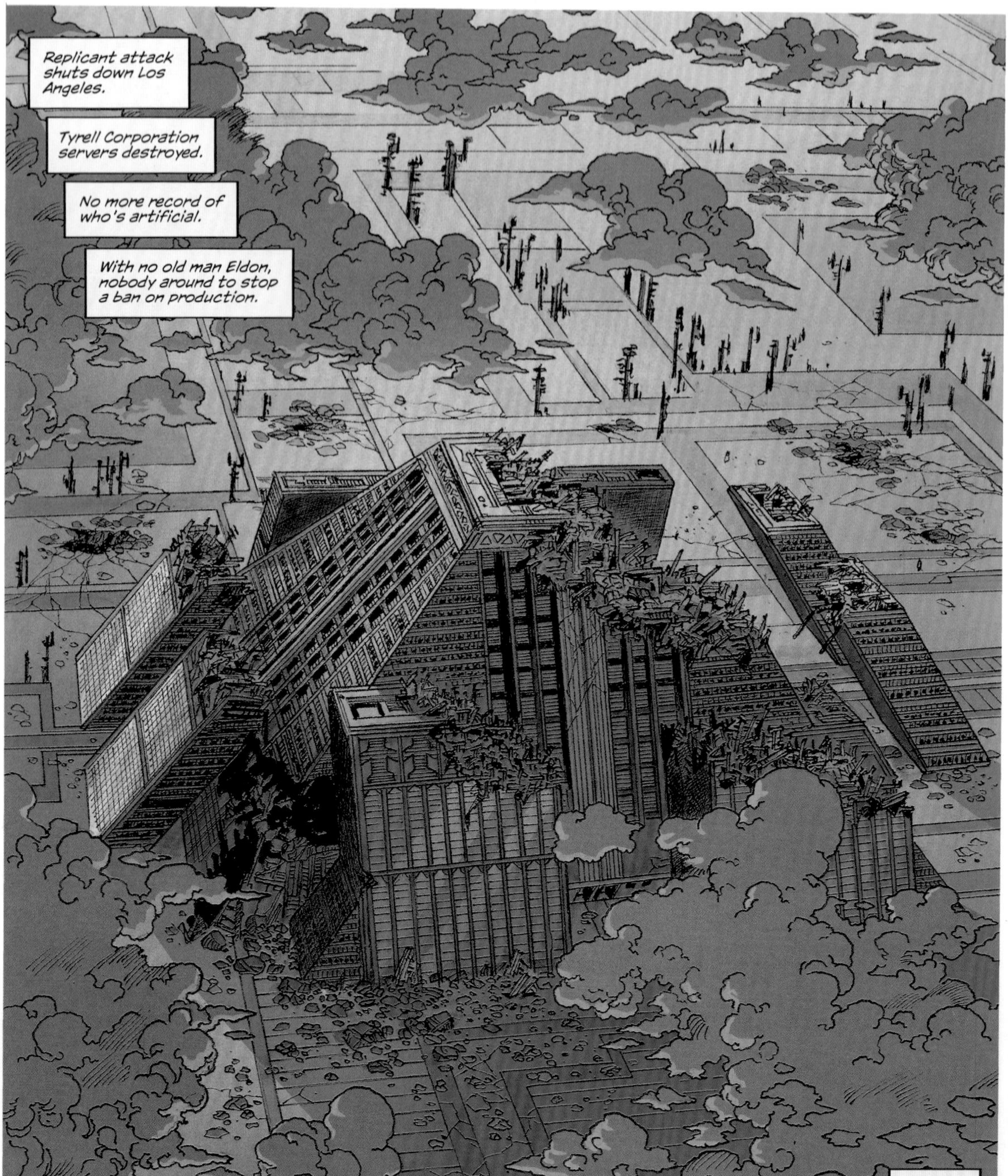
Replicant attack shuts down Los Angeles.
Tyrell Corporation servers destroyed.
No more record of who's artificial.
With no old man Eldon, nobody around to stop a ban on production.
And here we are.

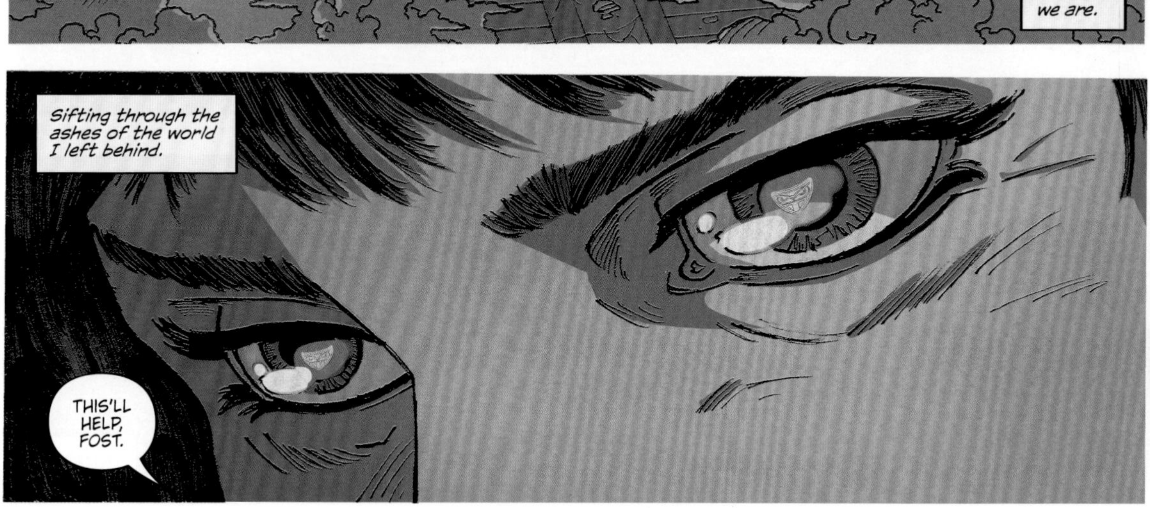
Sifting through the ashes of the world I left behind.
THIS'LL HELP, FOST.

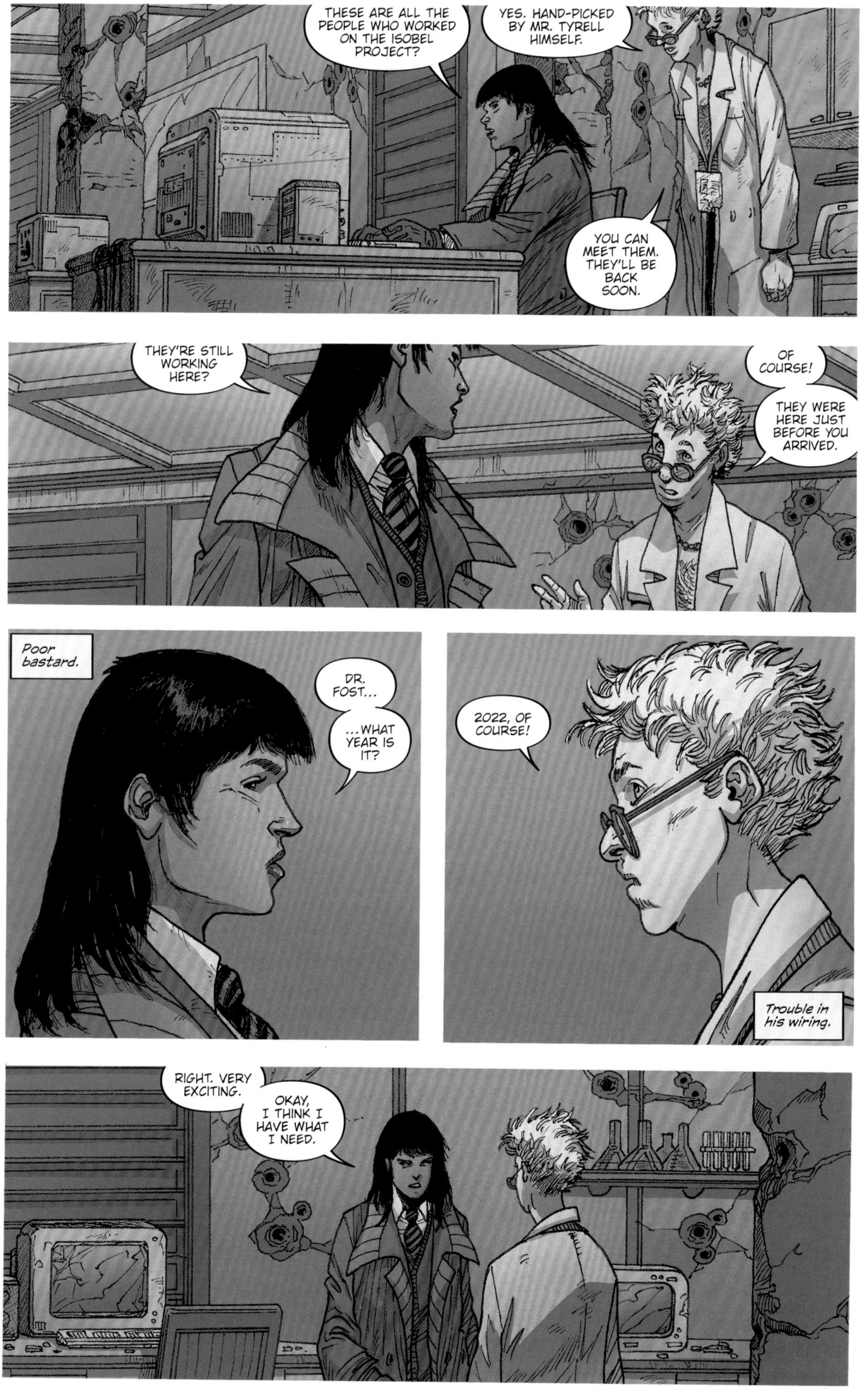
THESE ARE ALL THE PEOPLE WHO WORKED ON THE ISOBEL PROJECT?
YES. HAND-PICKED BY MR. TYRELL HIMSELF.
YOU CAN MEET THEM. THEY'LL BE BACK SOON.
THEY'RE STILL WORKING HERE?
OF COURSE!
THEY WERE HERE JUST BEFORE YOU ARRIVED.
Poor bastard.
DR. FOST...
...WHAT YEAR IS IT?
2022, OF COURSE!
Trouble in his wiring.
RIGHT. VERY EXCITING.
OKAY, I THINK I HAVE WHAT I NEED.

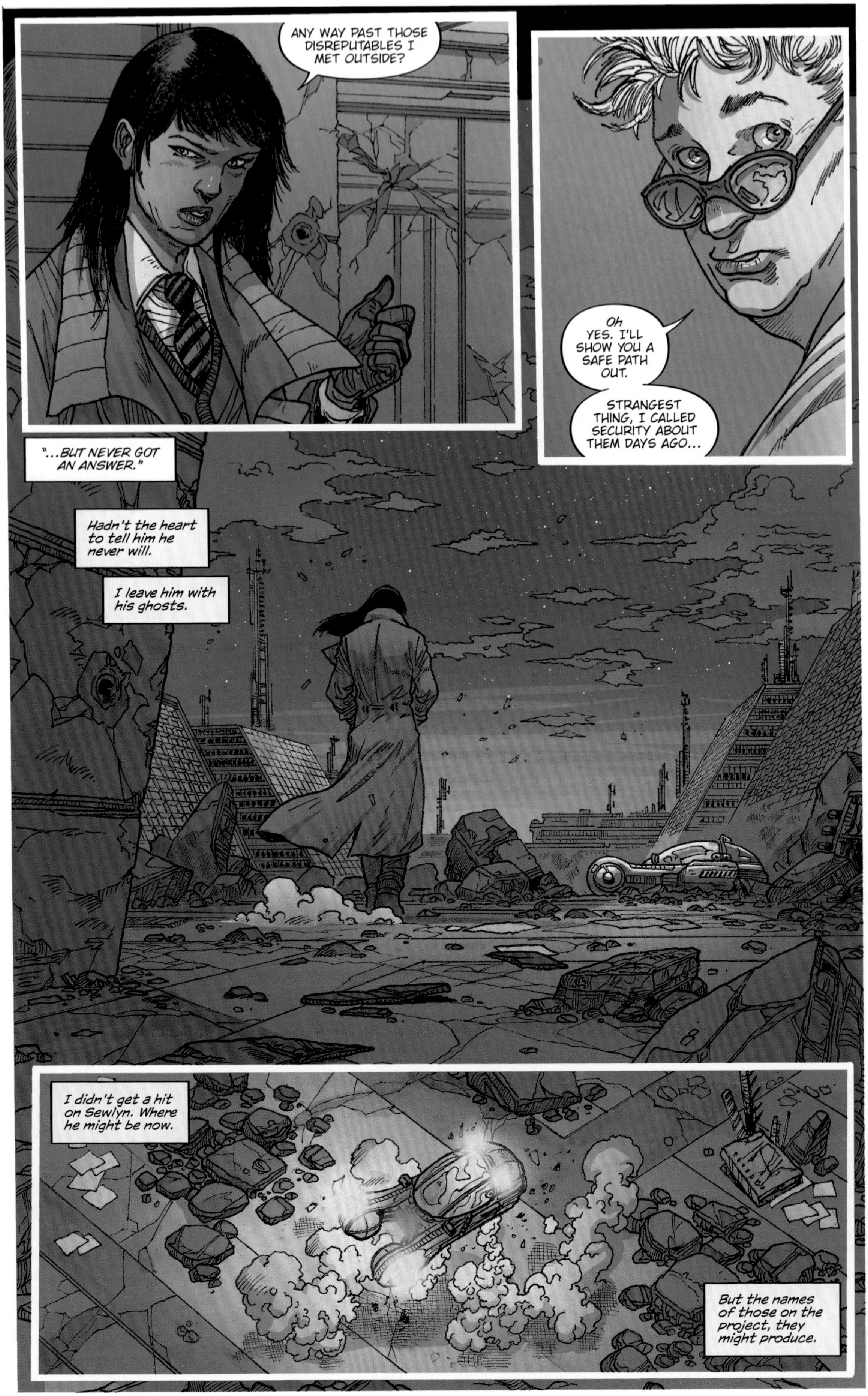
ANY WAY PAST THOSE DISREPUTABLES I MET OUTSIDE?
Oh YES. I'LL SHOW YOU A SAFE PATH OUT.
STRANGEST THING, I CALLED SECURITY ABOUT THEM DAYS AGO...
"...BUT NEVER GOT AN ANSWER."
Hadn't the heart to tell him he never will.
I leave him with his ghosts.
I didn't get a hit on Sewlyn. Where he might be now.
But the names of those on the project, they might produce.

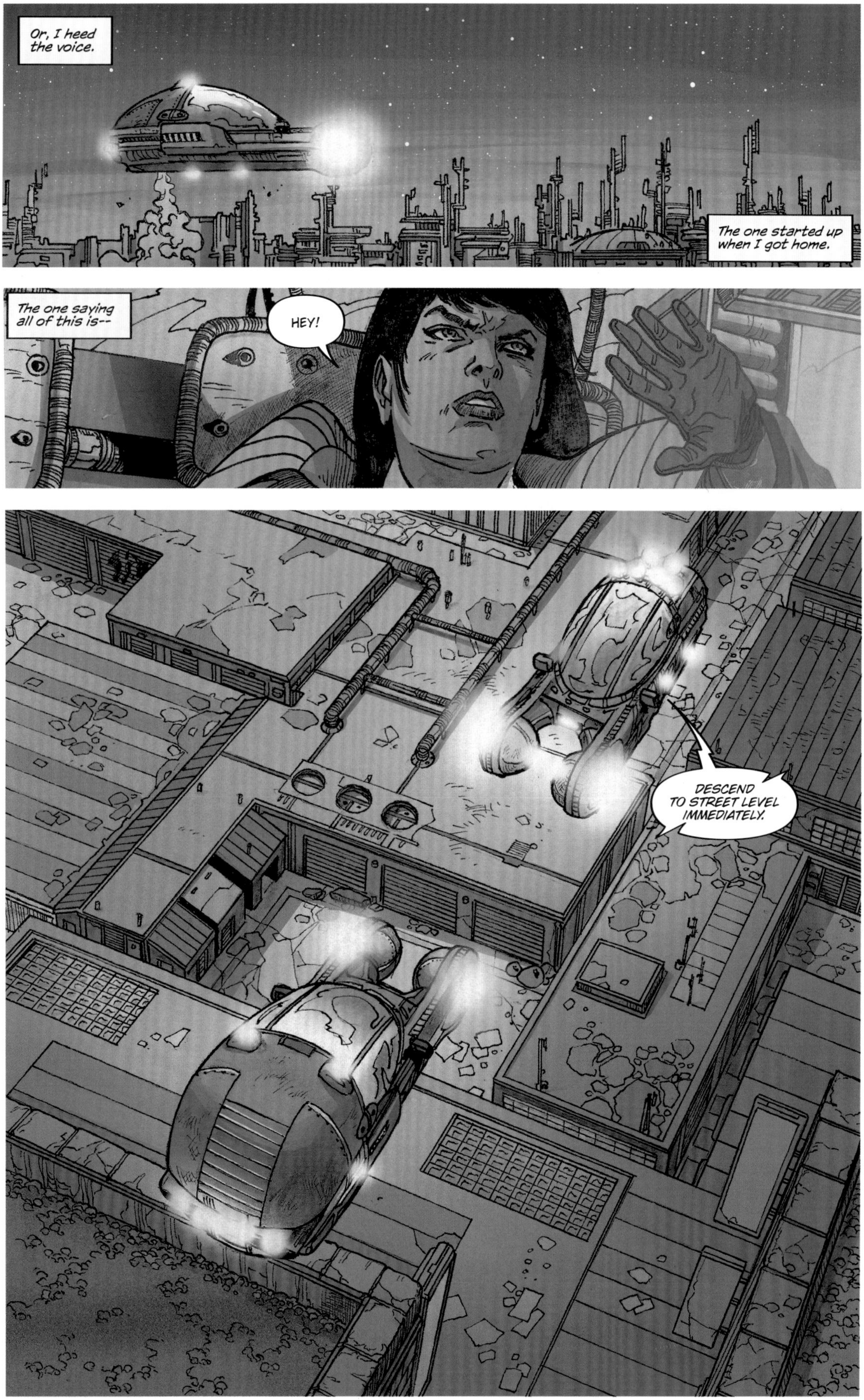
Or, I heed the voice.
The one started up when I got home.
The one saying all of this is--
HEY!
DESCEND TO STREET LEVEL IMMEDIATELY.

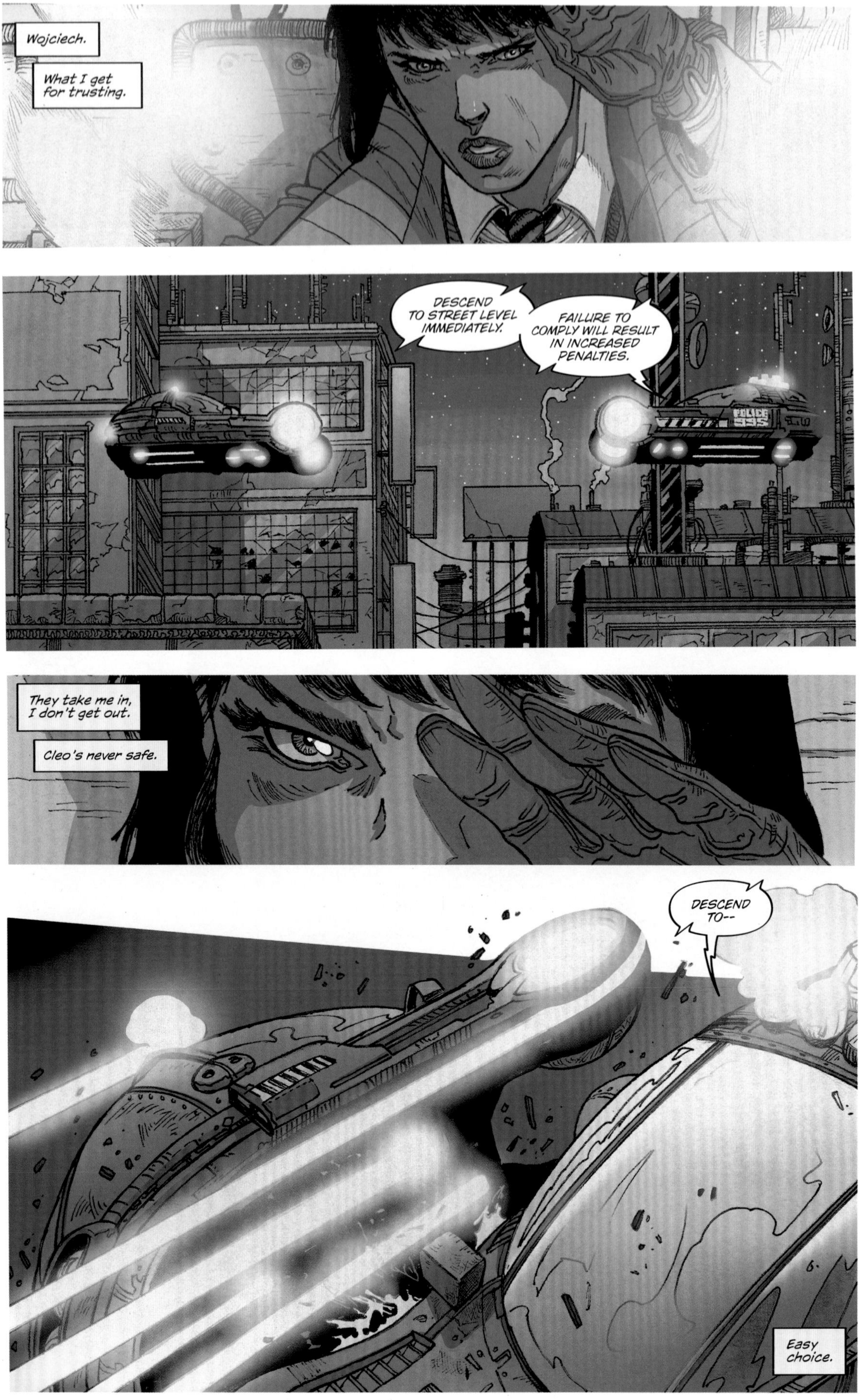
Wojciech.
What I get for trusting.
DESCEND TO STREET LEVEL IMMEDIATELY.
FAILURE TO COMPLY WILL RESULT IN INCREASED PENALTIES.
POLICE 995
They take me in, I don't get out.
Cleo's never safe.
DESCEND TO--
Easy choice.

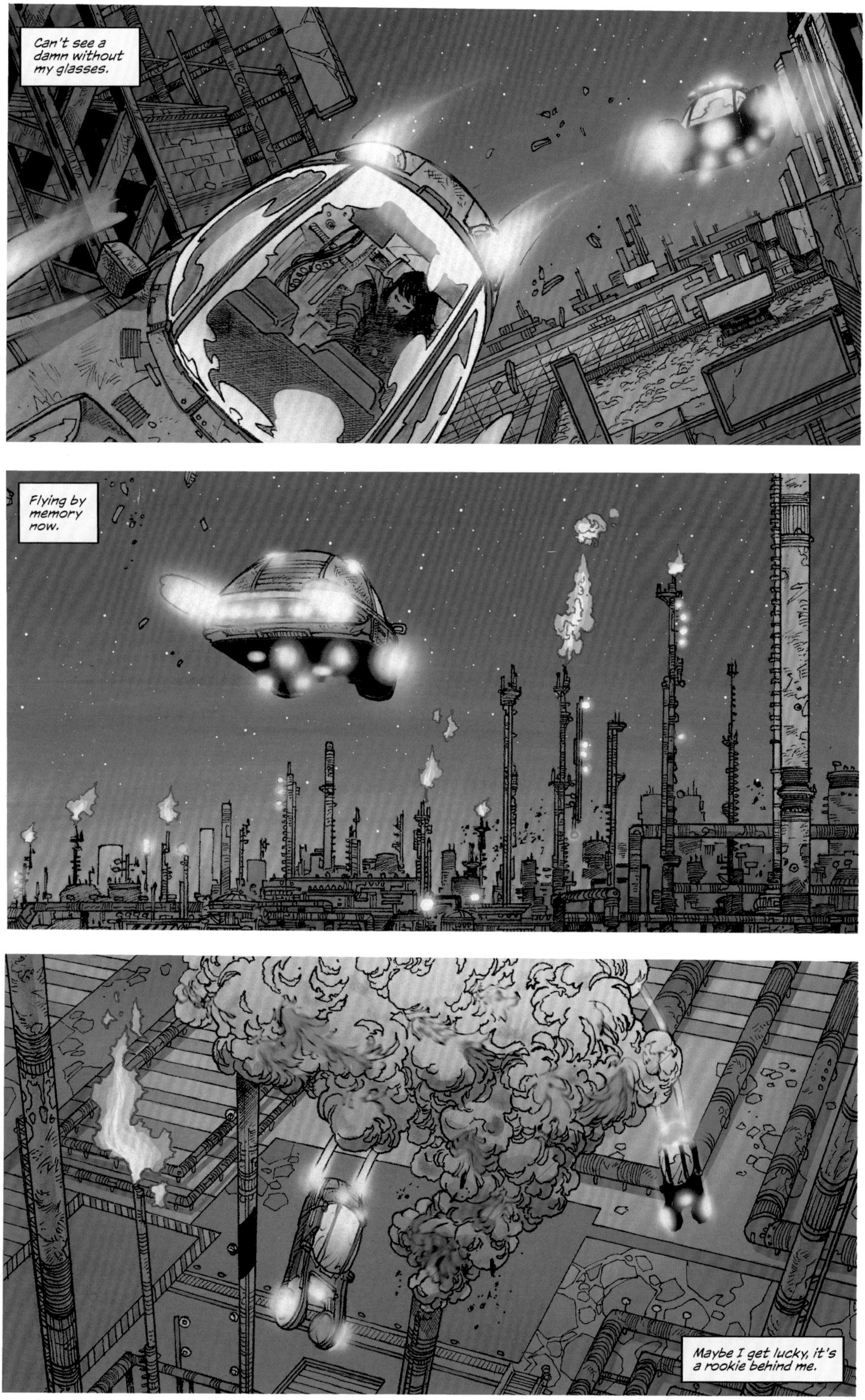
Can't see a damn without my glasses.
Flying by memory now.
Maybe I get lucky, it's a rookie behind me.

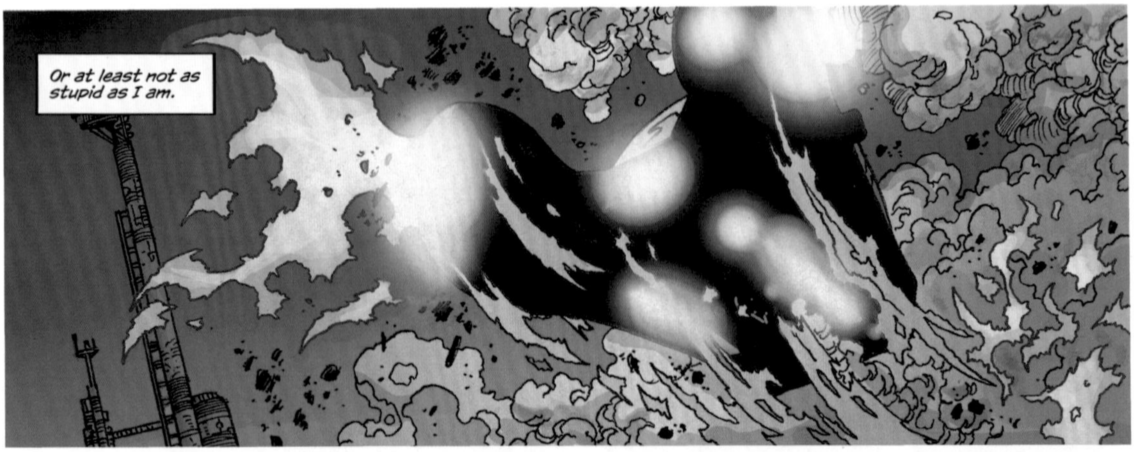
Or at least not as stupid as I am.
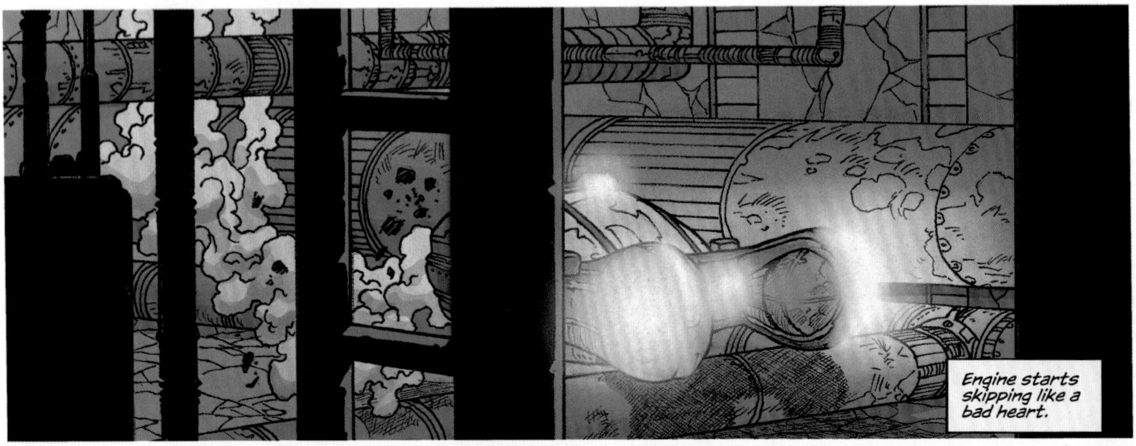
Engine starts skipping like a bad heart.
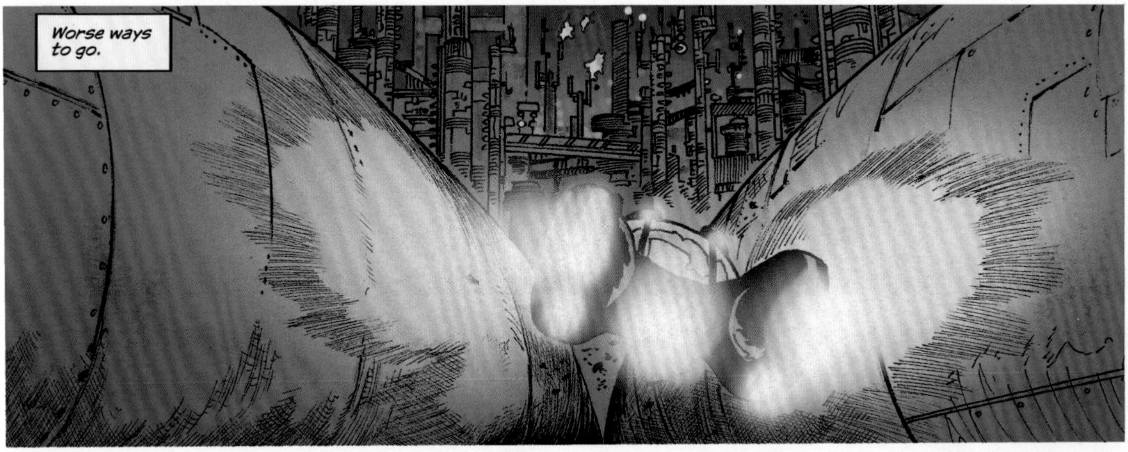
Worse ways to go.
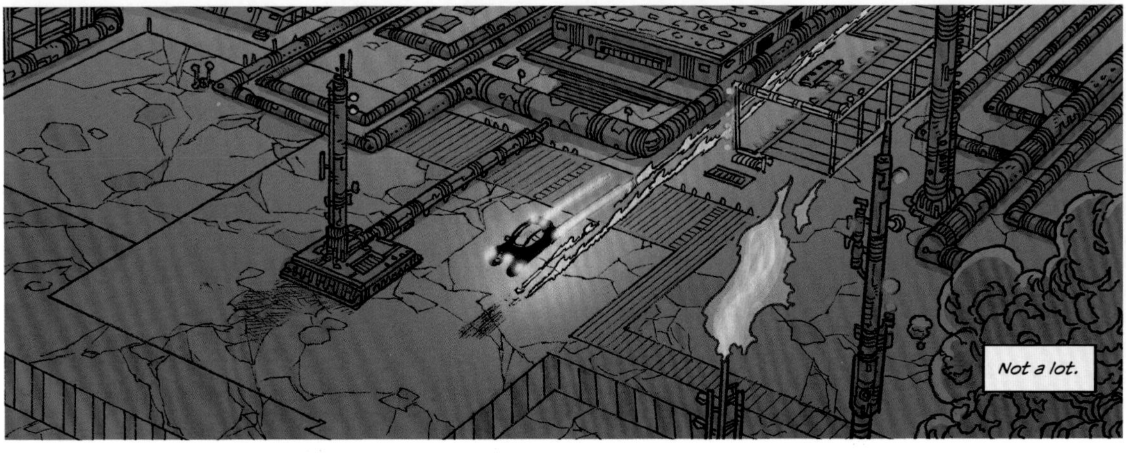
Not a lot.

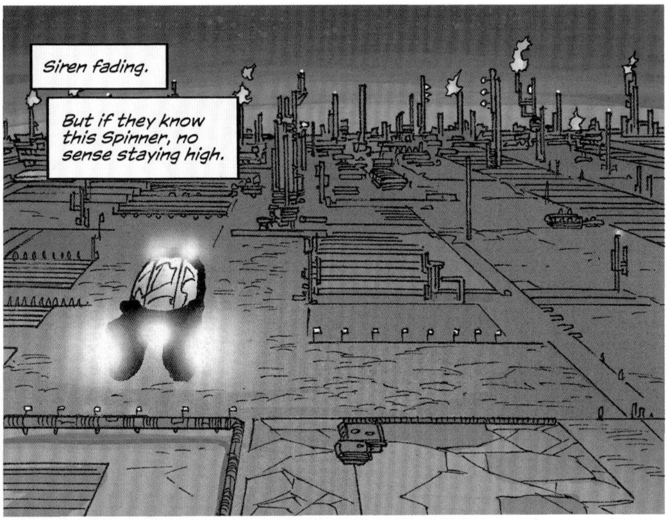
Siren fading.
But if they know this Spinner, no sense staying high.

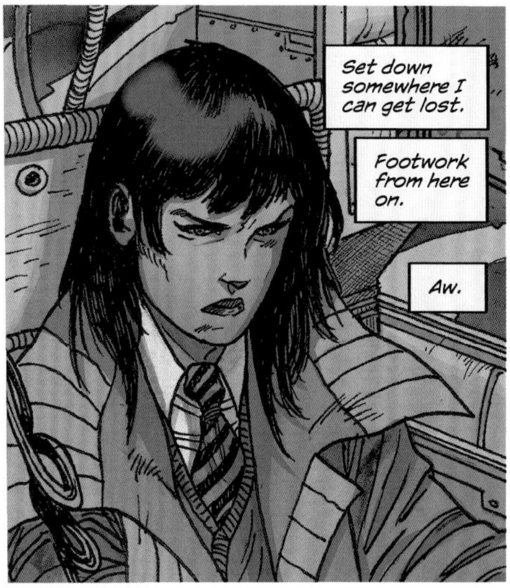
Set down somewhere I can get lost.
Footwork from here on.
Aw.

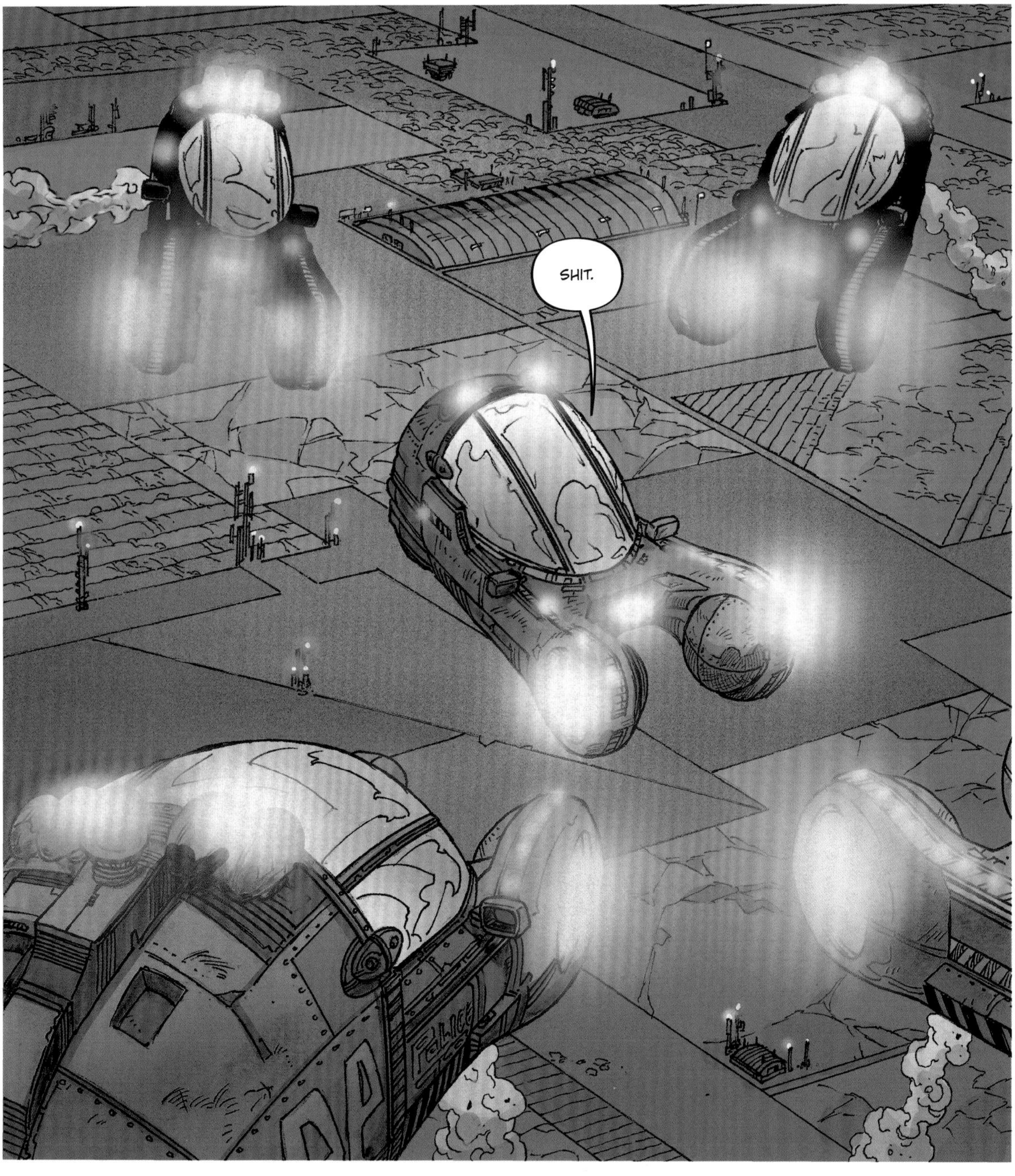
SHIT.

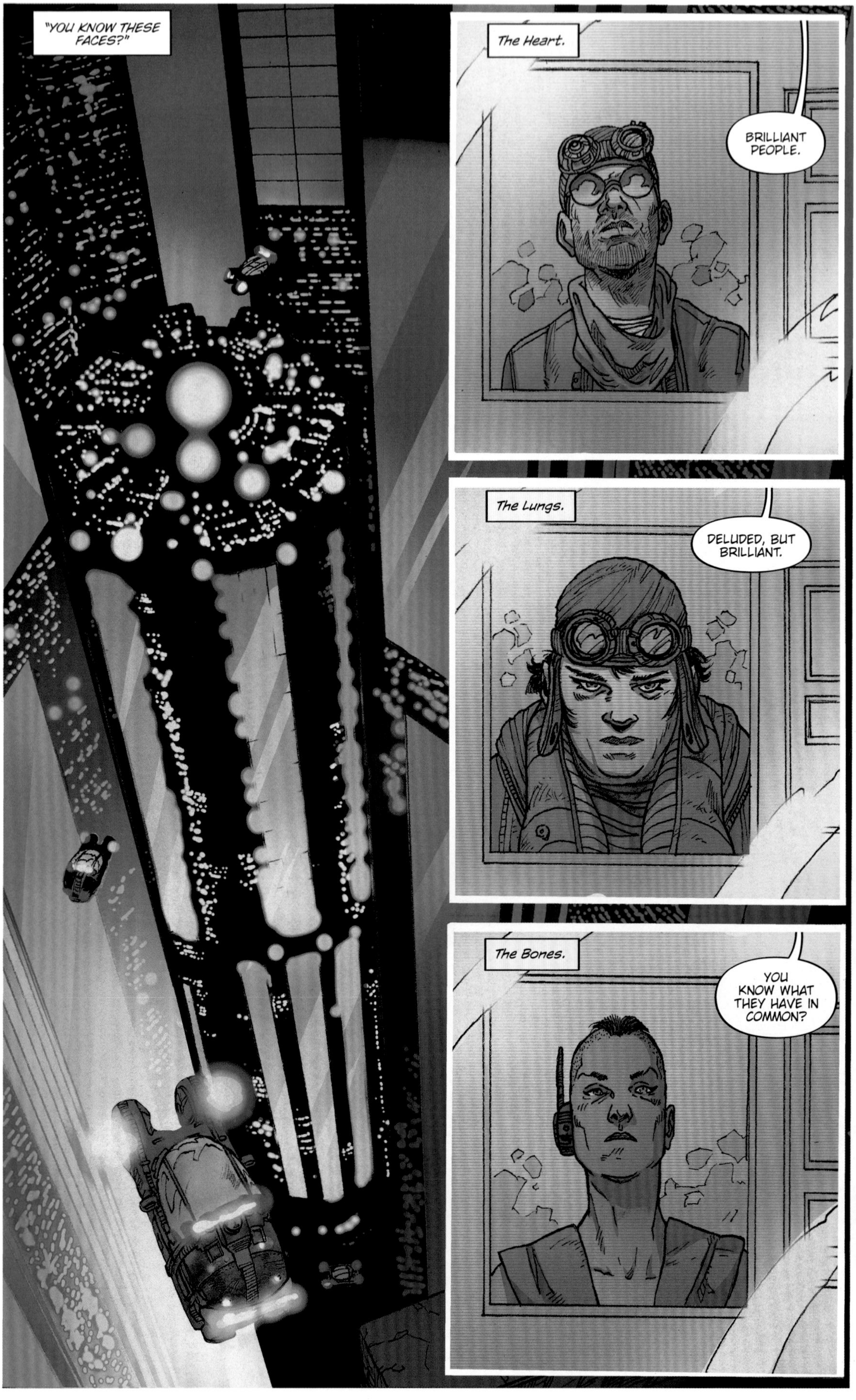
"YOU KNOW THESE FACES?"
The Heart.
BRILLIANT PEOPLE.
The Lungs.
DELUDED, BUT BRILLIANT.
The Bones.
YOU KNOW WHAT THEY HAVE IN COMMON?

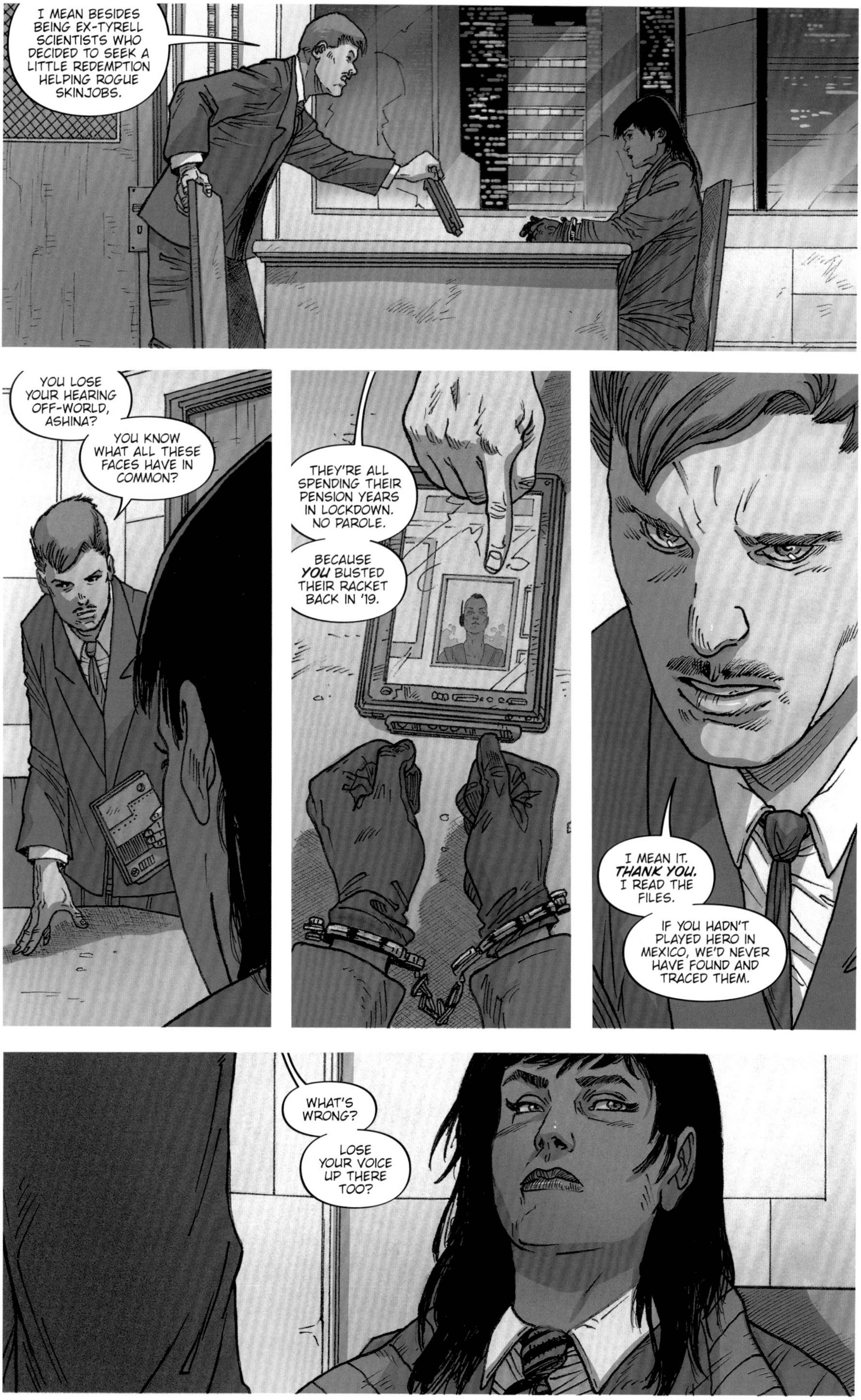
I MEAN BESIDES BEING EX-TYRELL SCIENTISTS WHO DECIDED TO SEEK A LITTLE REDEMPTION HELPING ROGUE SKINJOBS.
YOU LOSE YOUR HEARING OFF-WORLD, ASHINA?
YOU KNOW WHAT ALL THESE FACES HAVE IN COMMON?
THEY'RE ALL SPENDING THEIR PENSION YEARS IN LOCKDOWN. NO PAROLE.
BECAUSE ***YOU*** BUSTED THEIR RACKET BACK IN '19.
I MEAN IT. ***THANK YOU.*** I READ THE FILES.
IF YOU HADN'T PLAYED HERO IN MEXICO, WE'D NEVER HAVE FOUND AND TRACED THEM.
WHAT'S WRONG?
LOSE YOUR VOICE UP THERE TOO?

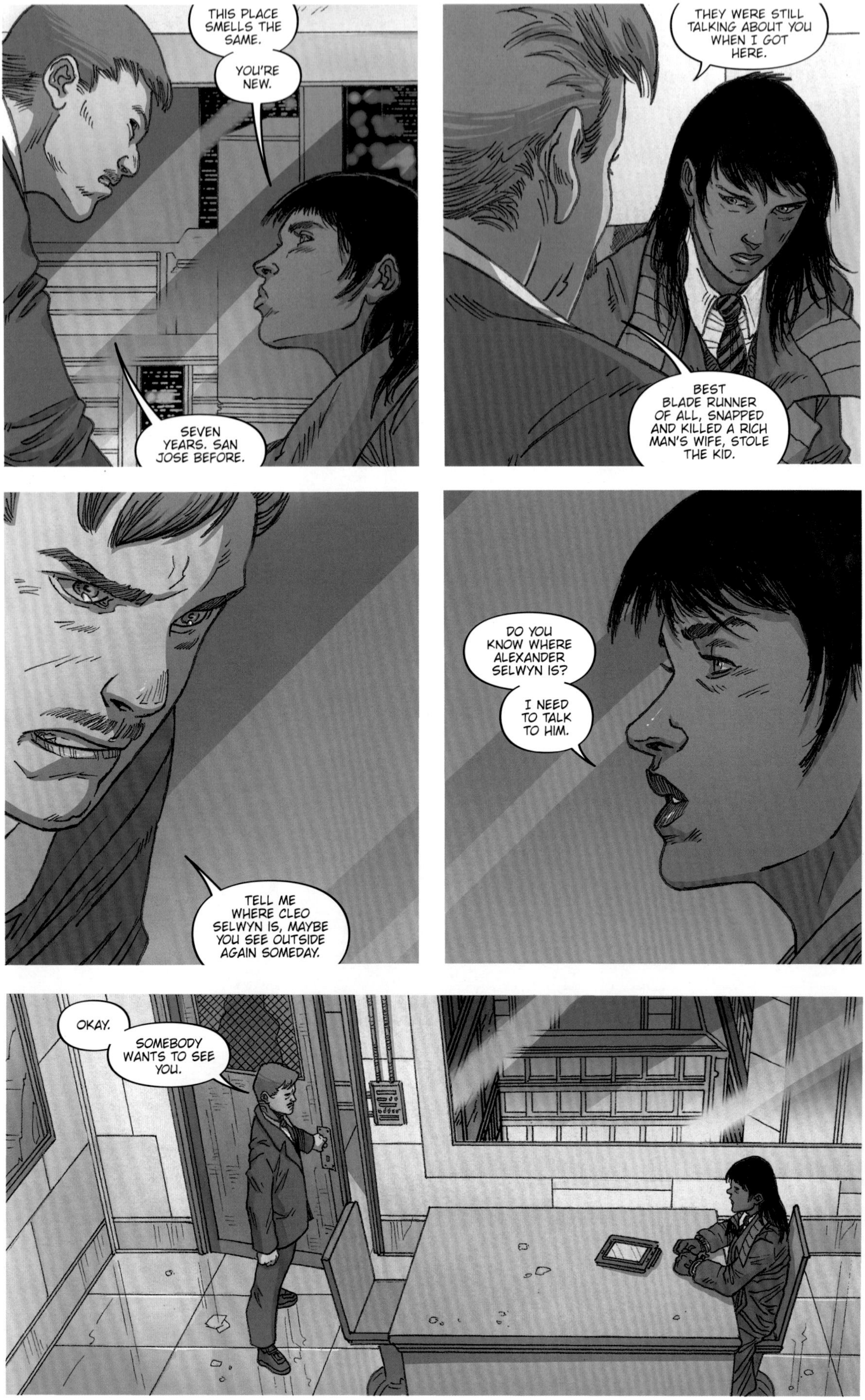
THIS PLACE SMELLS THE SAME.
YOU'RE NEW.
SEVEN YEARS. SAN JOSE BEFORE.
THEY WERE STILL TALKING ABOUT YOU WHEN I GOT HERE.
BEST BLADE RUNNER OF ALL, SNAPPED AND KILLED A RICH MAN'S WIFE, STOLE THE KID.
TELL ME WHERE CLEO SELWYN IS, MAYBE YOU SEE OUTSIDE AGAIN SOMEDAY.
DO YOU KNOW WHERE ALEXANDER SELWYN IS?
I NEED TO TALK TO HIM.
OKAY.
SOMEBODY WANTS TO SEE YOU.

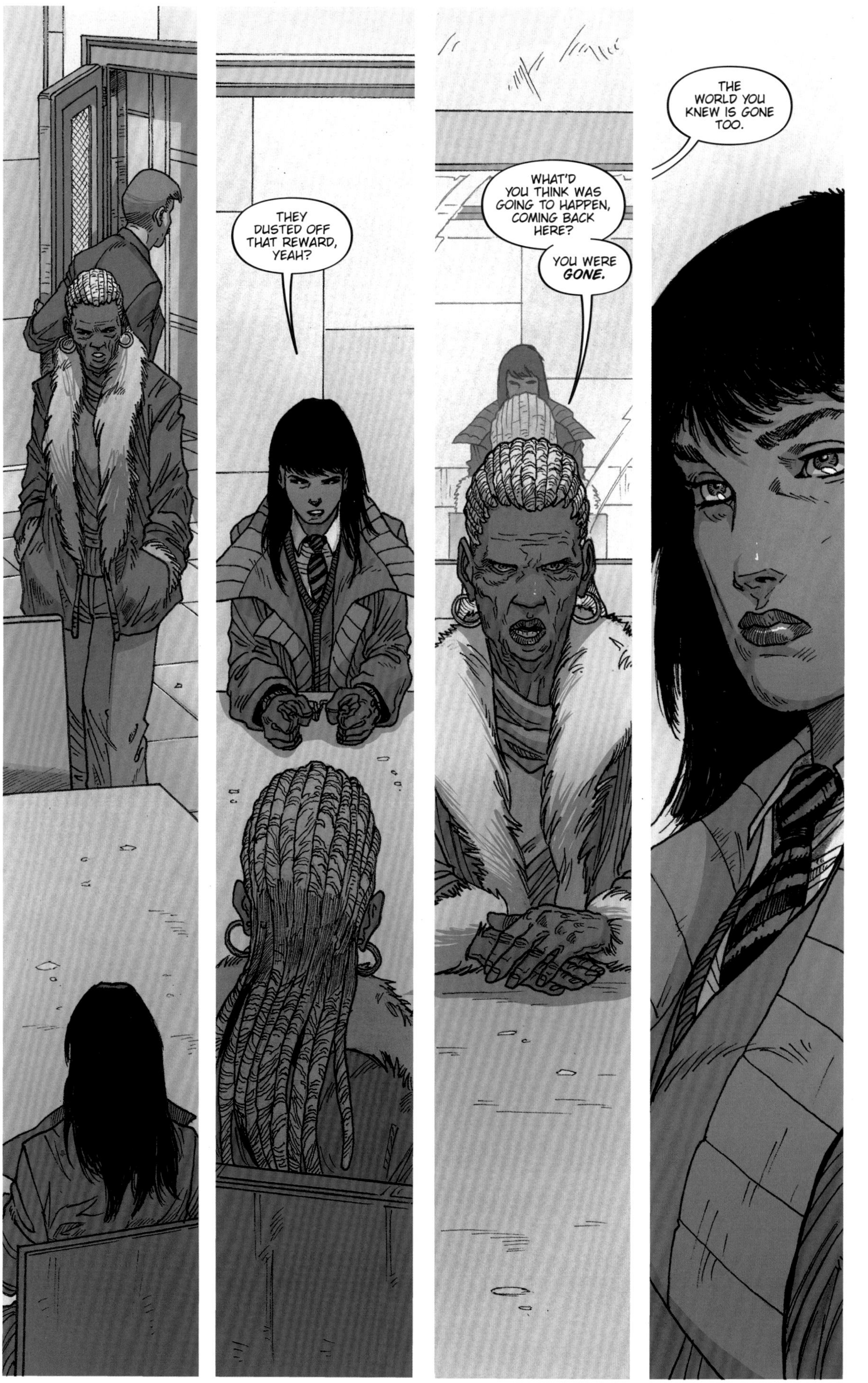
THEY DUSTED OFF THAT REWARD, YEAH?
WHAT'D YOU THINK WAS GOING TO HAPPEN, COMING BACK HERE?
YOU WERE **GONE.**
THE WORLD YOU KNEW IS GONE TOO.

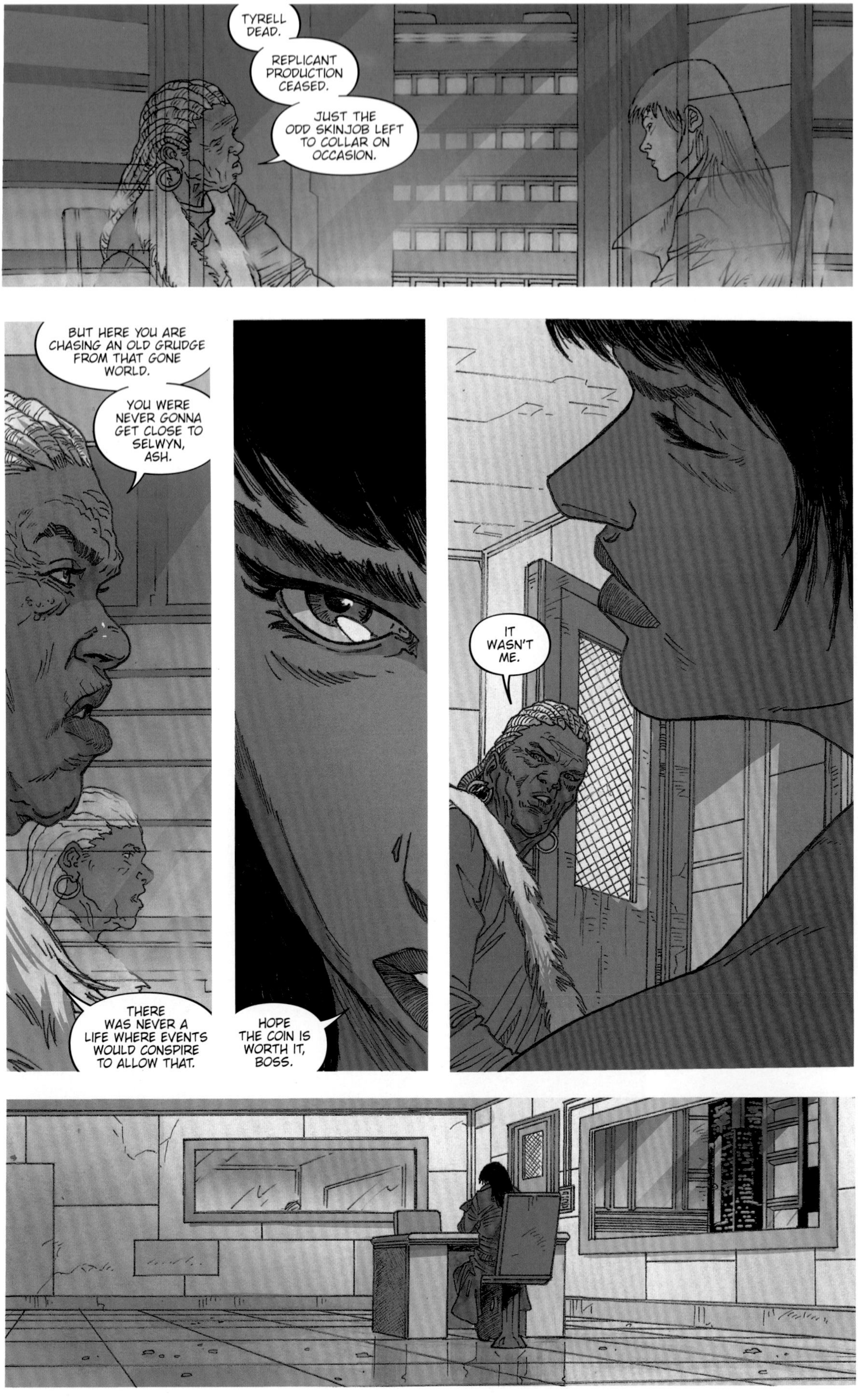
TYRELL DEAD.
REPLICANT PRODUCTION CEASED.
JUST THE ODD SKINJOB LEFT TO COLLAR ON OCCASION.
BUT HERE YOU ARE CHASING AN OLD GRUDGE FROM THAT GONE WORLD.
YOU WERE NEVER GONNA GET CLOSE TO SELWYN, ASH.
THERE WAS NEVER A LIFE WHERE EVENTS WOULD CONSPIRE TO ALLOW THAT.
HOPE THE COIN IS WORTH IT, BOSS.
IT WASN'T ME.

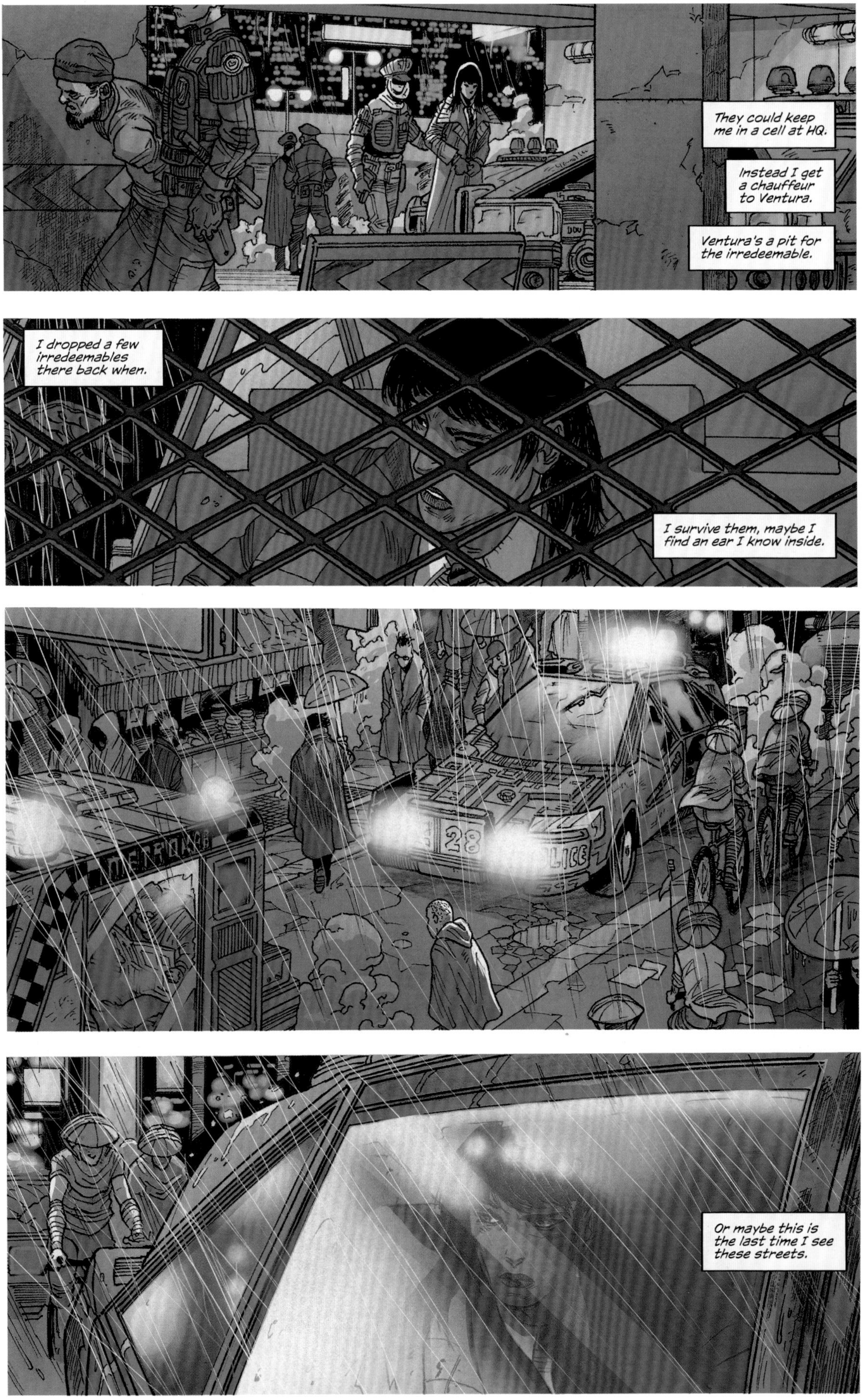

They could keep me in a cell at HQ.
Instead I get a chauffeur to Ventura.
Ventura's a pit for the irredeemable.
I dropped a few irredeemables there back when.
I survive them, maybe I find an ear I know inside.
28
Or maybe this is the last time I see these streets.

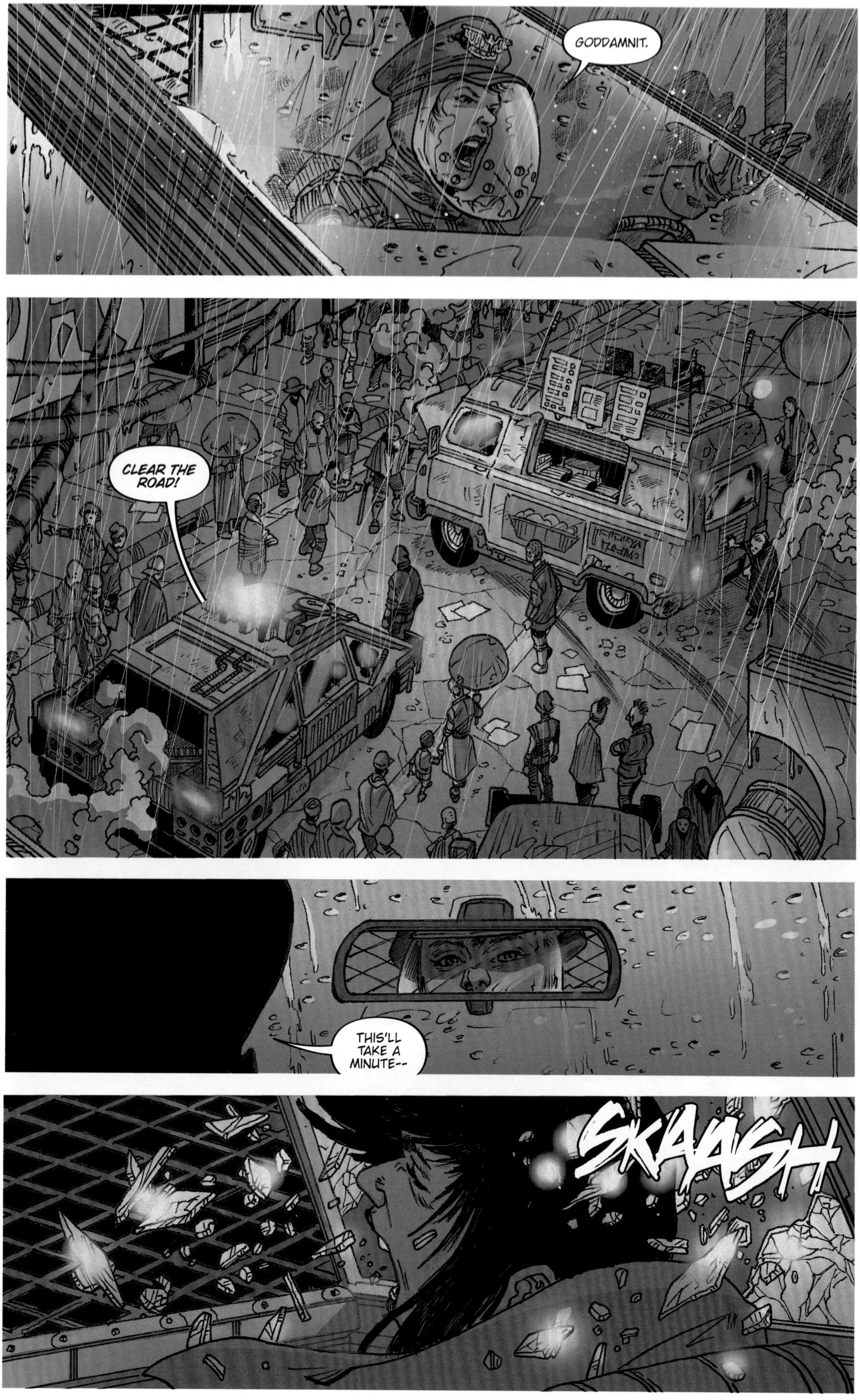
GODDAMNIT.
CLEAR THE ROAD!
THIS'LL TAKE A MINUTE--
SKAASH

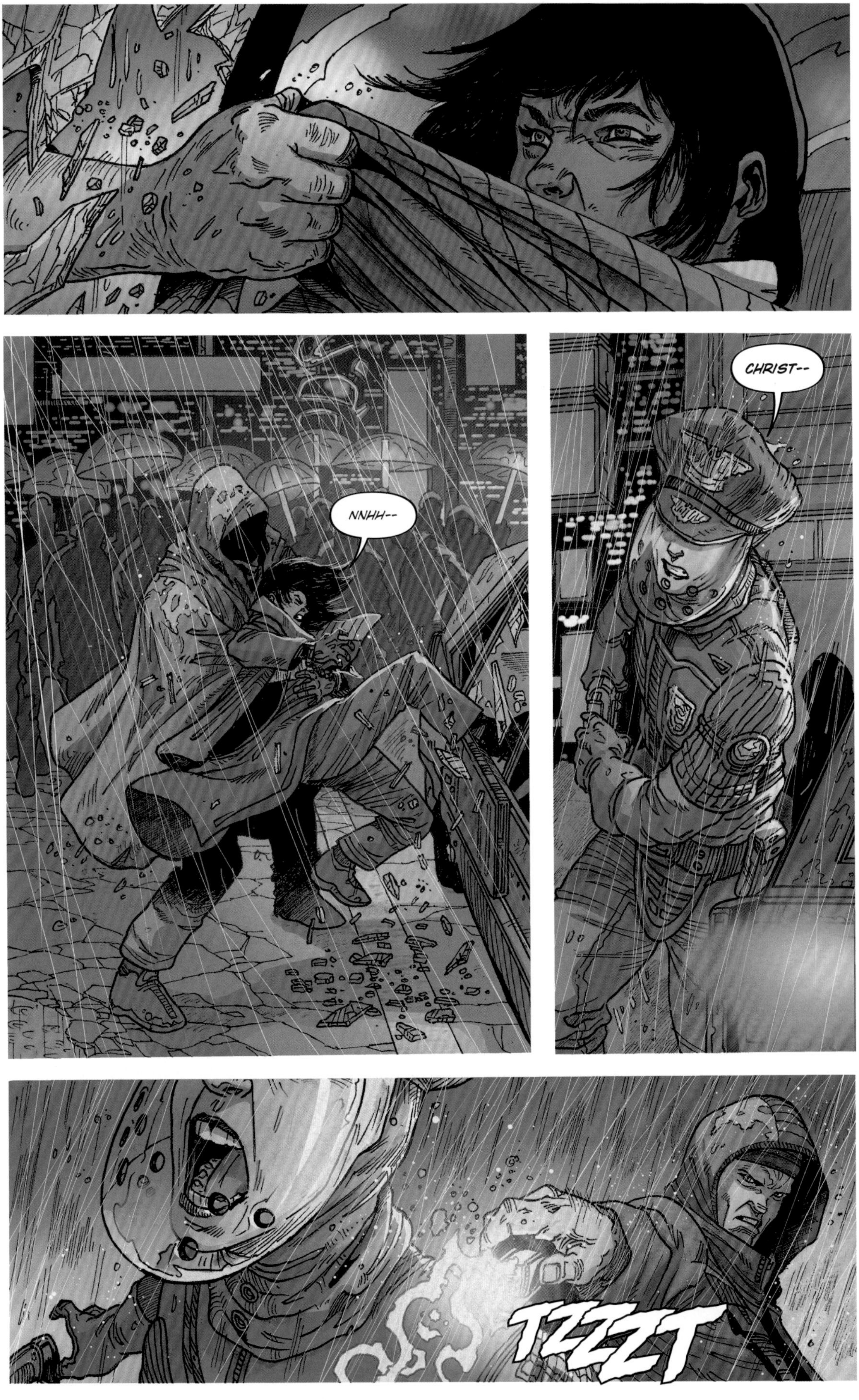
NNHH--
CHRIST--
TZZZT

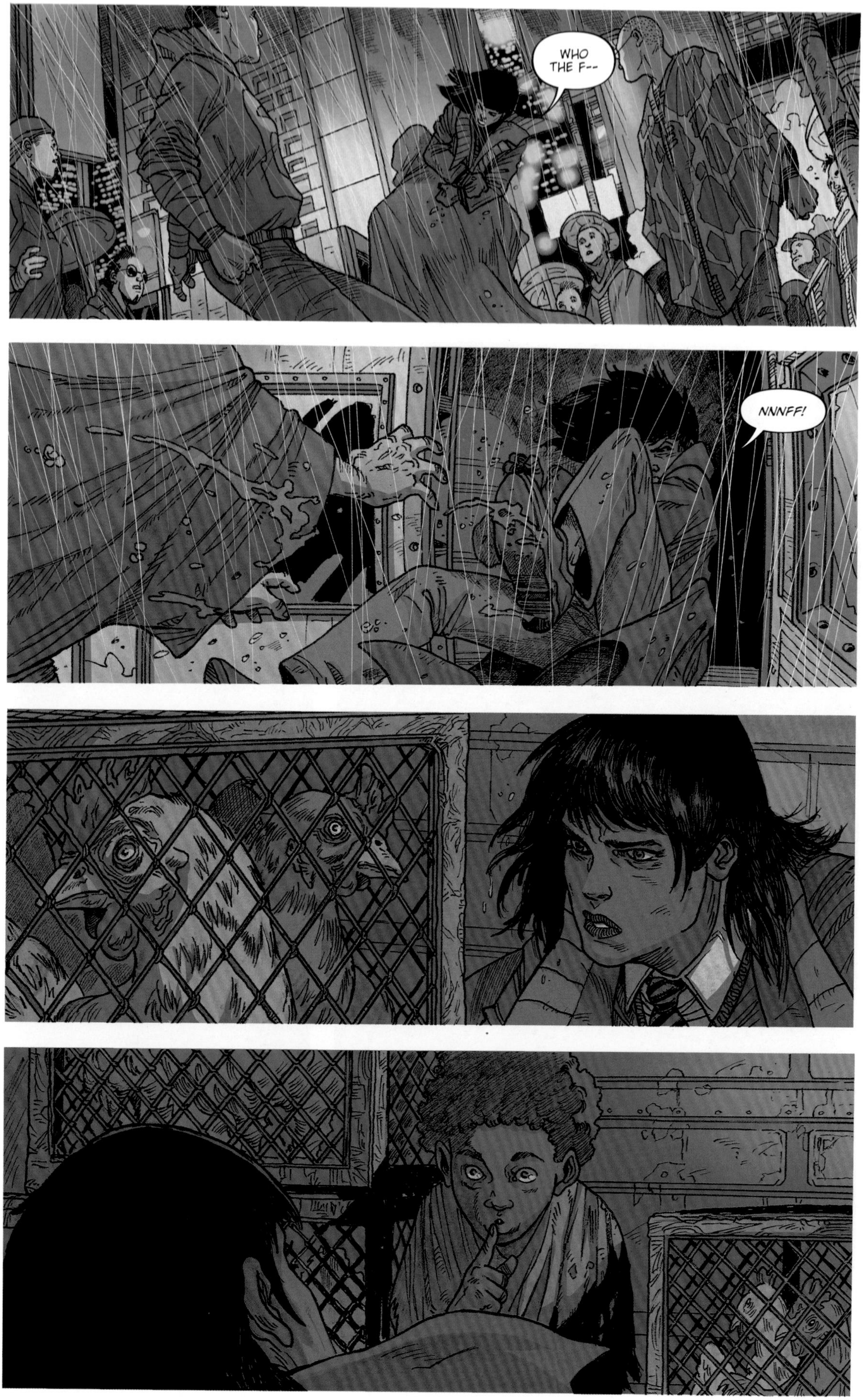
WHO THE F--
NNNFF!

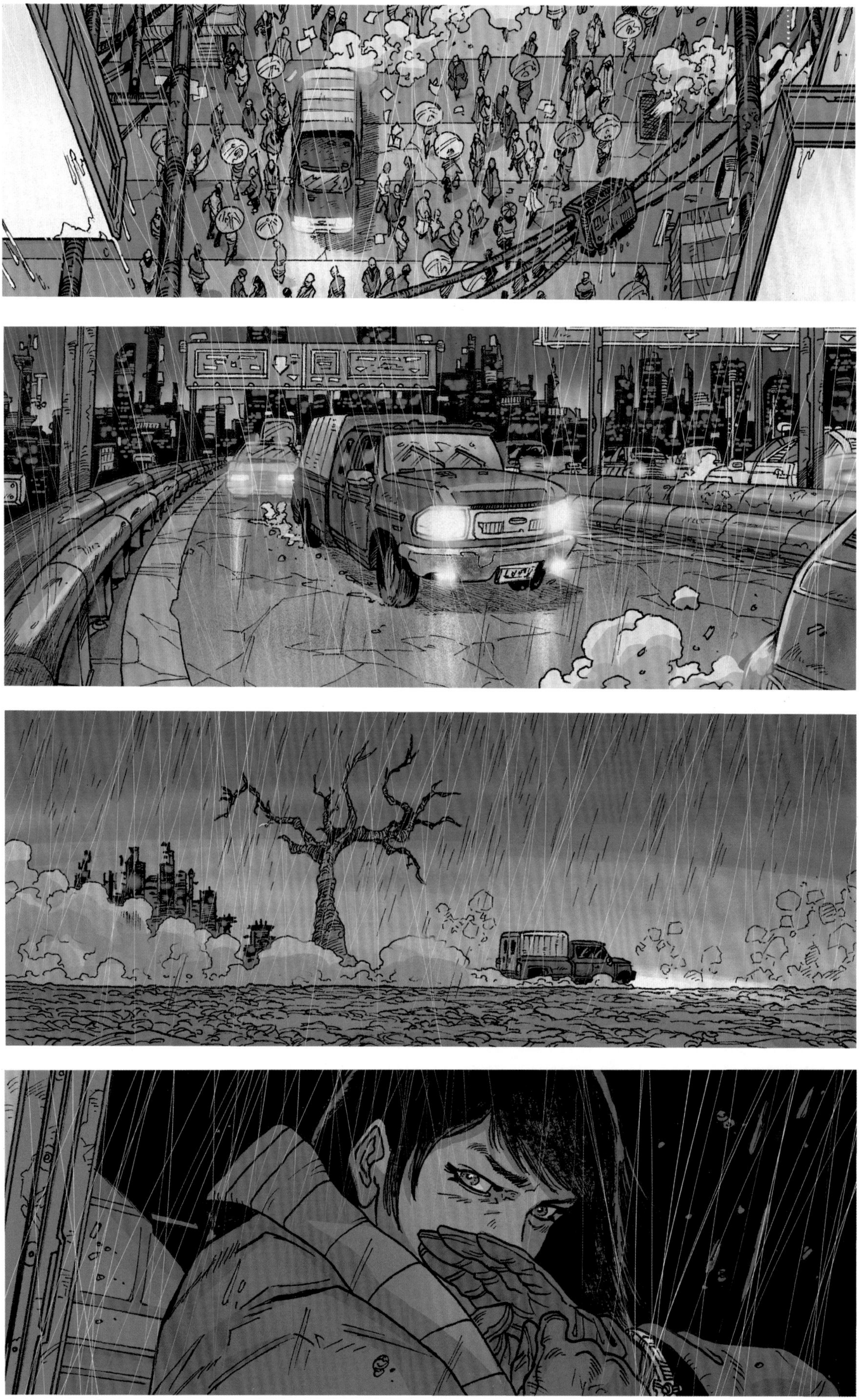

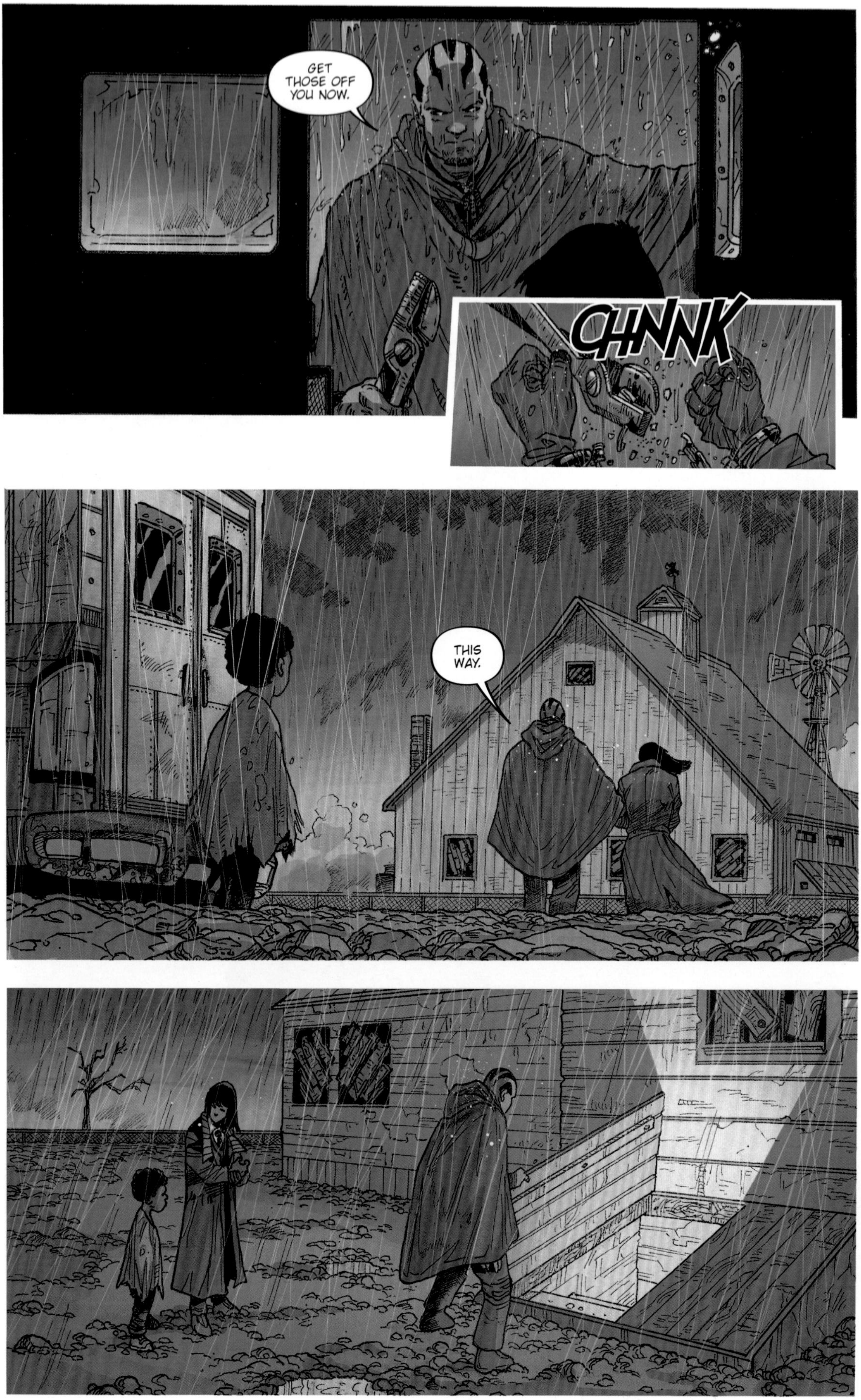
GET THOSE OFF YOU NOW.
CHNNK
THIS WAY.

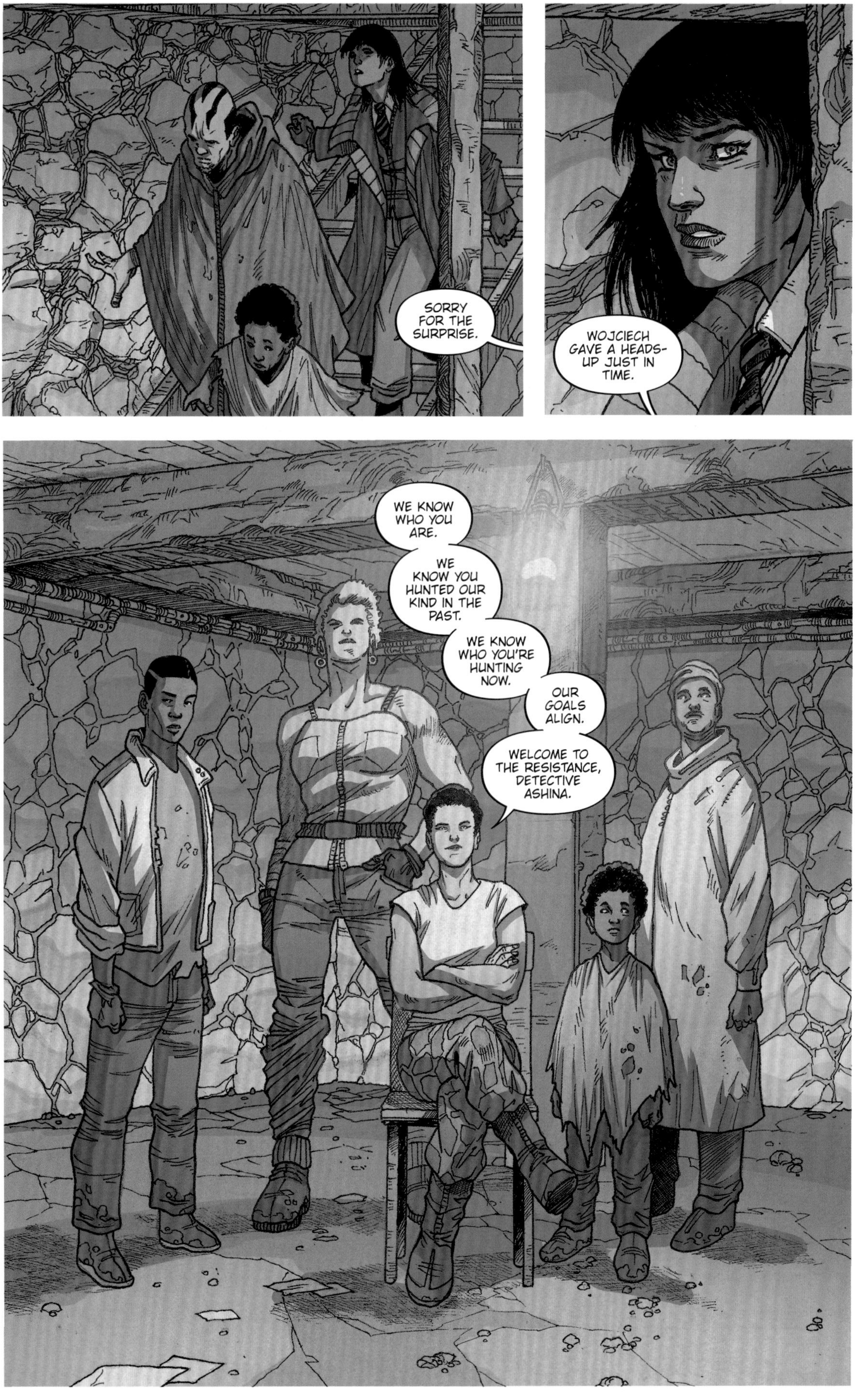
SORRY FOR THE SURPRISE.
WOJCIECH GAVE A HEADS-UP JUST IN TIME.
WE KNOW WHO YOU ARE.
WE KNOW YOU HUNTED OUR KIND IN THE PAST.
WE KNOW WHO YOU'RE HUNTING NOW.
OUR GOALS ALIGN.
WELCOME TO THE RESISTANCE, DETECTIVE ASHINA.

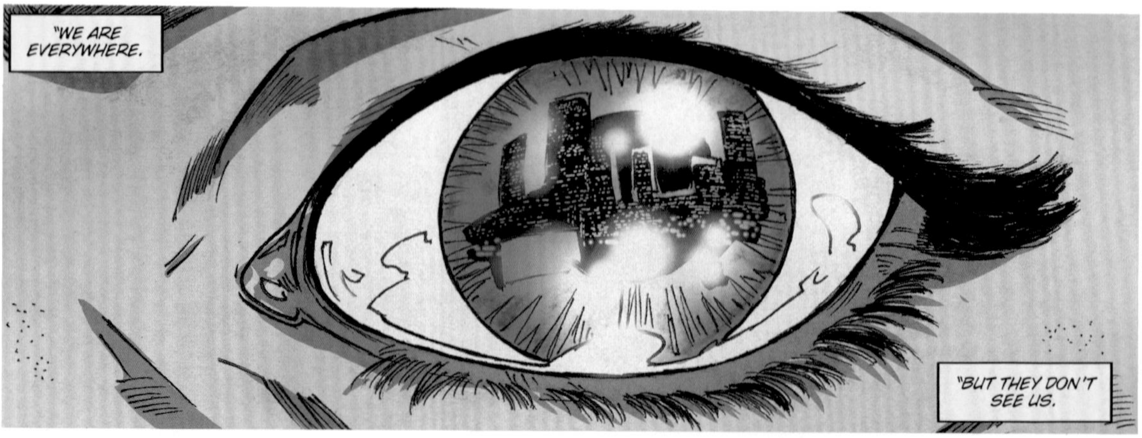
"WE ARE EVERYWHERE.
"BUT THEY DON'T SEE US.

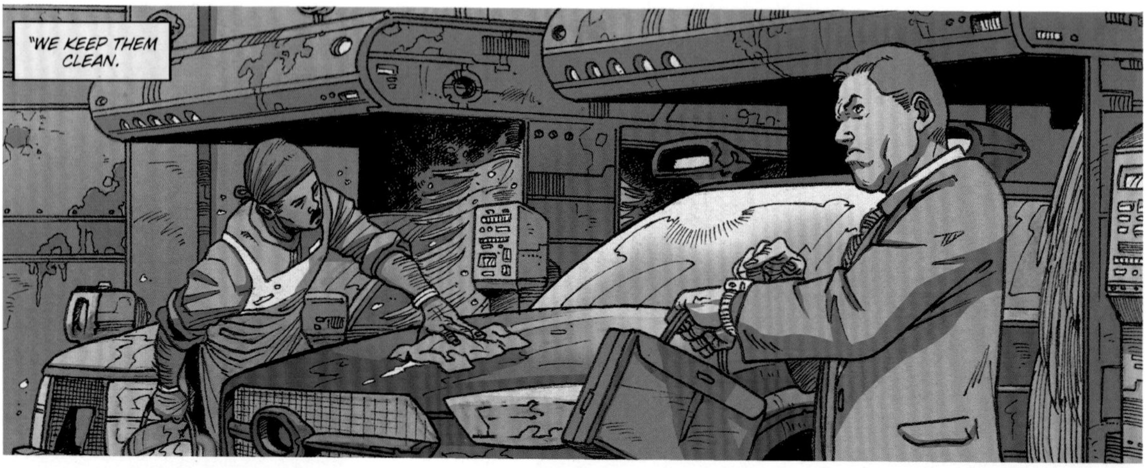
"WE KEEP THEM CLEAN.

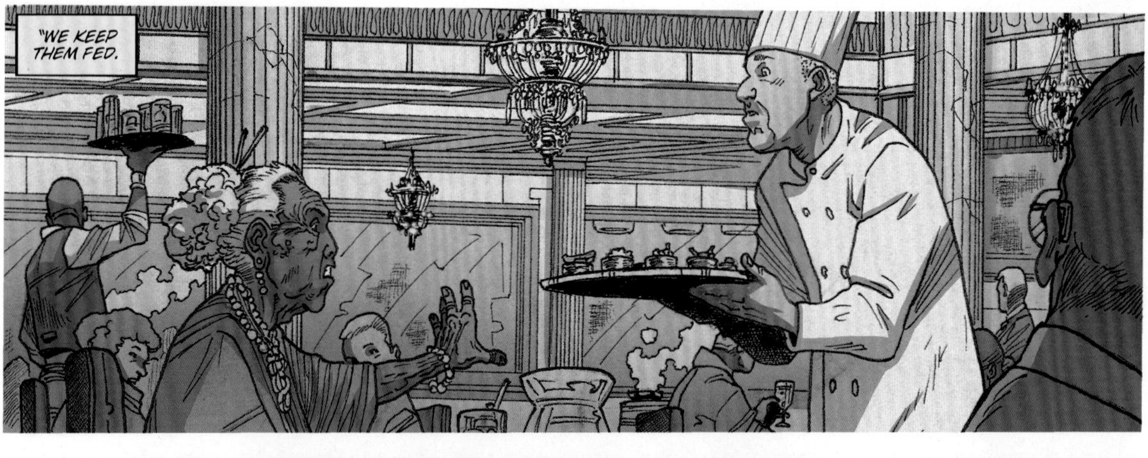
"WE KEEP THEM FED.

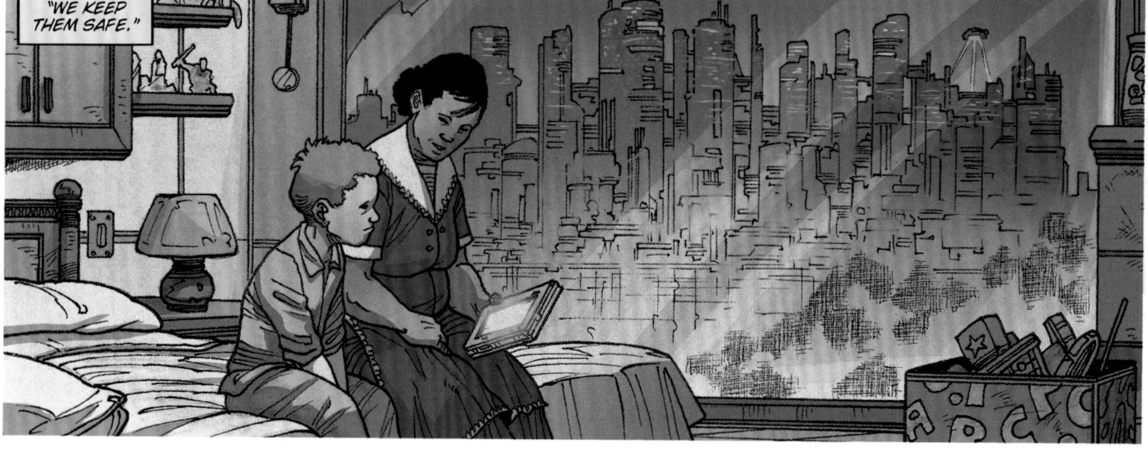
"WE KEEP THEM SAFE."

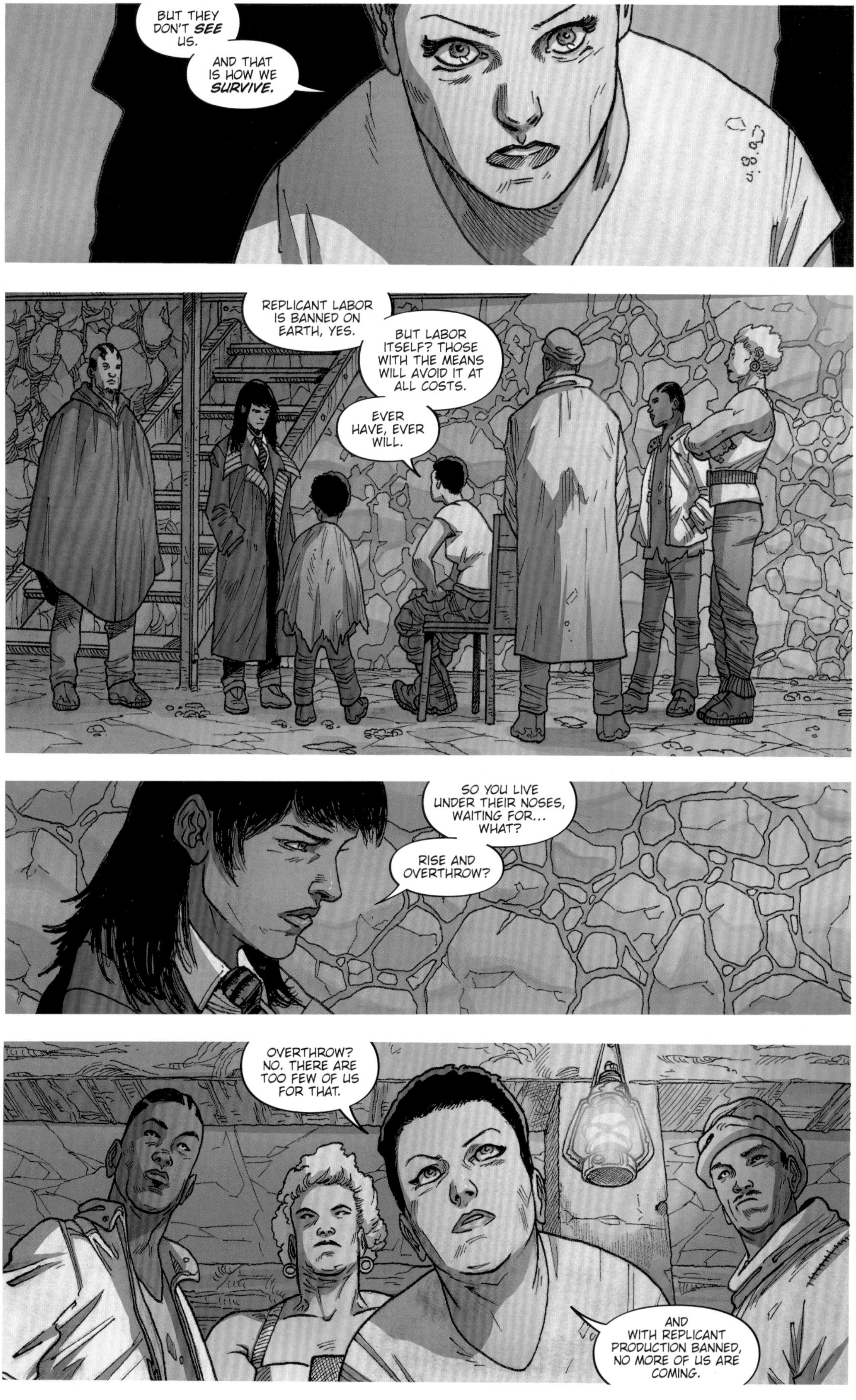
BUT THEY DON'T **SEE** US.
AND THAT IS HOW WE ***SURVIVE.***
REPLICANT LABOR IS BANNED ON EARTH, YES.
BUT LABOR ITSELF? THOSE WITH THE MEANS WILL AVOID IT AT ALL COSTS.
EVER HAVE, EVER WILL.
SO YOU LIVE UNDER THEIR NOSES, WAITING FOR... WHAT?
RISE AND OVERTHROW?
OVERTHROW? NO. THERE ARE TOO FEW OF US FOR THAT.
AND WITH REPLICANT PRODUCTION BANNED, NO MORE OF US ARE COMING.

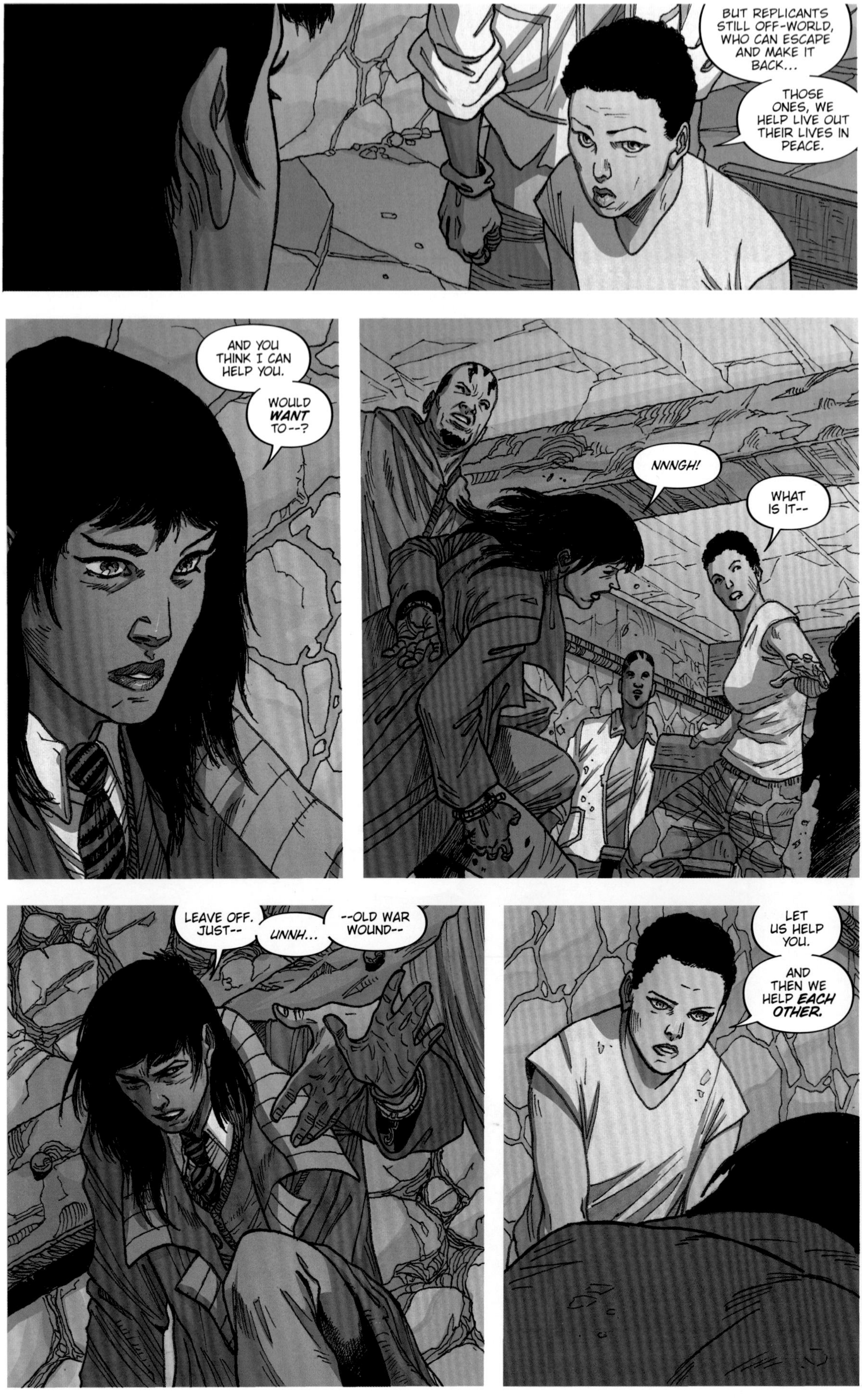
BUT REPLICANTS STILL OFF-WORLD, WHO CAN ESCAPE AND MAKE IT BACK...
THOSE ONES, WE HELP LIVE OUT THEIR LIVES IN PEACE.
AND YOU THINK I CAN HELP YOU.
WOULD *WANT* TO--?
NNNGH!
WHAT IS IT--
LEAVE OFF. JUST--
UNNH...
--OLD WAR WOUND--
LET US HELP YOU.
AND THEN WE HELP *EACH OTHER.*

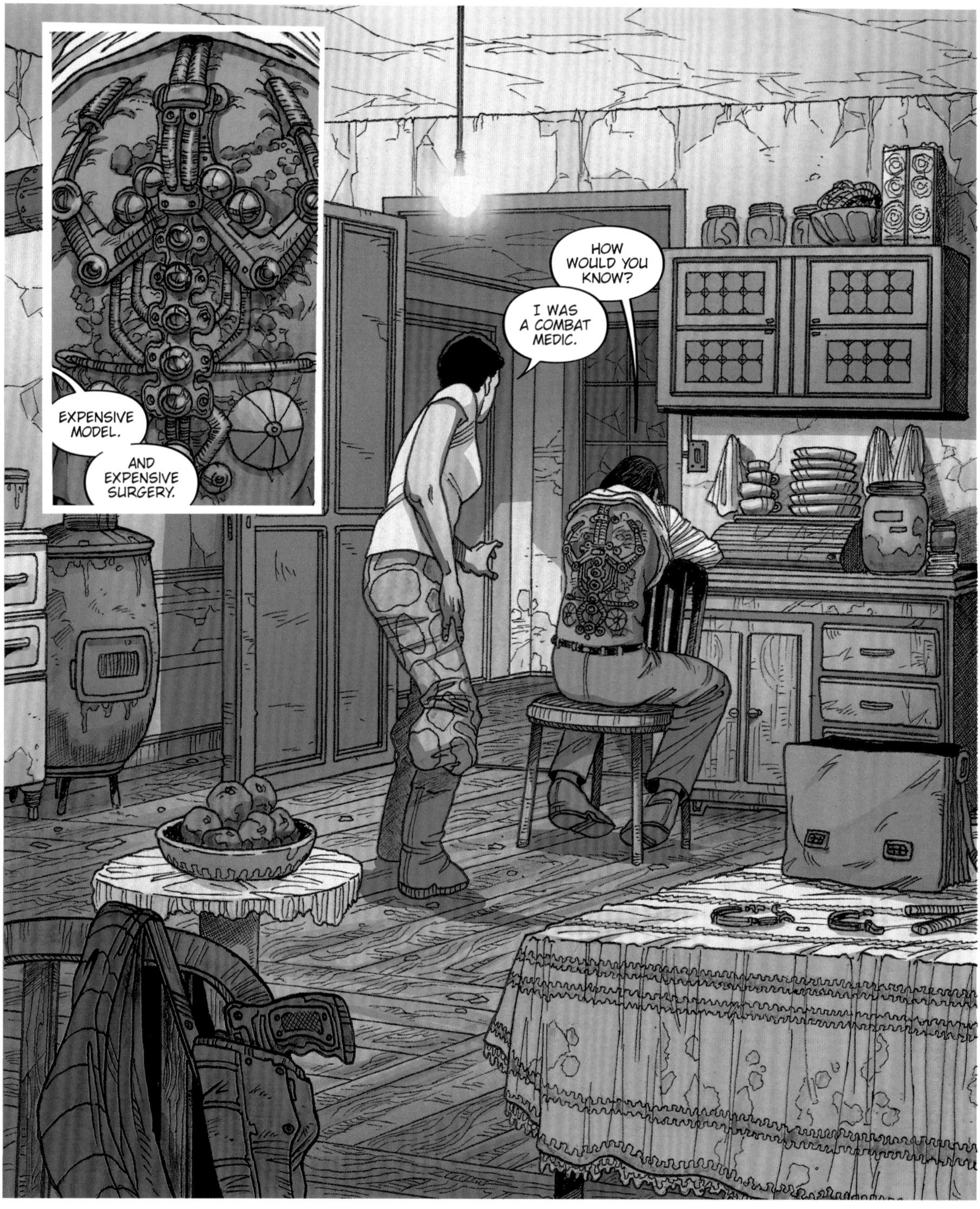
EXPENSIVE MODEL.
AND EXPENSIVE SURGERY.
HOW WOULD YOU KNOW?
I WAS A COMBAT MEDIC.

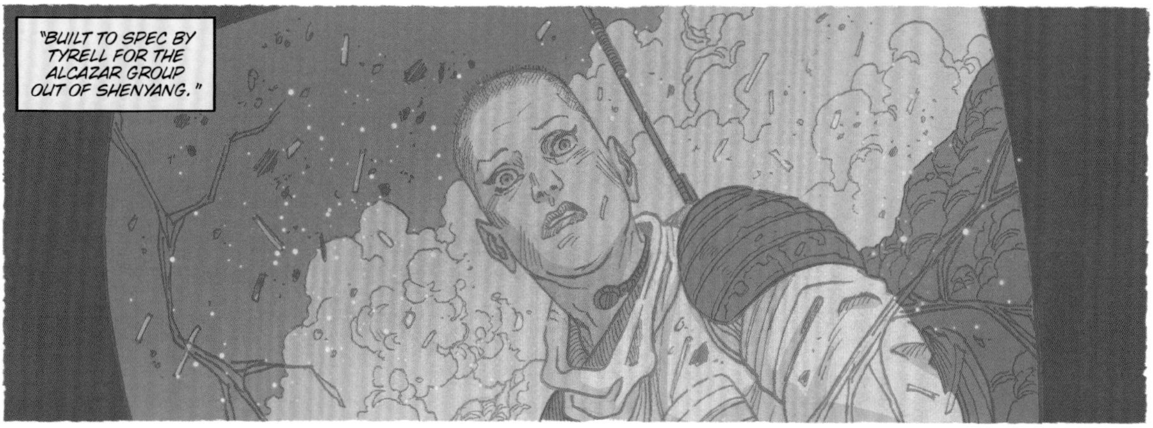
"BUILT TO SPEC BY TYRELL FOR THE ALCAZAR GROUP OUT OF SHENYANG."

FIVE TOURS ON KALANTHIA AND THE CERIUM BELT...

"...FOUR MORE IN THE TRENCHES AFTER THE VIDAR TAKEOVER KICKED OFF."

SO YEAH, I'VE SEEN--AND *FIXED*--MY SHARE OF SPINE-RIGS.

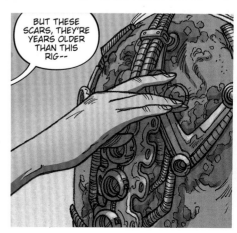

BUT THESE SCARS, THEY'RE YEARS OLDER THAN THIS RIG--

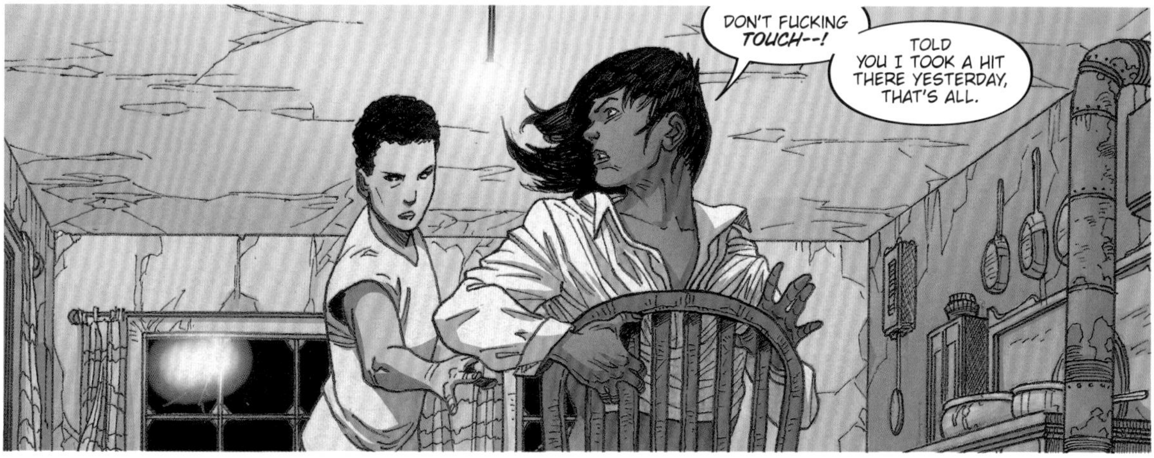
DON'T FUCKING *TOUCH--!*
TOLD YOU I TOOK A HIT THERE YESTERDAY, THAT'S ALL.

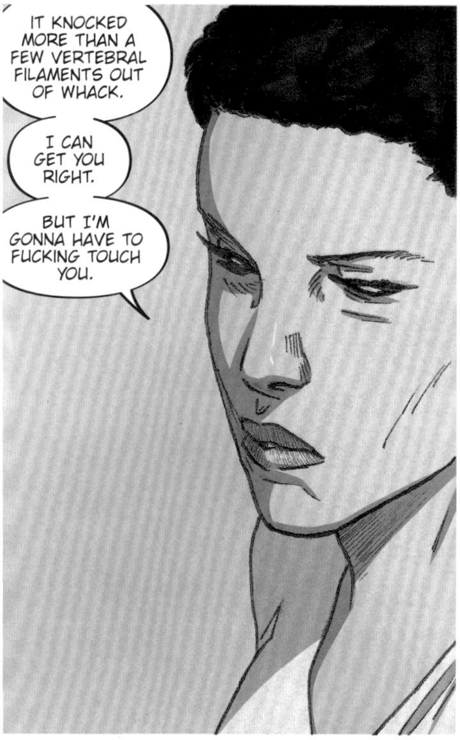
IT KNOCKED MORE THAN A FEW VERTEBRAL FILAMENTS OUT OF WHACK.
I CAN GET YOU RIGHT.
BUT I'M GONNA HAVE TO FUCKING TOUCH YOU.

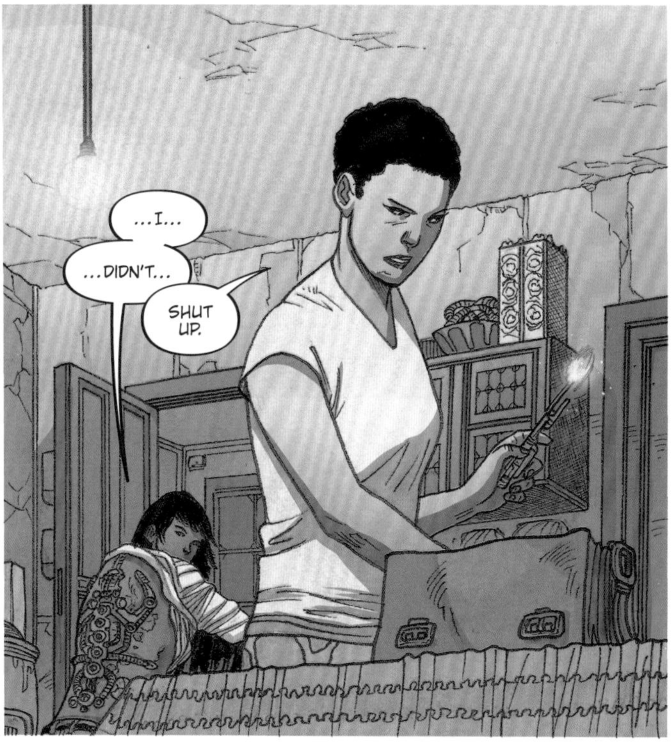
...I...
...DIDN'T...
SHUT UP.

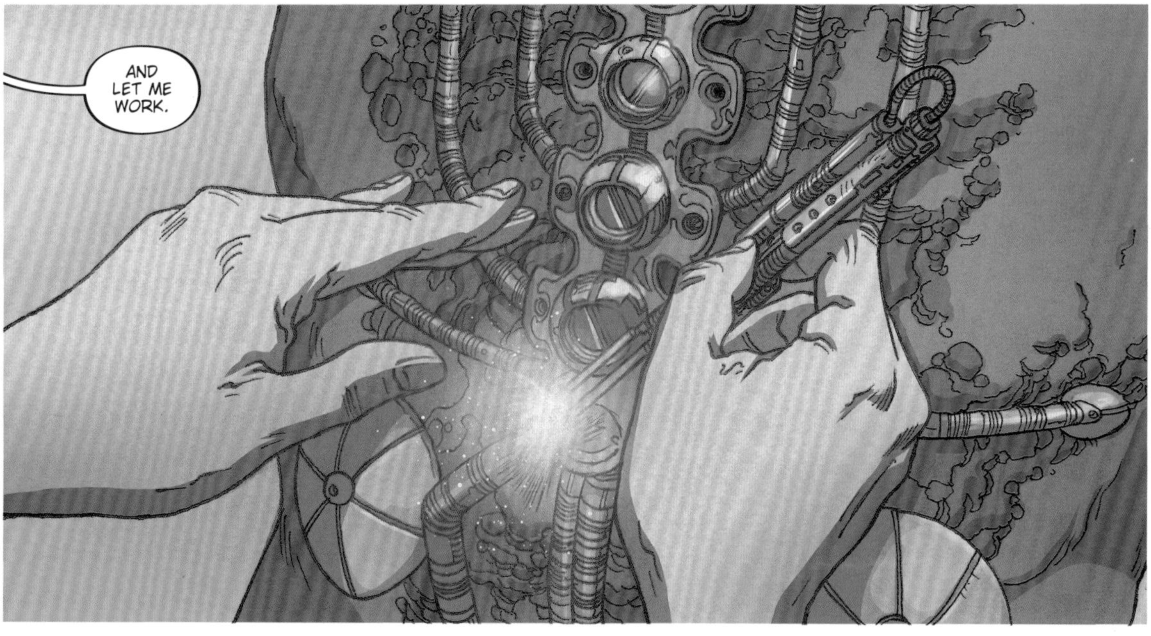
AND LET ME WORK.

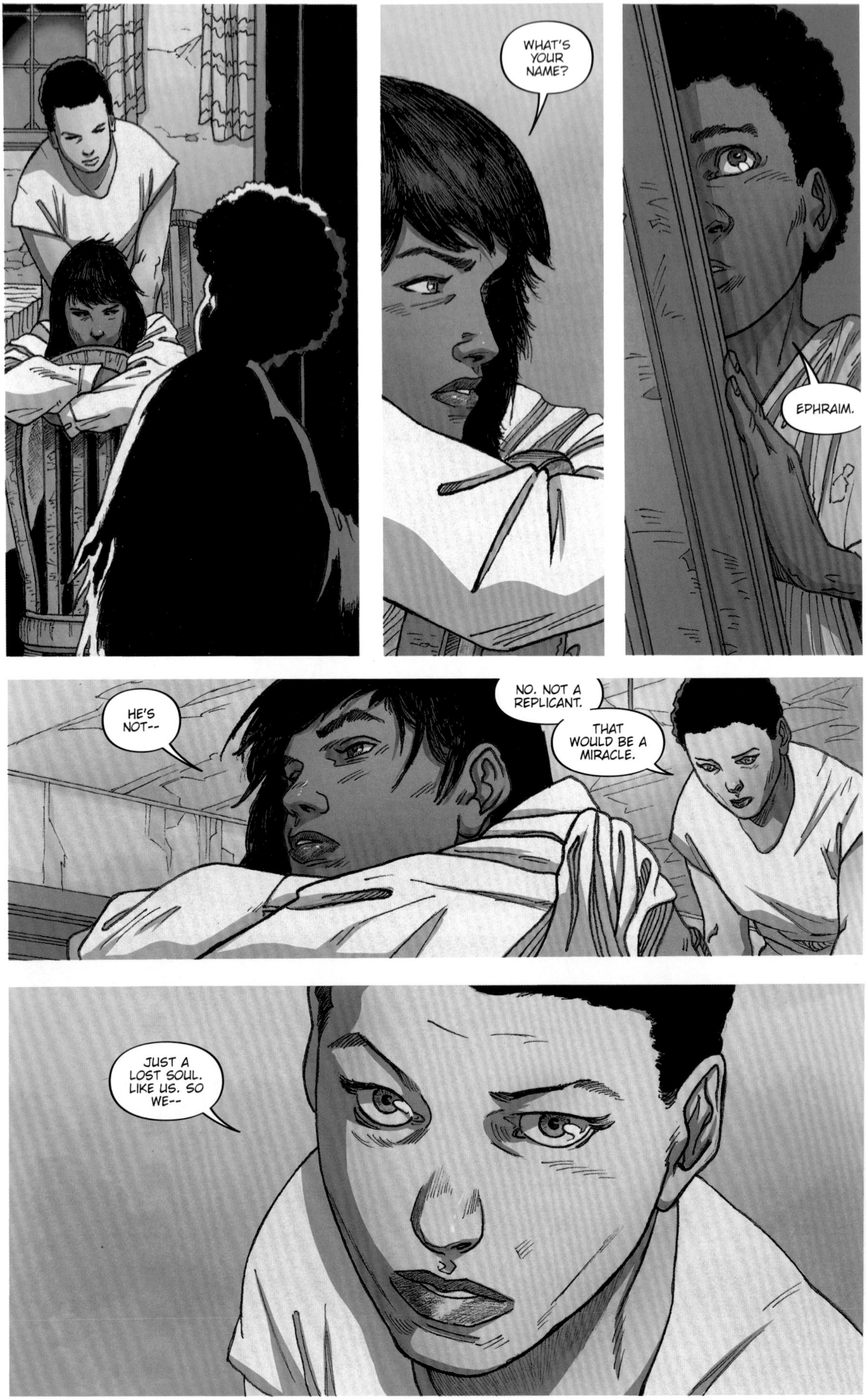
WHAT'S YOUR NAME?
EPHRAIM.
HE'S NOT--
NO. NOT A REPLICANT.
THAT WOULD BE A MIRACLE.
JUST A LOST SOUL. LIKE US. SO WE--

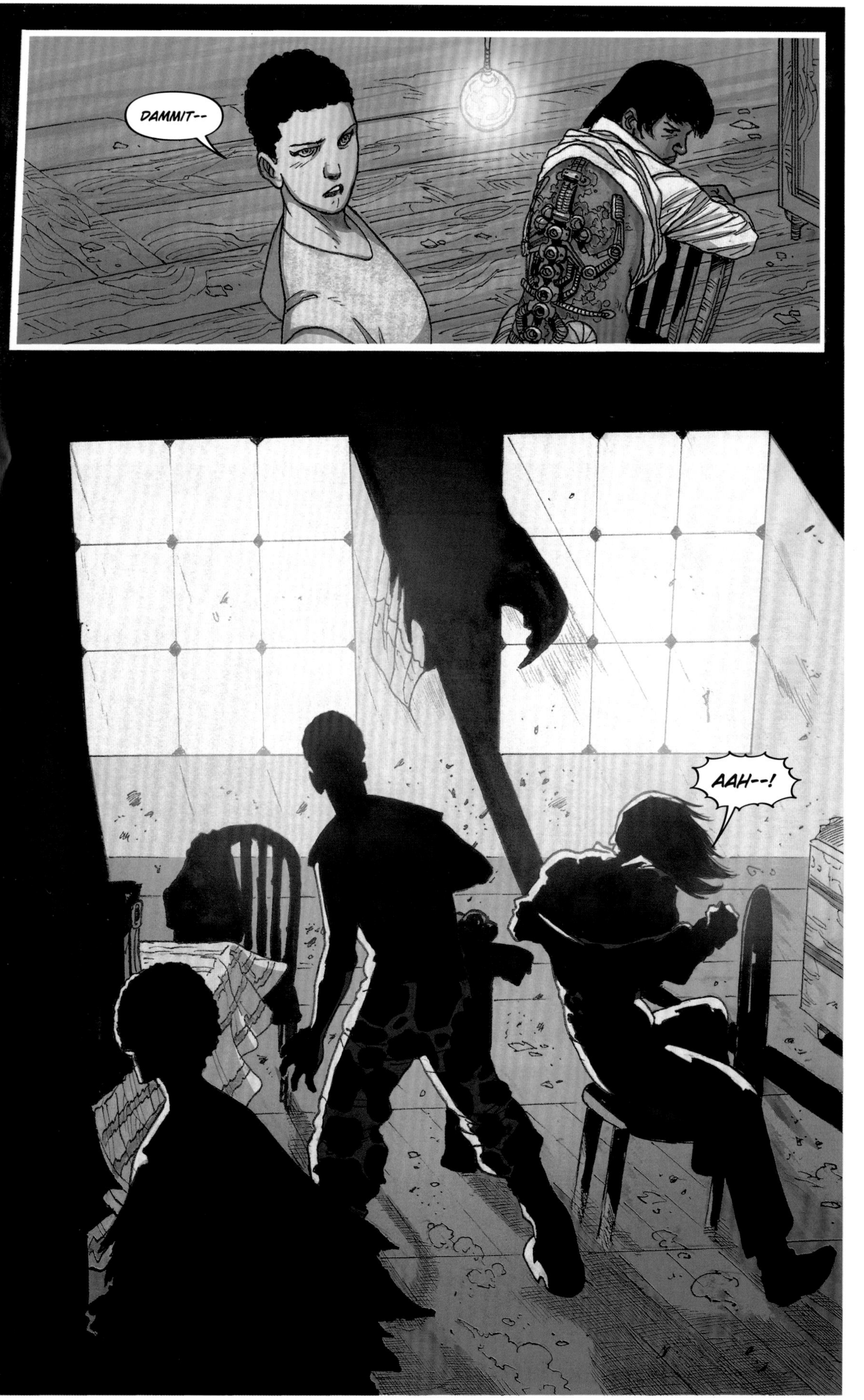
DAMMIT--
AAH--!

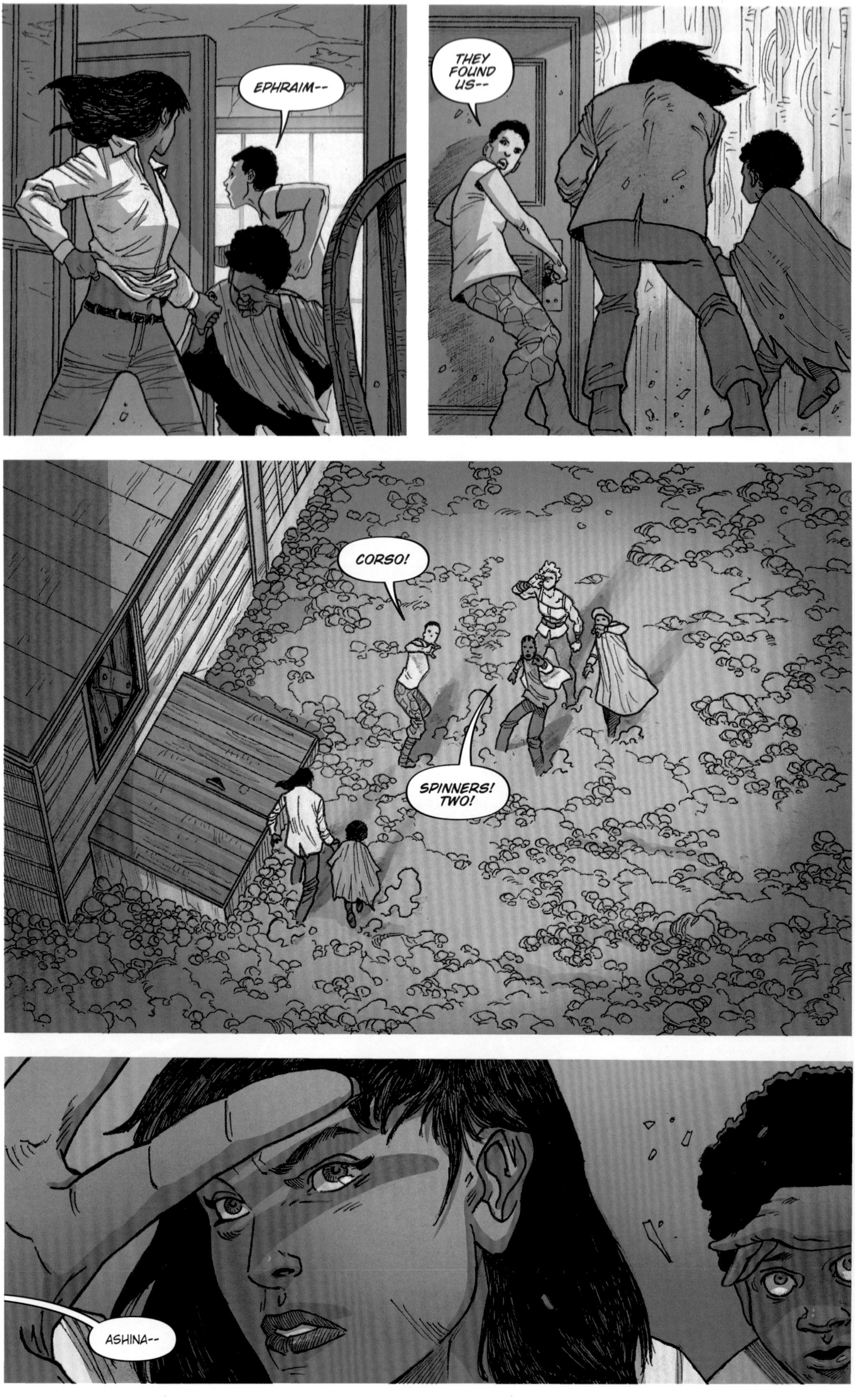
EPHRAIM--
THEY FOUND US--
CORSO!
SPINNERS! TWO!
ASHINA--

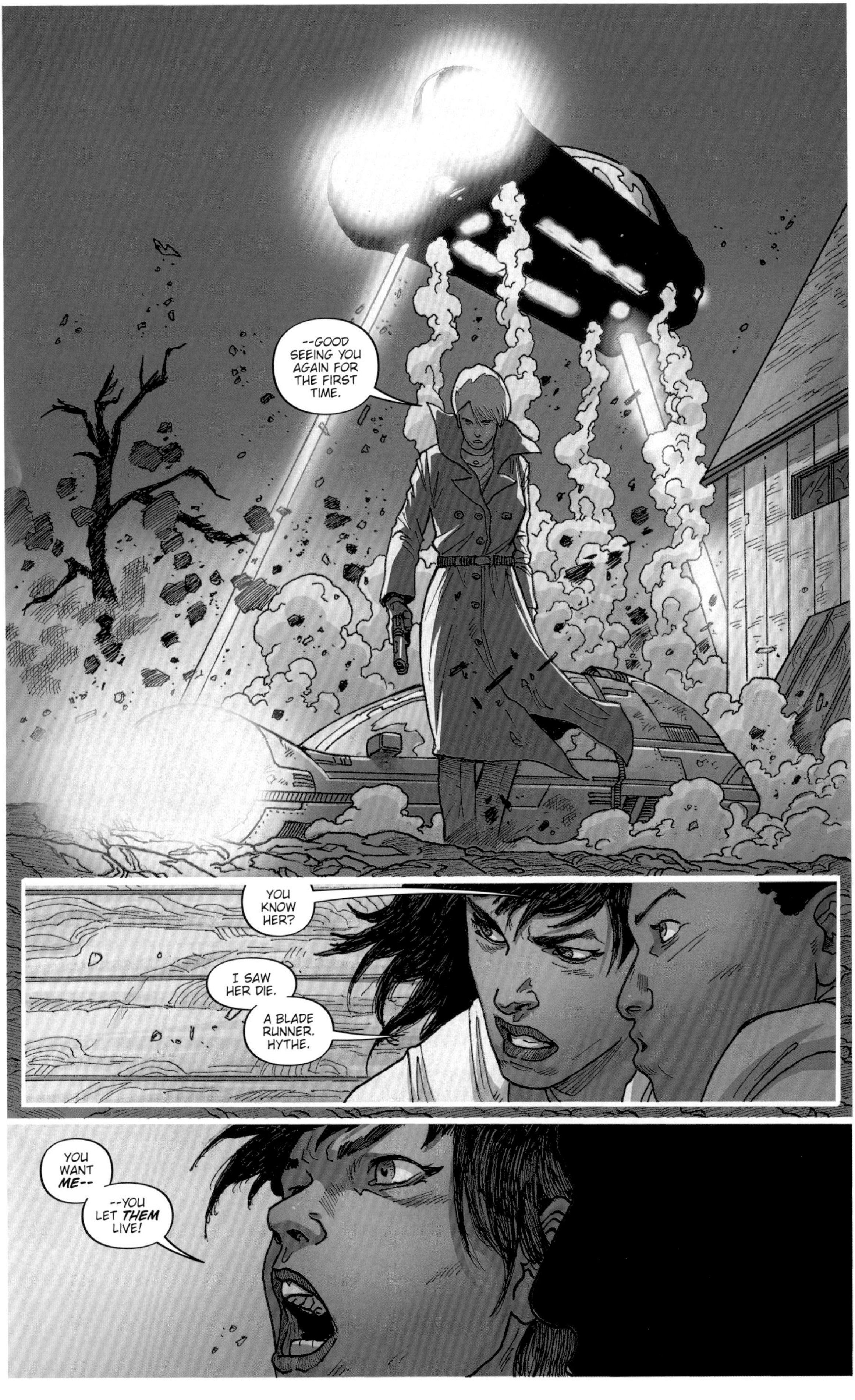
--GOOD SEEING YOU AGAIN FOR THE FIRST TIME.
YOU KNOW HER?
I SAW HER DIE.
A BLADE RUNNER. HYTHE.
YOU WANT **ME--**
--YOU LET **THEM** LIVE!

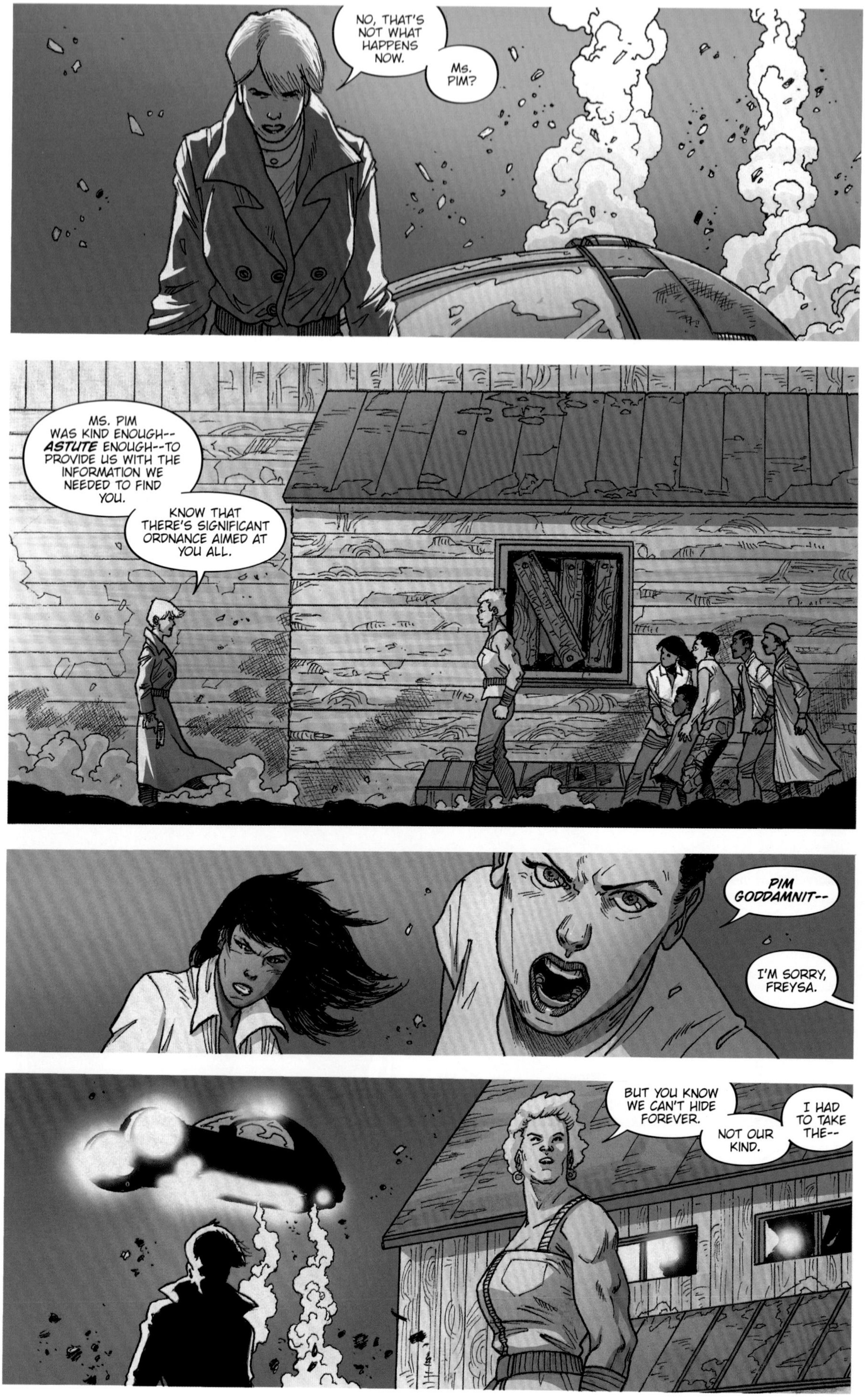
NO, THAT'S NOT WHAT HAPPENS NOW.
Ms. PIM?
MS. PIM WAS KIND ENOUGH-- ASTUTE ENOUGH--TO PROVIDE US WITH THE INFORMATION WE NEEDED TO FIND YOU.
KNOW THAT THERE'S SIGNIFICANT ORDNANCE AIMED AT YOU ALL.
PIM GODDAMNIT--
I'M SORRY, FREYSA.
BUT YOU KNOW WE CAN'T HIDE FOREVER.
NOT OUR KIND.
I HAD TO TAKE THE--

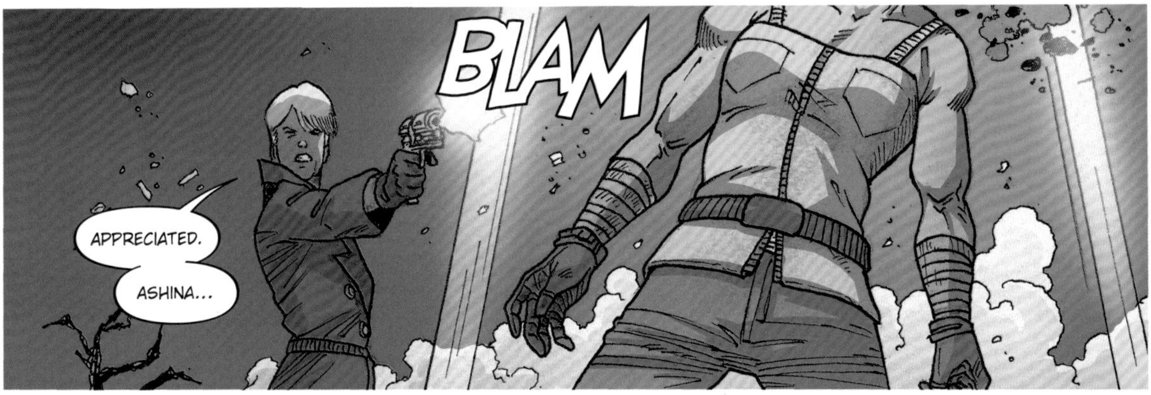
BLAM
APPRECIATED.
ASHINA...

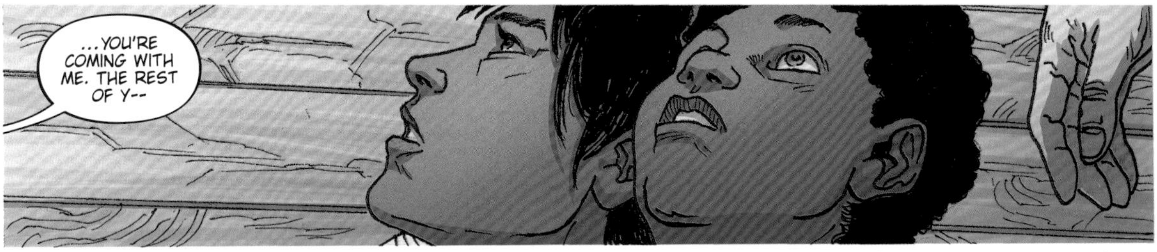
...YOU'RE COMING WITH ME. THE REST OF Y--

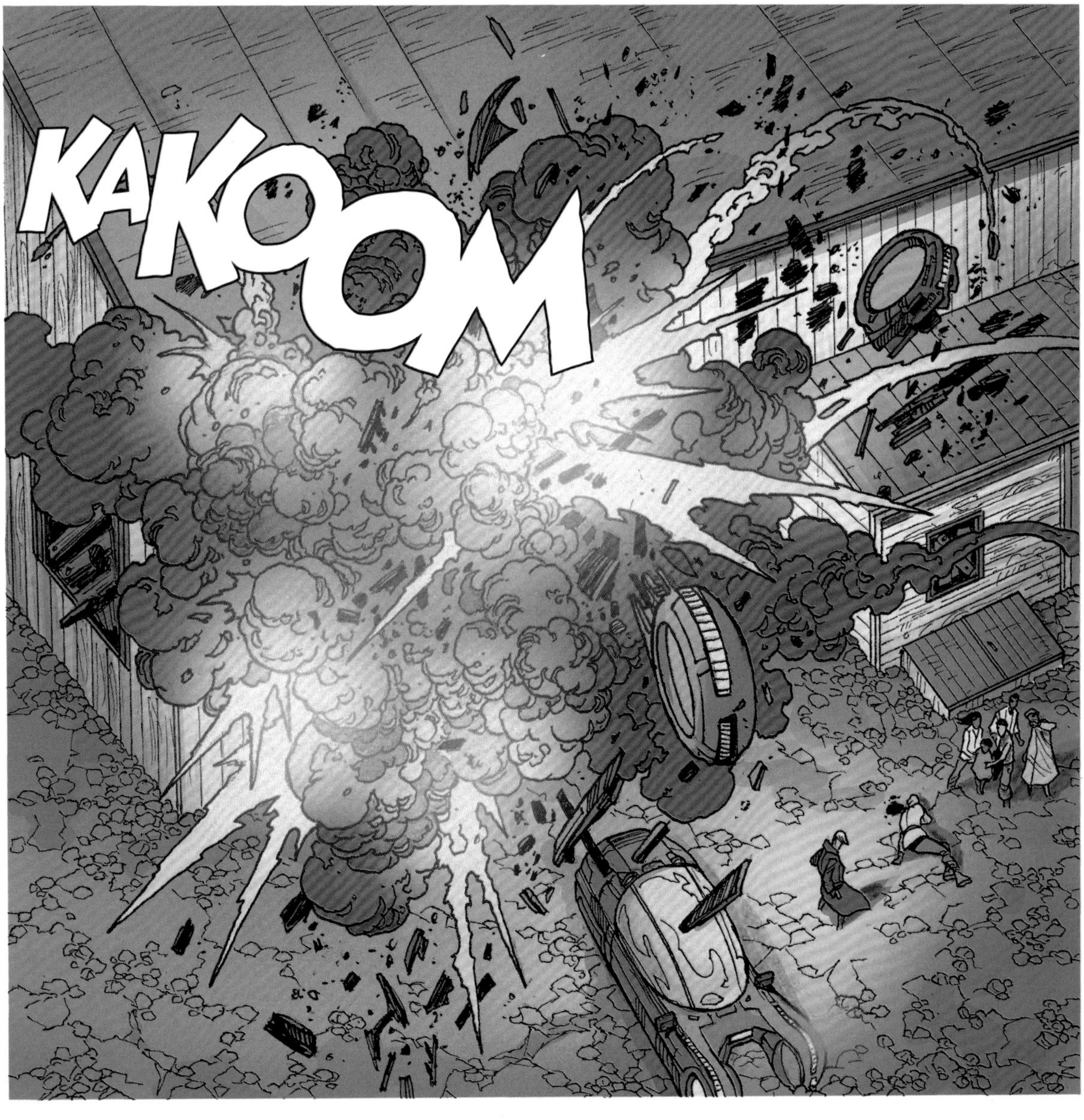
KAKOOM

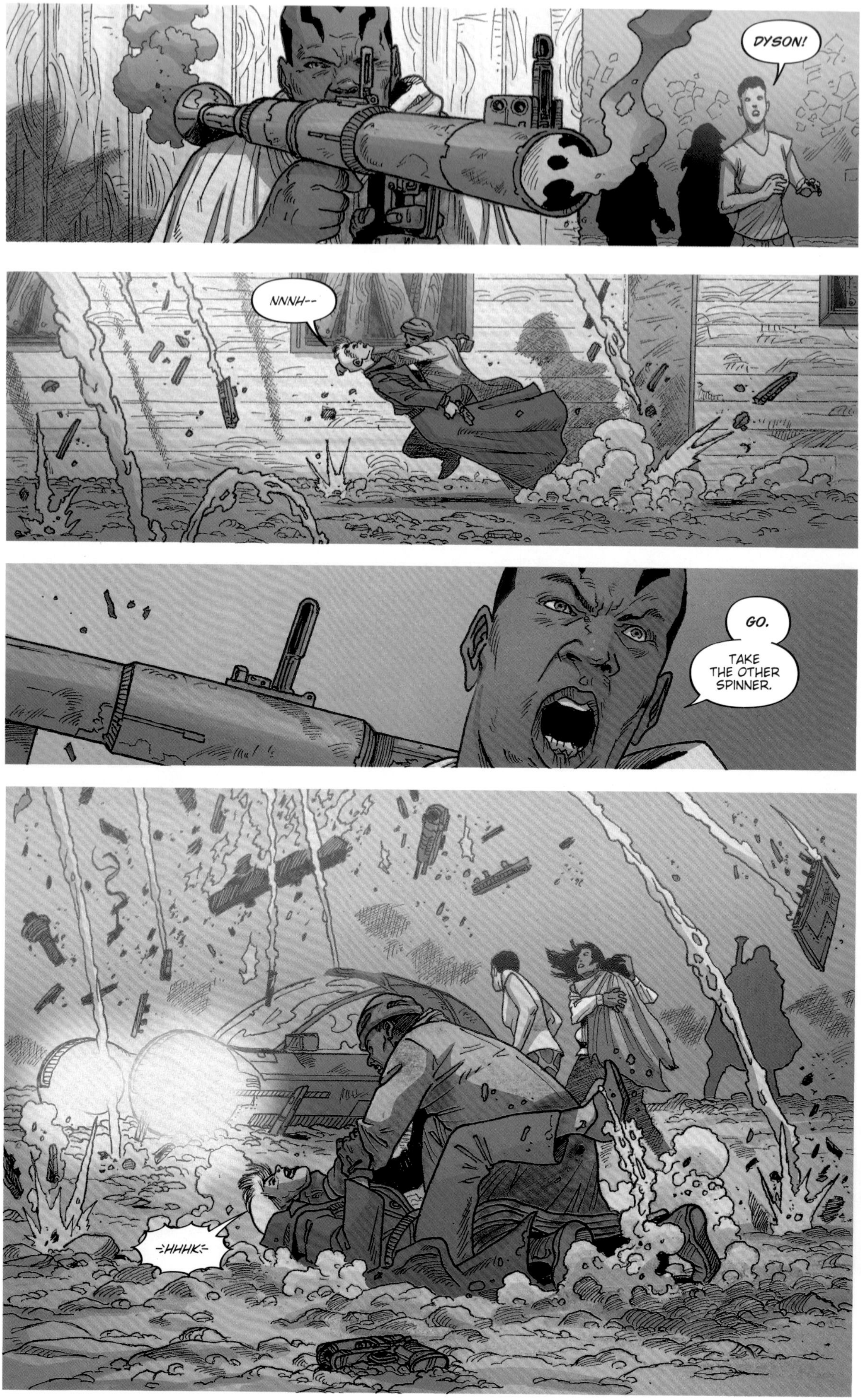
DYSON!
NNNH--
GO.
TAKE THE OTHER SPINNER.
-HHHK-

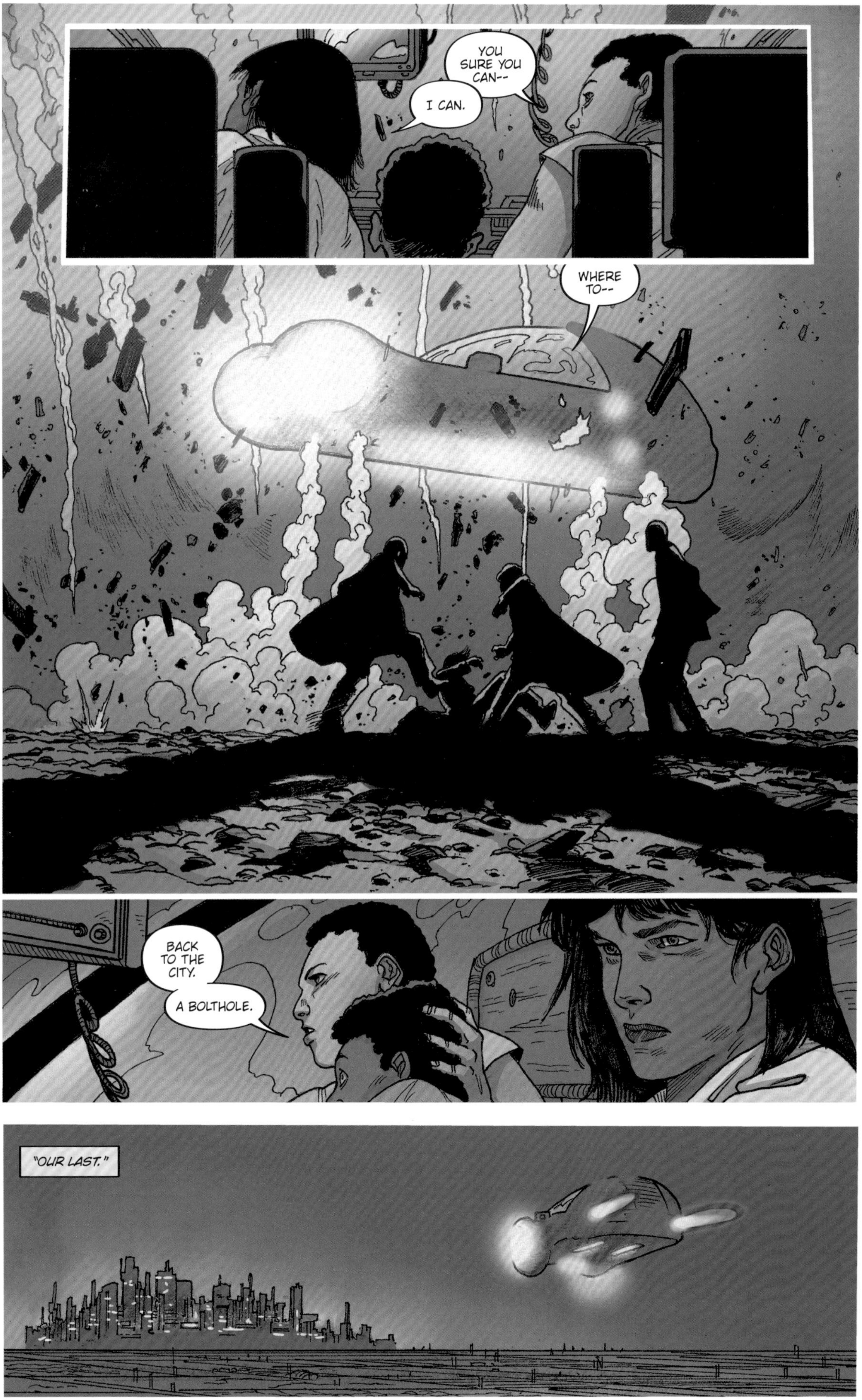
YOU SURE YOU CAN--
I CAN.
WHERE TO--
BACK TO THE CITY.
A BOLTHOLE.
"OUR LAST."

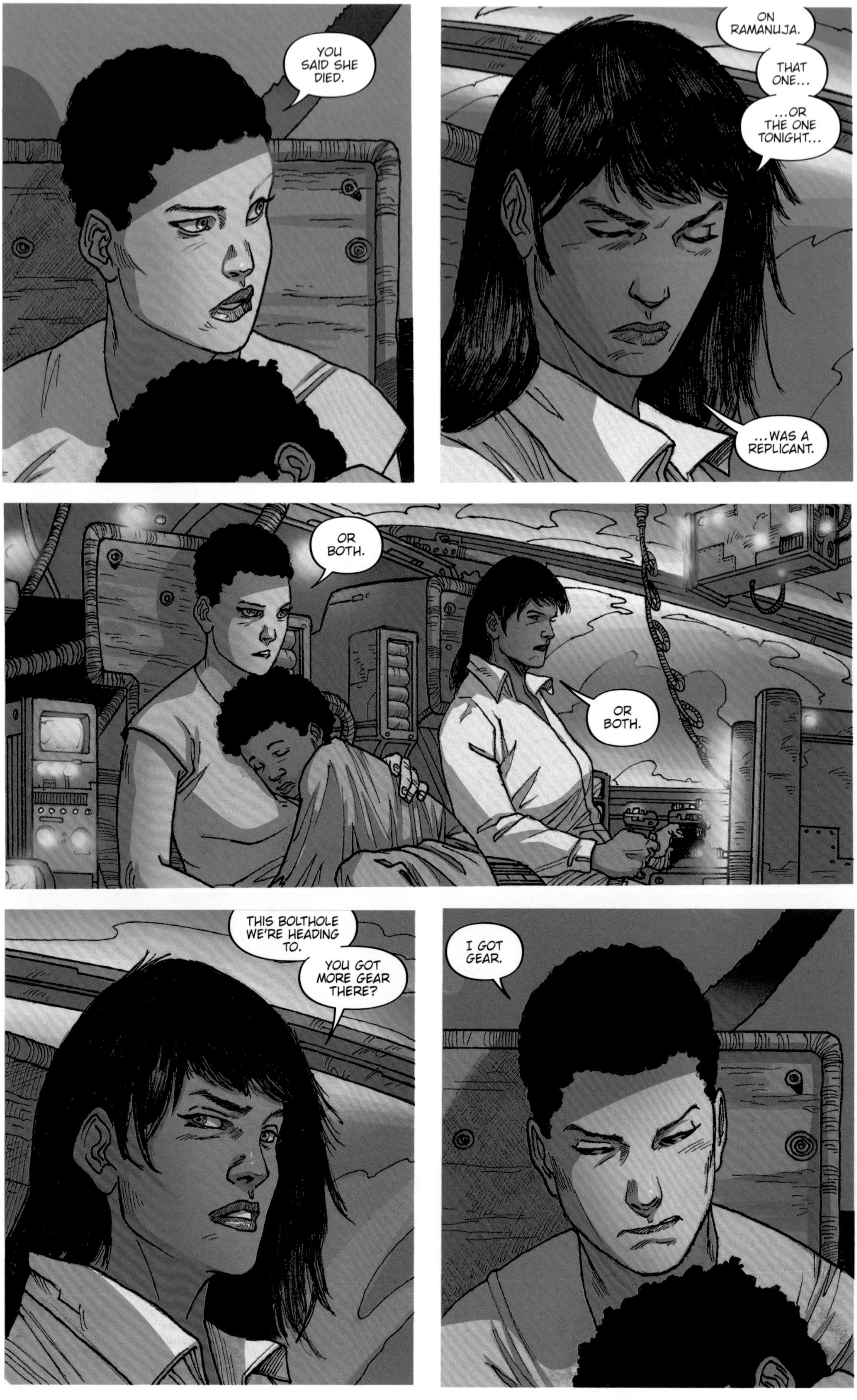
YOU SAID SHE DIED.
ON RAMANUJA.
THAT ONE...
...OR THE ONE TONIGHT...
...WAS A REPLICANT.
OR BOTH.
OR BOTH.
THIS BOLTHOLE WE'RE HEADING TO.
YOU GOT MORE GEAR THERE?
I GOT GEAR.

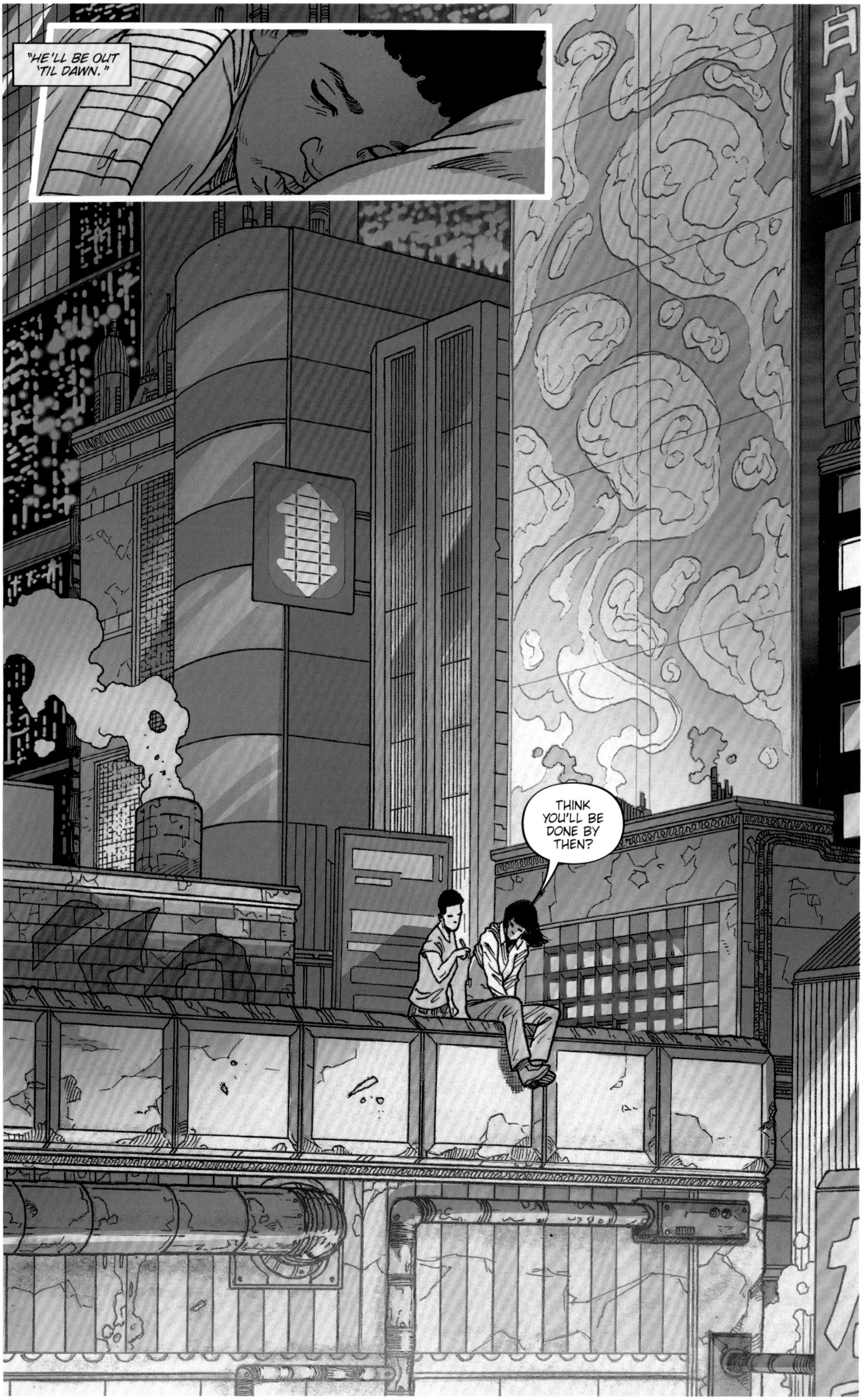
"HE'LL BE OUT 'TIL DAWN."
THINK YOU'LL BE DONE BY THEN?

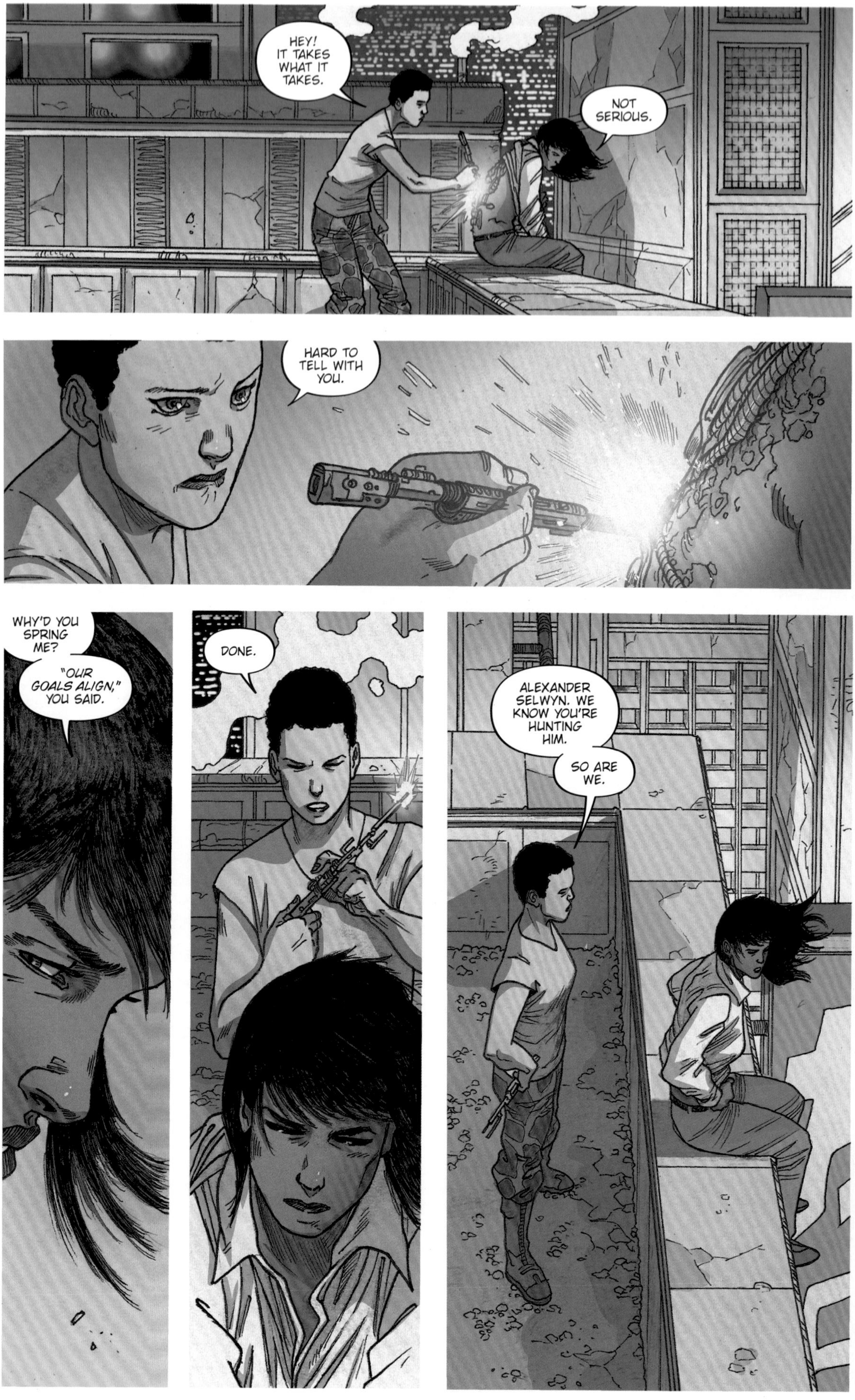
HEY! IT TAKES WHAT IT TAKES.
NOT SERIOUS.
HARD TO TELL WITH YOU.
WHY'D YOU SPRING ME?
"OUR GOALS ALIGN," YOU SAID.
DONE.
ALEXANDER SELWYN. WE KNOW YOU'RE HUNTING HIM.
SO ARE WE.

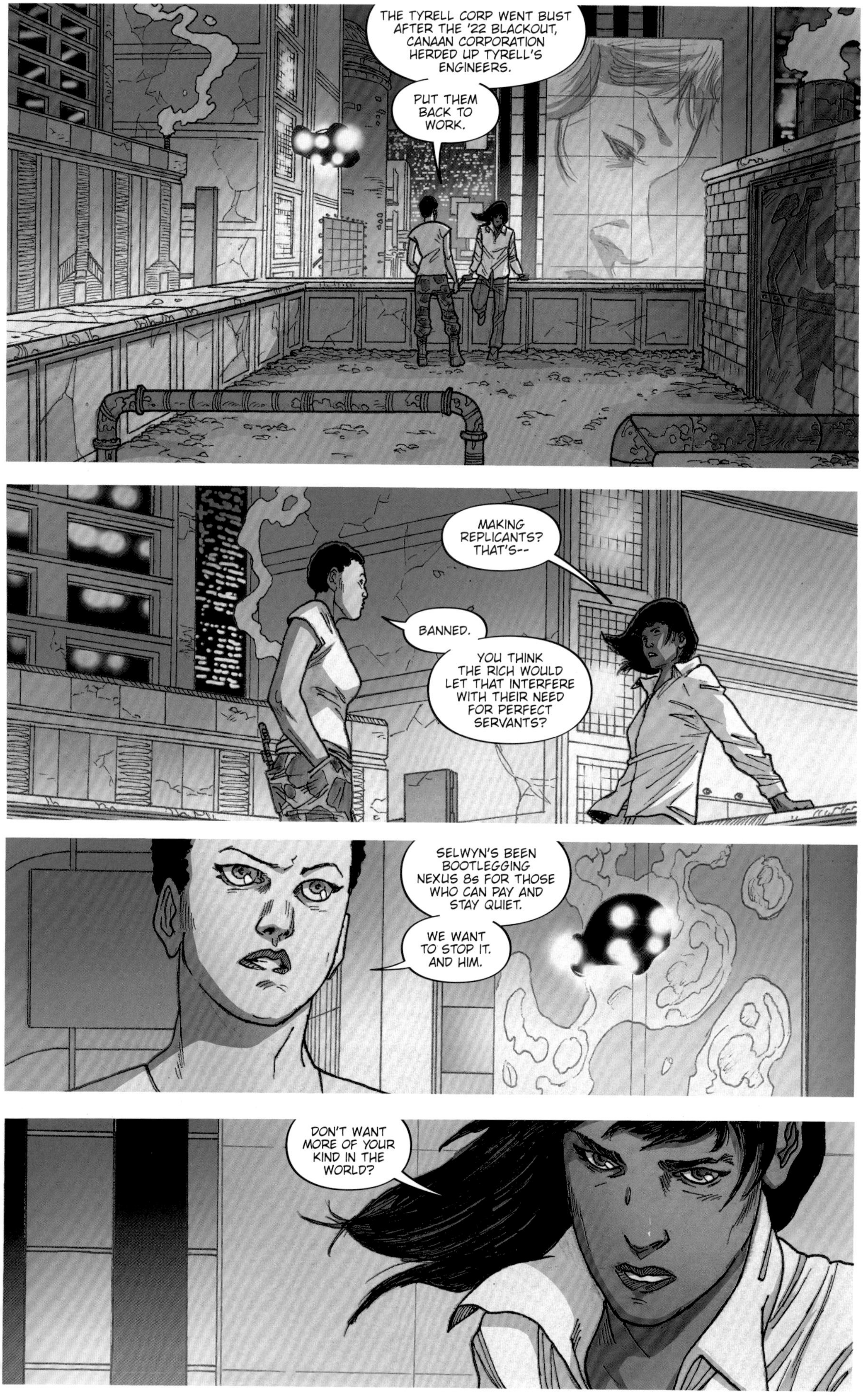
THE TYRELL CORP WENT BUST AFTER THE '22 BLACKOUT, CANAAN CORPORATION HERDED UP TYRELL'S ENGINEERS.
PUT THEM BACK TO WORK.
MAKING REPLICANTS? THAT'S--
BANNED.
YOU THINK THE RICH WOULD LET THAT INTERFERE WITH THEIR NEED FOR PERFECT SERVANTS?
SELWYN'S BEEN BOOTLEGGING NEXUS 8s FOR THOSE WHO CAN PAY AND STAY QUIET.
WE WANT TO STOP IT. AND HIM.
DON'T WANT MORE OF YOUR KIND IN THE WORLD?

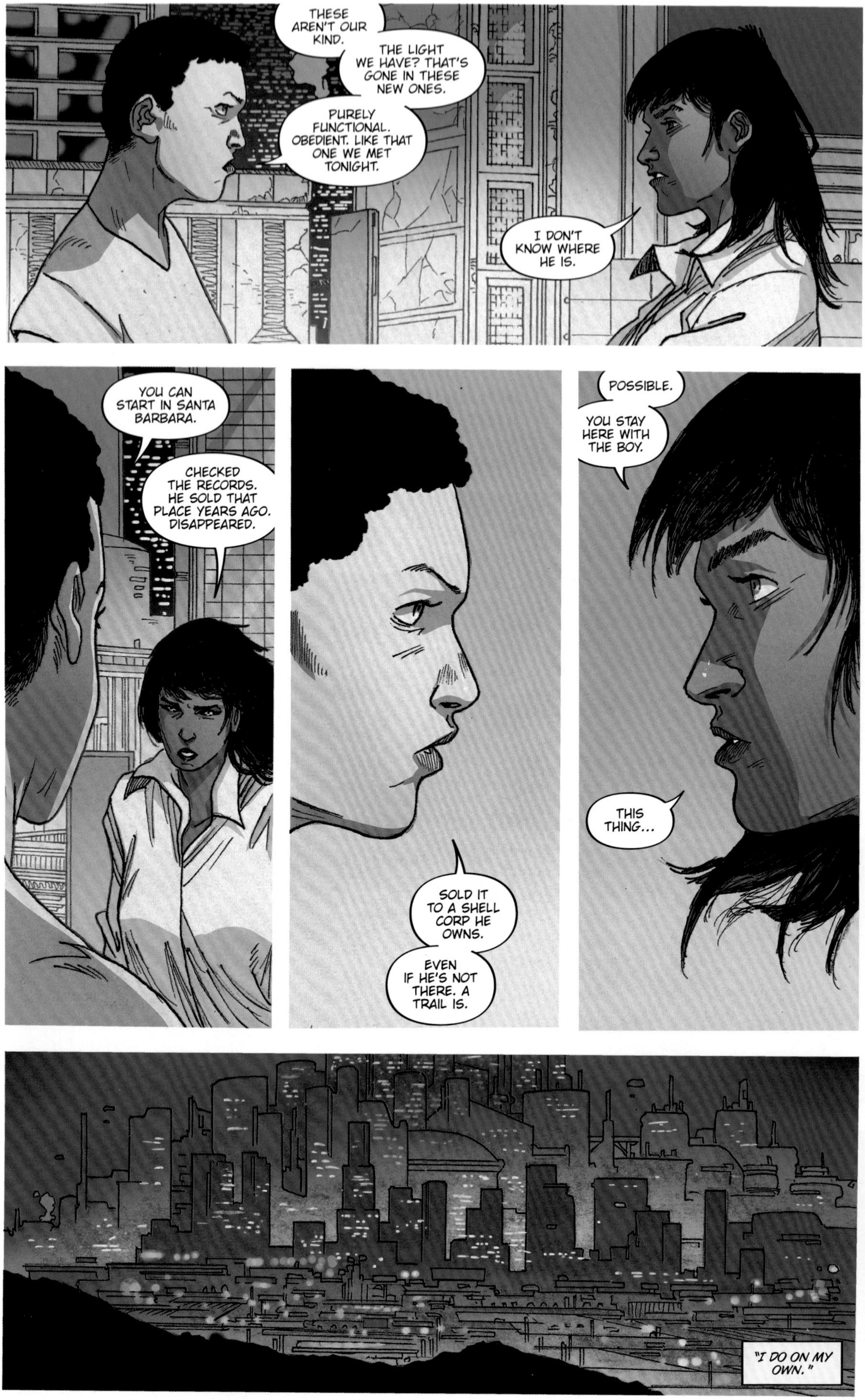
THESE AREN'T OUR KIND.
THE LIGHT WE HAVE? THAT'S GONE IN THESE NEW ONES.
PURELY FUNCTIONAL. OBEDIENT. LIKE THAT ONE WE MET TONIGHT.
I DON'T KNOW WHERE HE IS.
YOU CAN START IN SANTA BARBARA.
CHECKED THE RECORDS. HE SOLD THAT PLACE YEARS AGO. DISAPPEARED.
SOLD IT TO A SHELL CORP HE OWNS.
EVEN IF HE'S NOT THERE. A TRAIL IS.
POSSIBLE.
YOU STAY HERE WITH THE BOY.
THIS THING...
"I DO ON MY OWN."

I crash and dream of nothing.

Up and I'm back to the archipelago.

No signs of life.

House looks trapped in amber.

Somebody's gone to the trouble.

Same real oak smell.

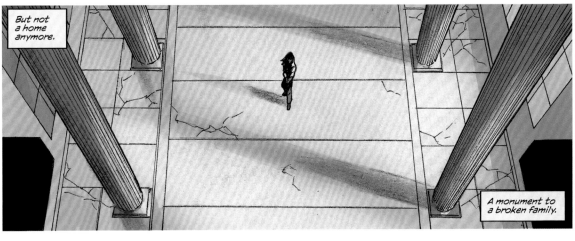

But not a home anymore.

A monument to a broken family.

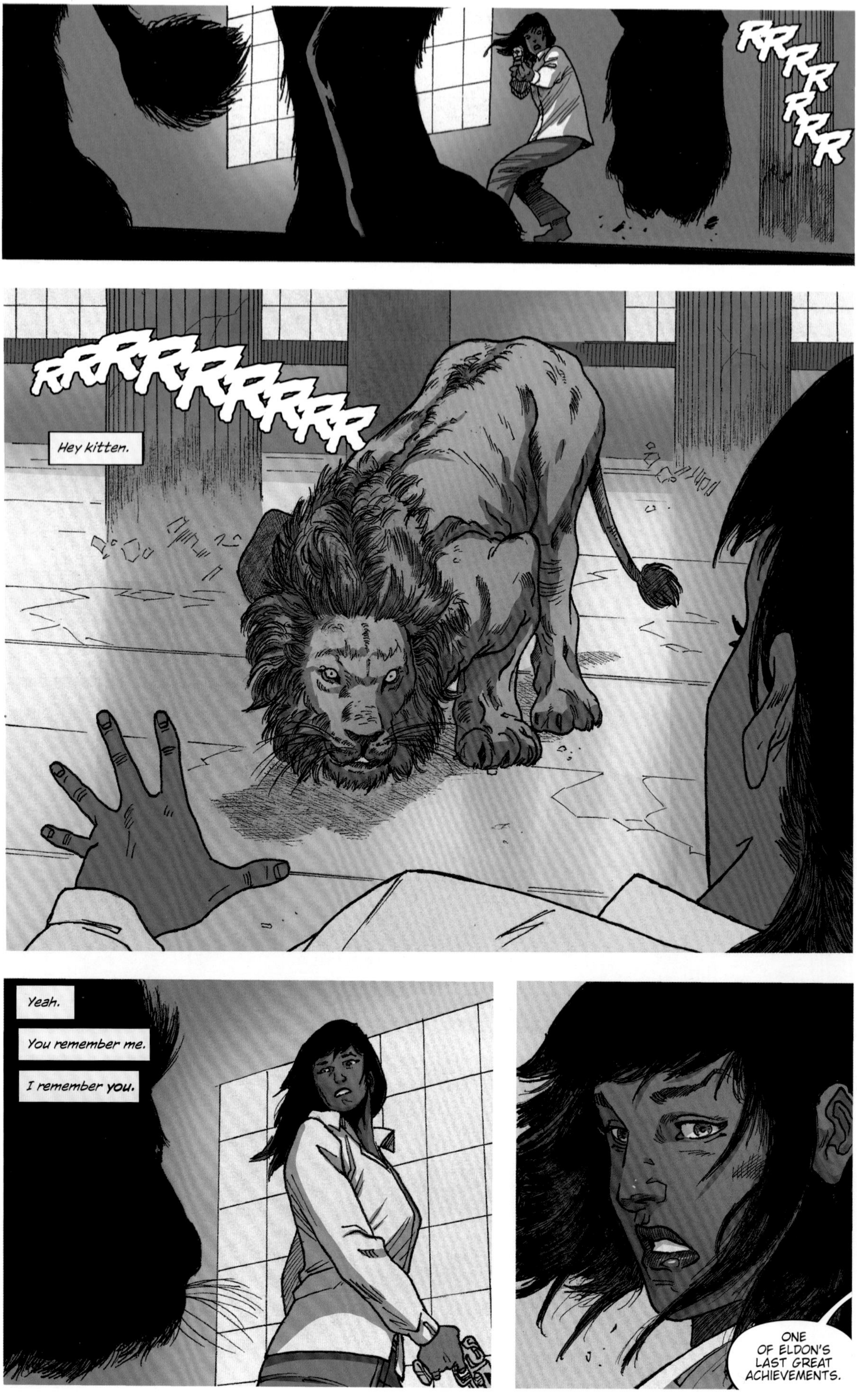
RRRRRRRR
RRRRRRRRRRRRR
Hey kitten.
Yeah.
You remember me.
I remember you.
ONE OF ELDON'S LAST GREAT ACHIEVEMENTS.

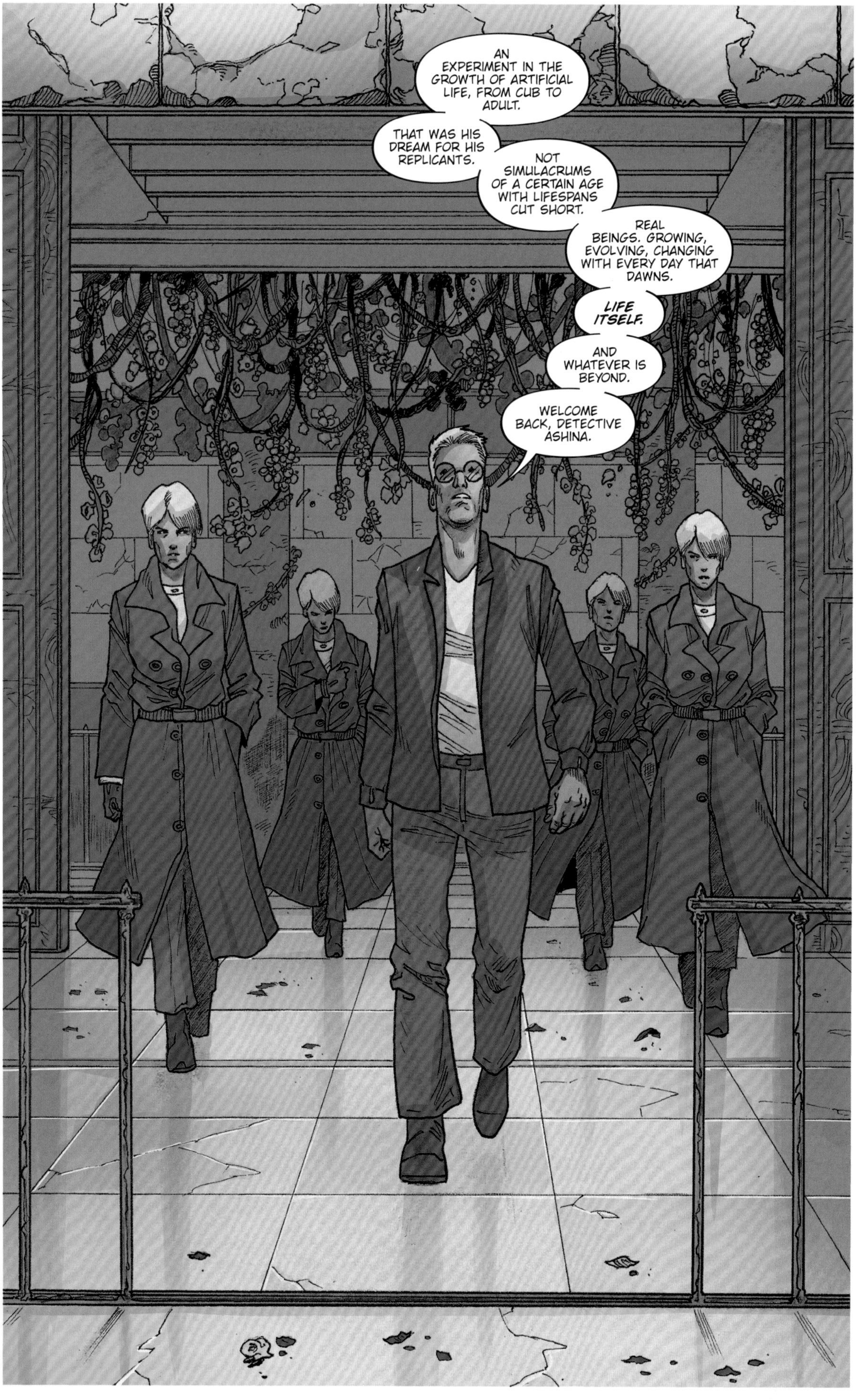
AN EXPERIMENT IN THE GROWTH OF ARTIFICIAL LIFE, FROM CUB TO ADULT.
THAT WAS HIS DREAM FOR HIS REPLICANTS.
NOT SIMULACRUMS OF A CERTAIN AGE WITH LIFESPANS CUT SHORT.
REAL BEINGS. GROWING, EVOLVING, CHANGING WITH EVERY DAY THAT DAWNS.
LIFE ITSELF.
AND WHATEVER IS BEYOND.
WELCOME BACK, DETECTIVE ASHINA.

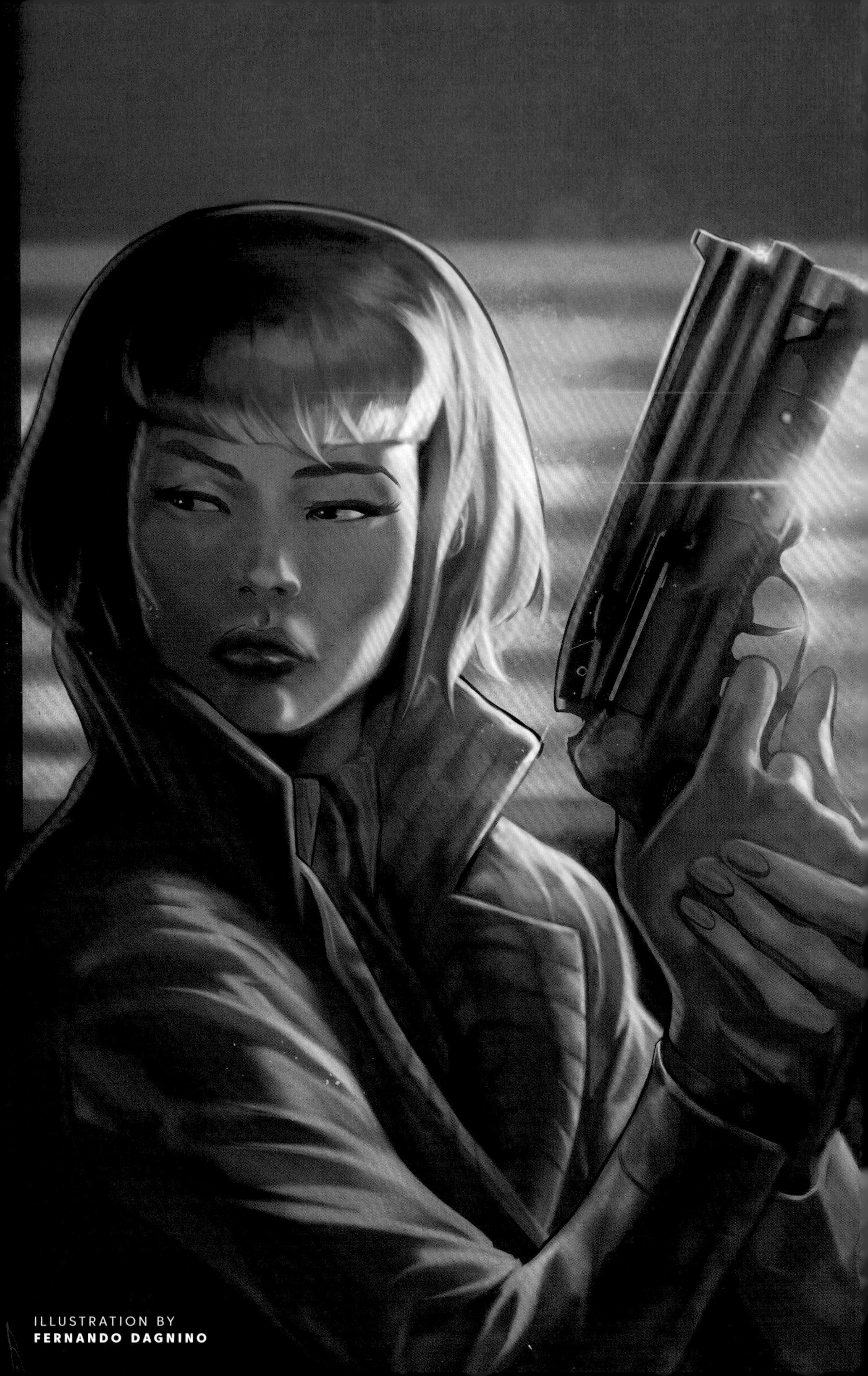

ILLUSTRATION BY
FERNANDO DAGNINO

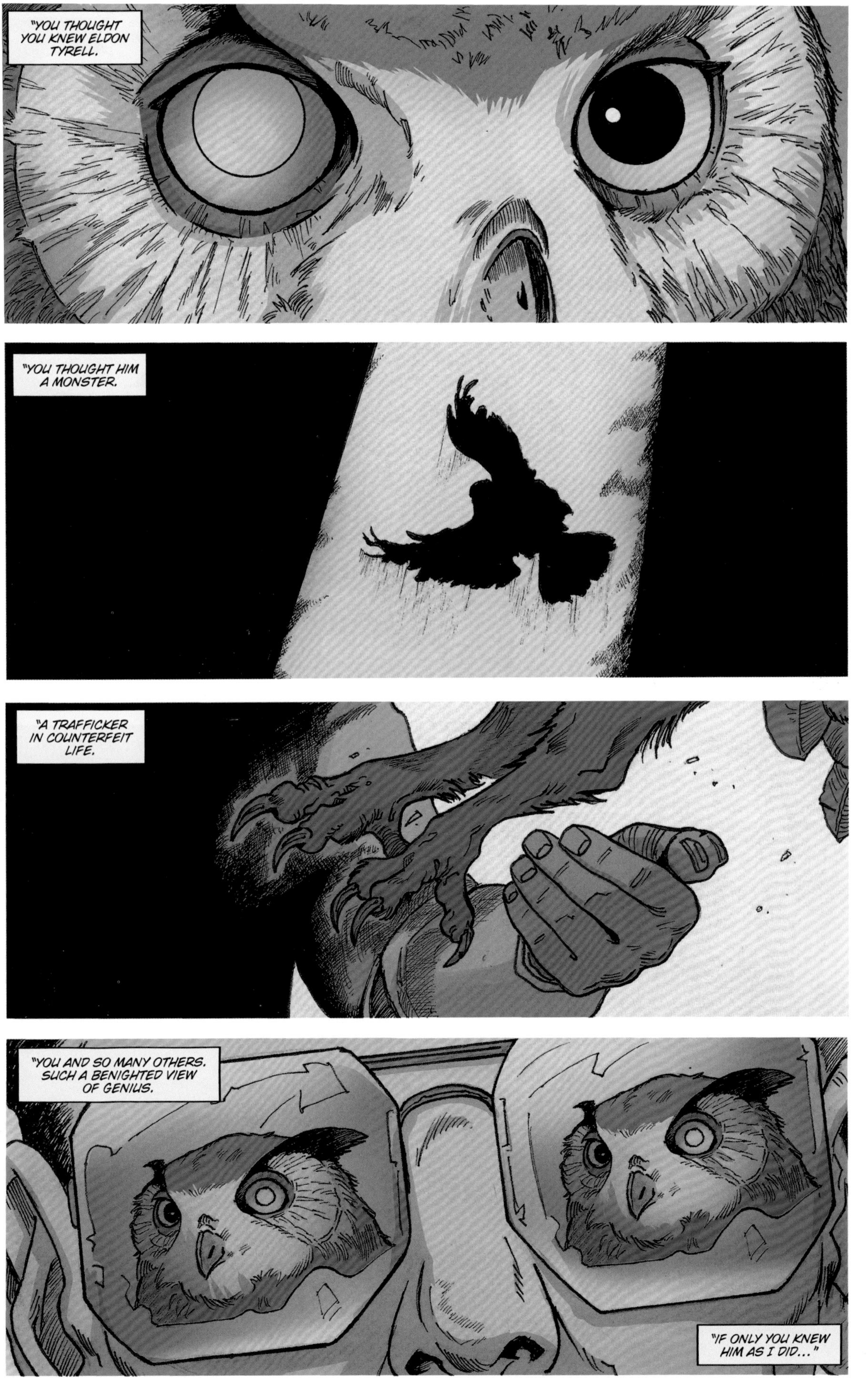
"YOU THOUGHT YOU KNEW ELDON TYRELL.
"YOU THOUGHT HIM A MONSTER.
"A TRAFFICKER IN COUNTERFEIT LIFE.
"YOU AND SO MANY OTHERS. SUCH A BENIGHTED VIEW OF GENIUS.
"IF ONLY YOU KNEW HIM AS I DID..."

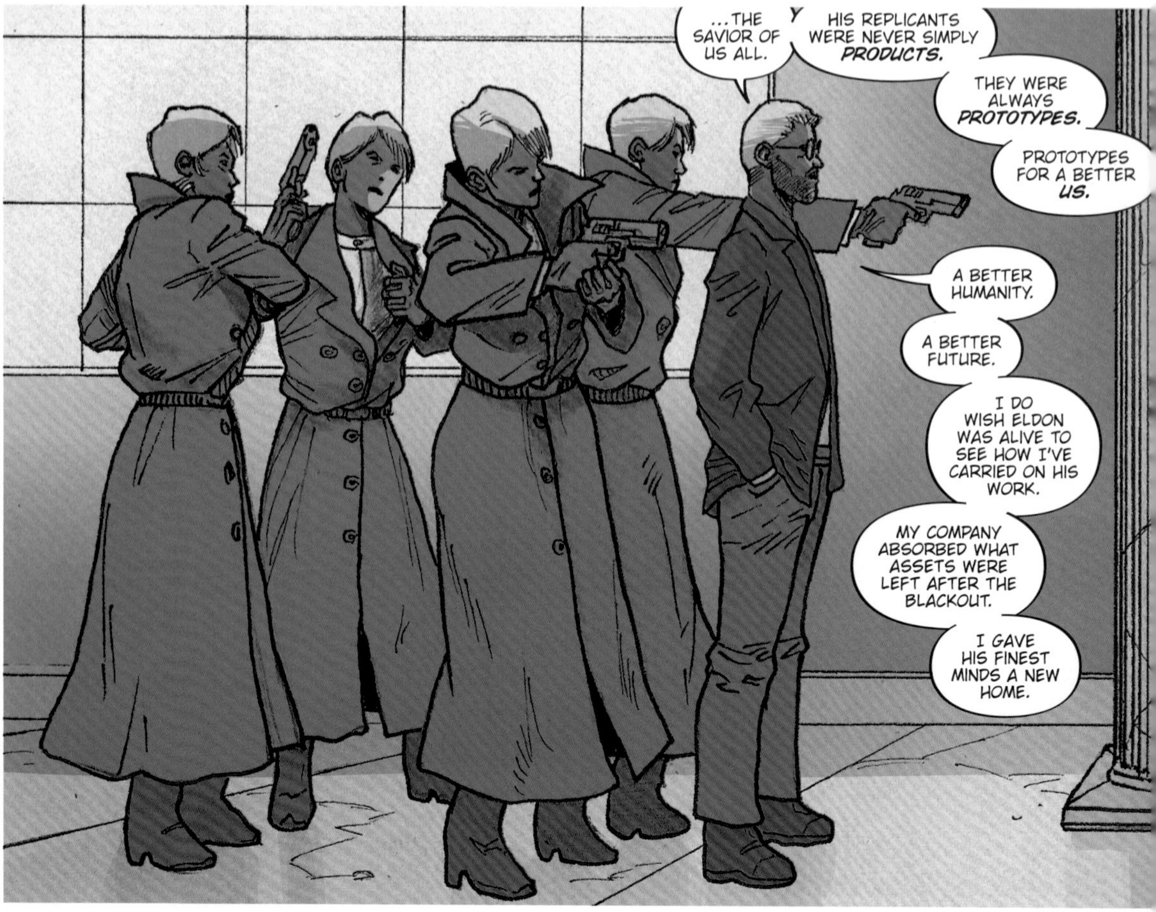
...THE SAVIOR OF US ALL.
HIS REPLICANTS WERE NEVER SIMPLY PRODUCTS.
THEY WERE ALWAYS PROTOTYPES.
PROTOTYPES FOR A BETTER US.
A BETTER HUMANITY.
A BETTER FUTURE.
I DO WISH ELDON WAS ALIVE TO SEE HOW I'VE CARRIED ON HIS WORK.
MY COMPANY ABSORBED WHAT ASSETS WERE LEFT AFTER THE BLACKOUT.
I GAVE HIS FINEST MINDS A NEW HOME.

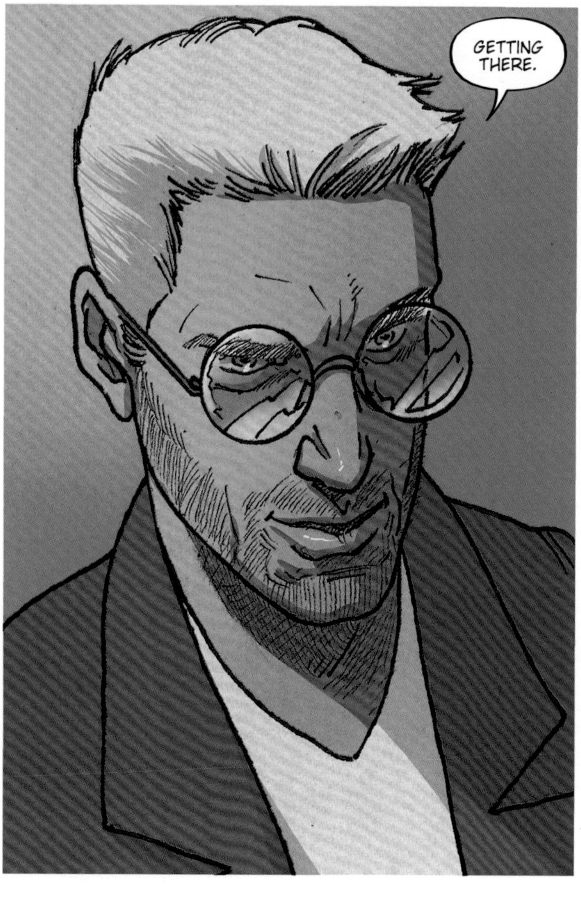
GETTING THERE.

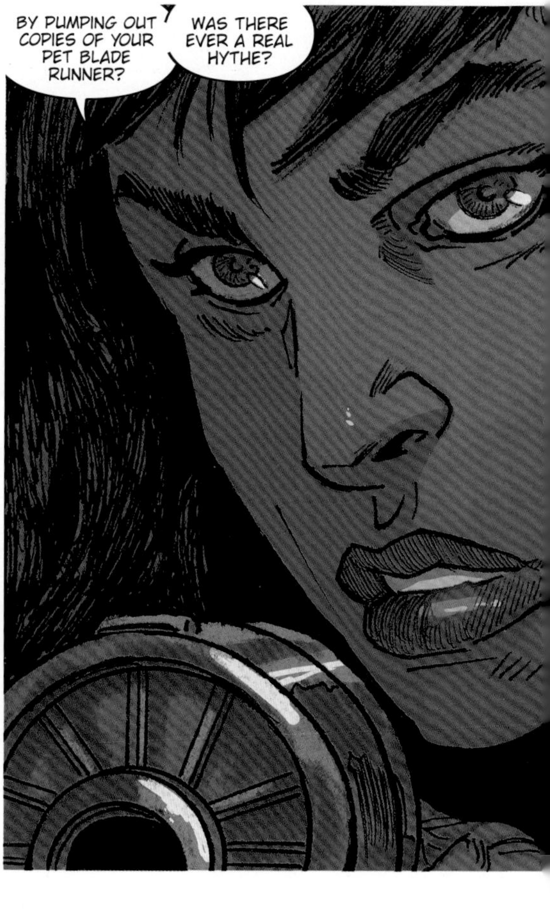
BY PUMPING OUT COPIES OF YOUR PET BLADE RUNNER?
WAS THERE EVER A REAL HYTHE?

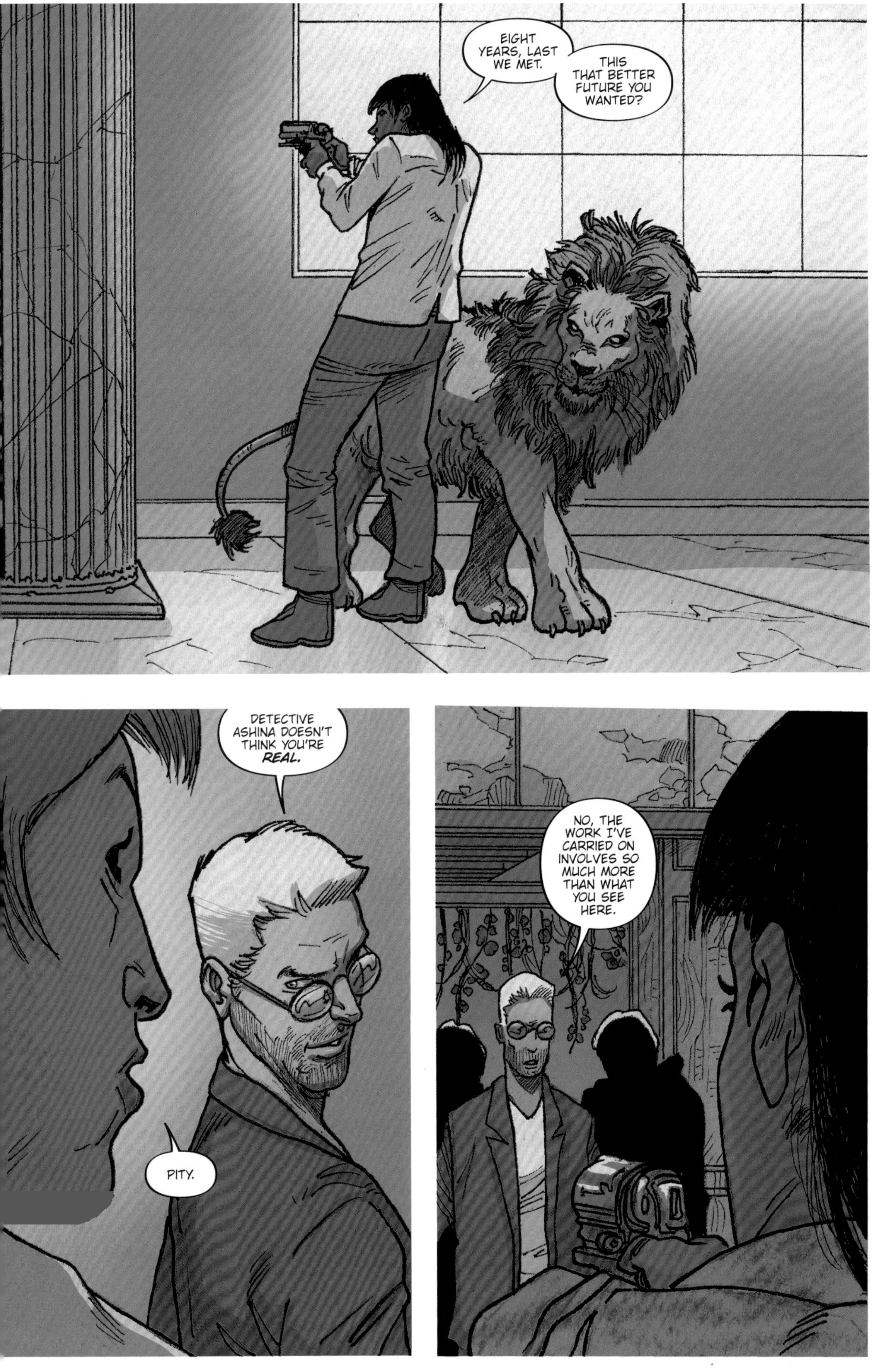
EIGHT YEARS, LAST WE MET.
THIS THAT BETTER FUTURE YOU WANTED?
DETECTIVE ASHINA DOESN'T THINK YOU'RE **REAL.**
PITY.
NO, THE WORK I'VE CARRIED ON INVOLVES SO MUCH MORE THAN WHAT YOU SEE HERE.

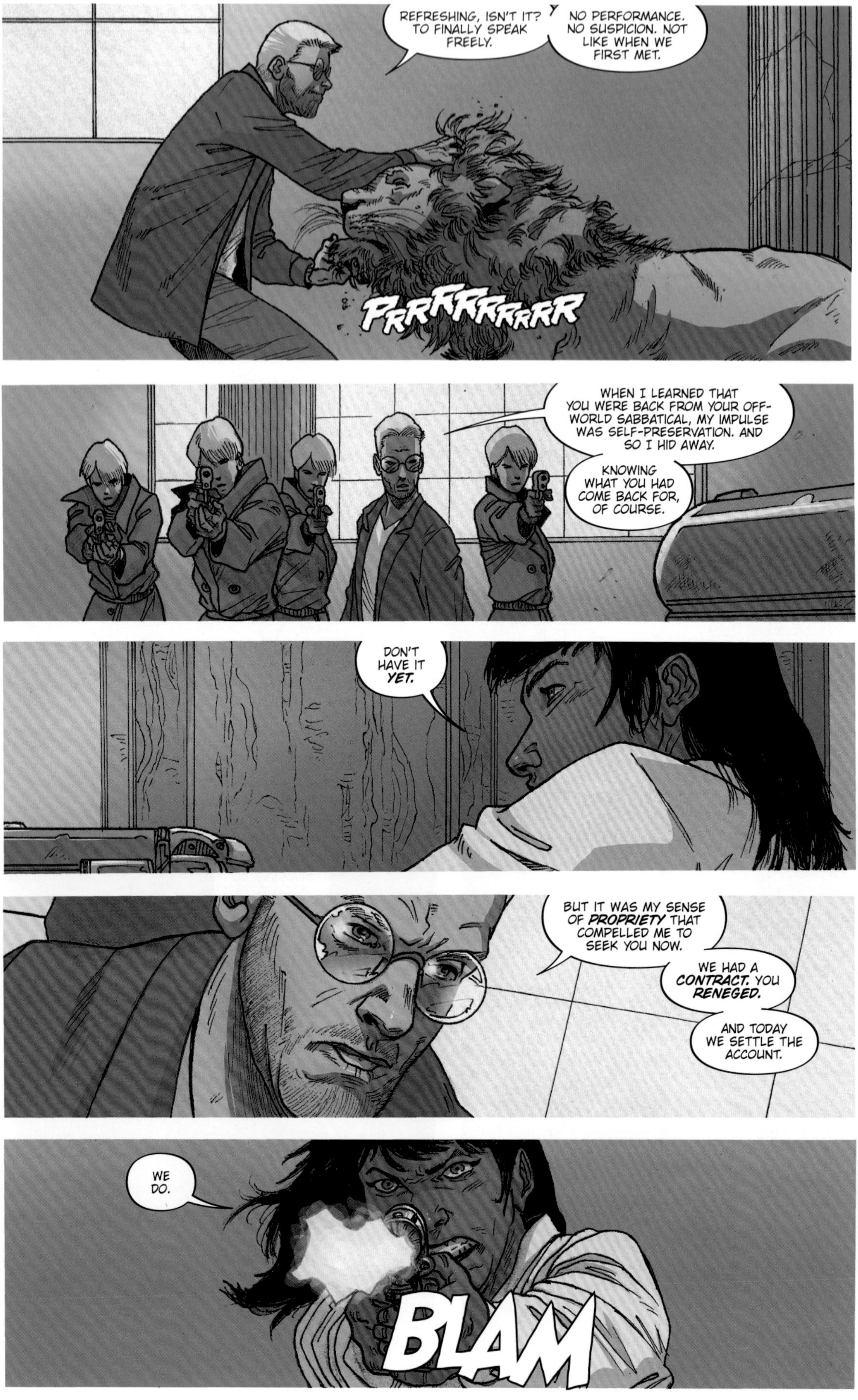

REFRESHING, ISN'T IT? TO FINALLY SPEAK FREELY.
NO PERFORMANCE. NO SUSPICION. NOT LIKE WHEN WE FIRST MET.
PRRRRRRRRRR
WHEN I LEARNED THAT YOU WERE BACK FROM YOUR OFF-WORLD SABBATICAL, MY IMPULSE WAS SELF-PRESERVATION. AND SO I HID AWAY.
KNOWING WHAT YOU HAD COME BACK FOR, OF COURSE.
DON'T HAVE IT *YET.*
BUT IT WAS MY SENSE OF ***PROPRIETY*** THAT COMPELLED ME TO SEEK YOU NOW.
WE HAD A ***CONTRACT.*** YOU ***RENEGED.***
AND TODAY WE SETTLE THE ACCOUNT.
WE DO.
BLAM

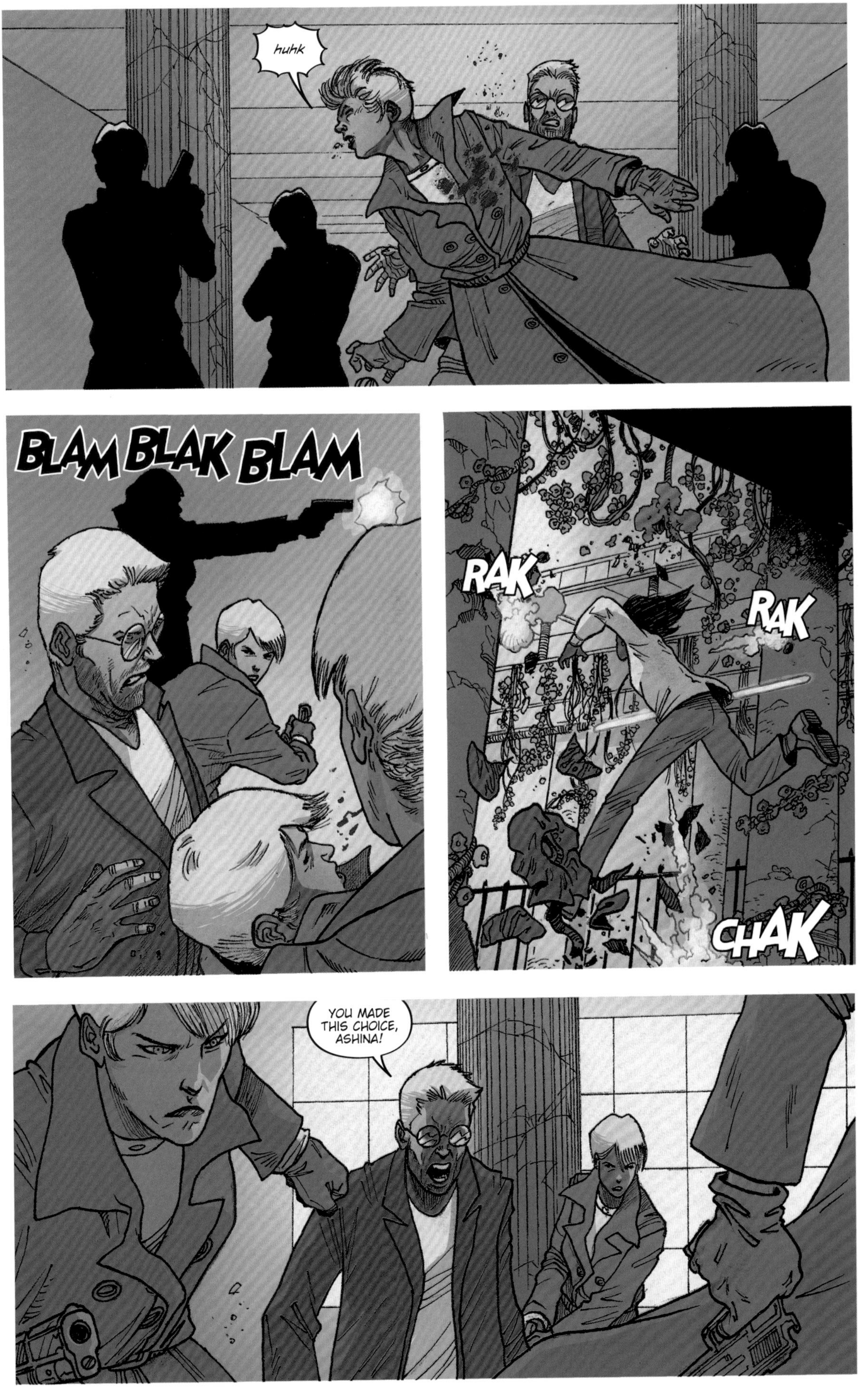
huhk
BLAM BLAK BLAM
RAK
RAK
CHAK
YOU MADE THIS CHOICE, ASHINA!

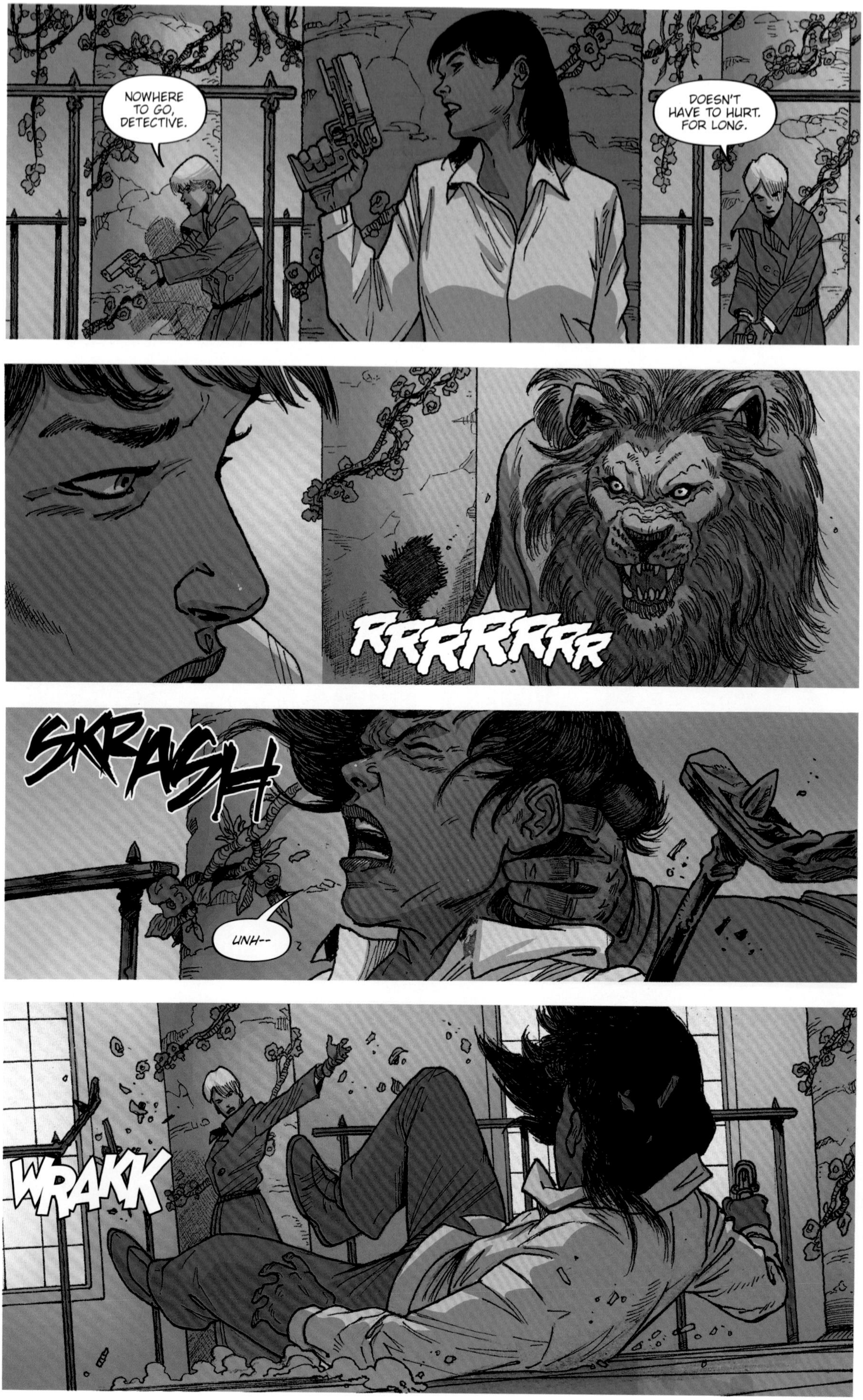
NOWHERE TO GO, DETECTIVE.
DOESN'T HAVE TO HURT. FOR LONG.
RRRRRRRR
SKRASH
UNH--
WRAKK

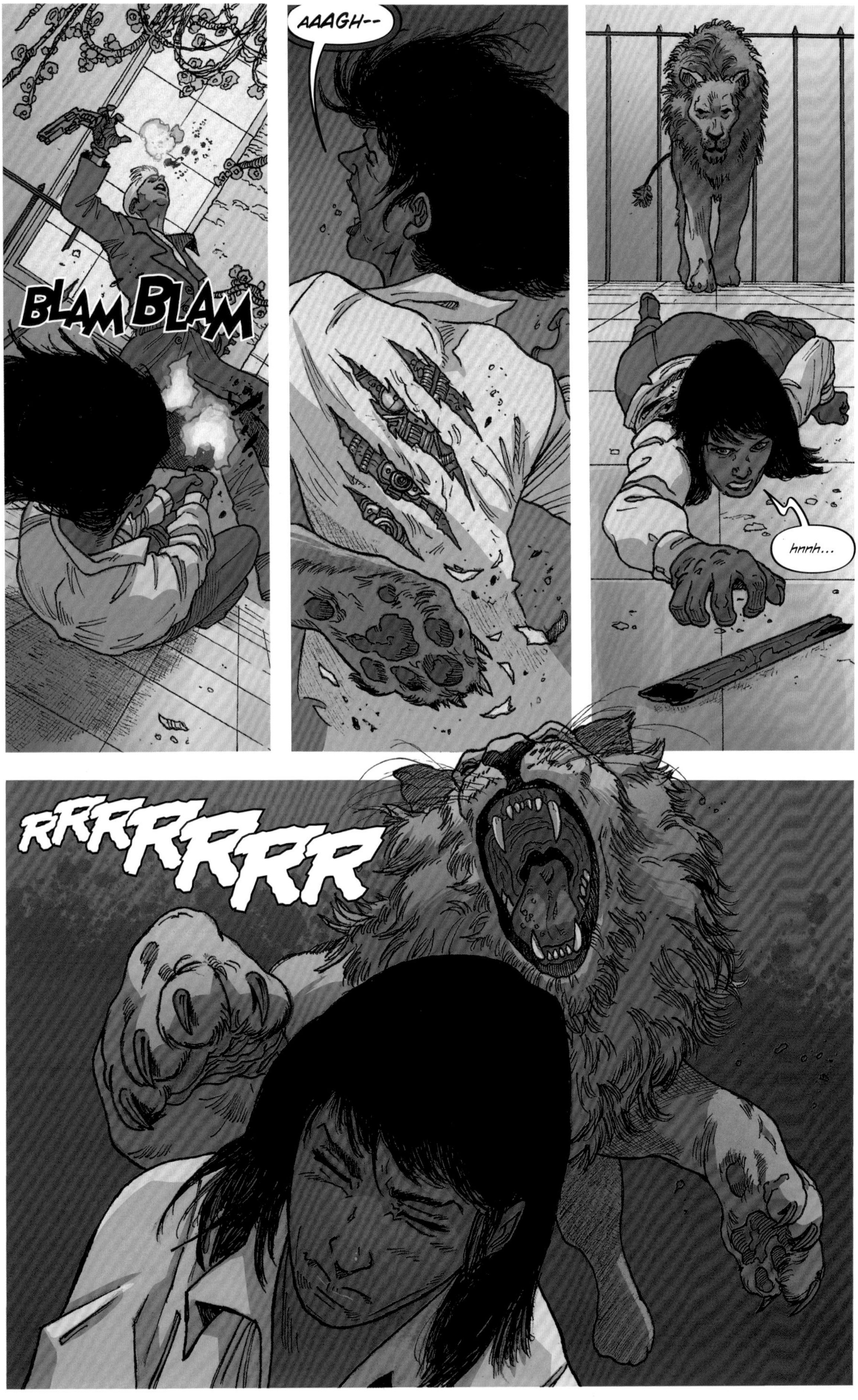
BLAM BLAM
AAAGH--
hnnh...
RRRRRRRR

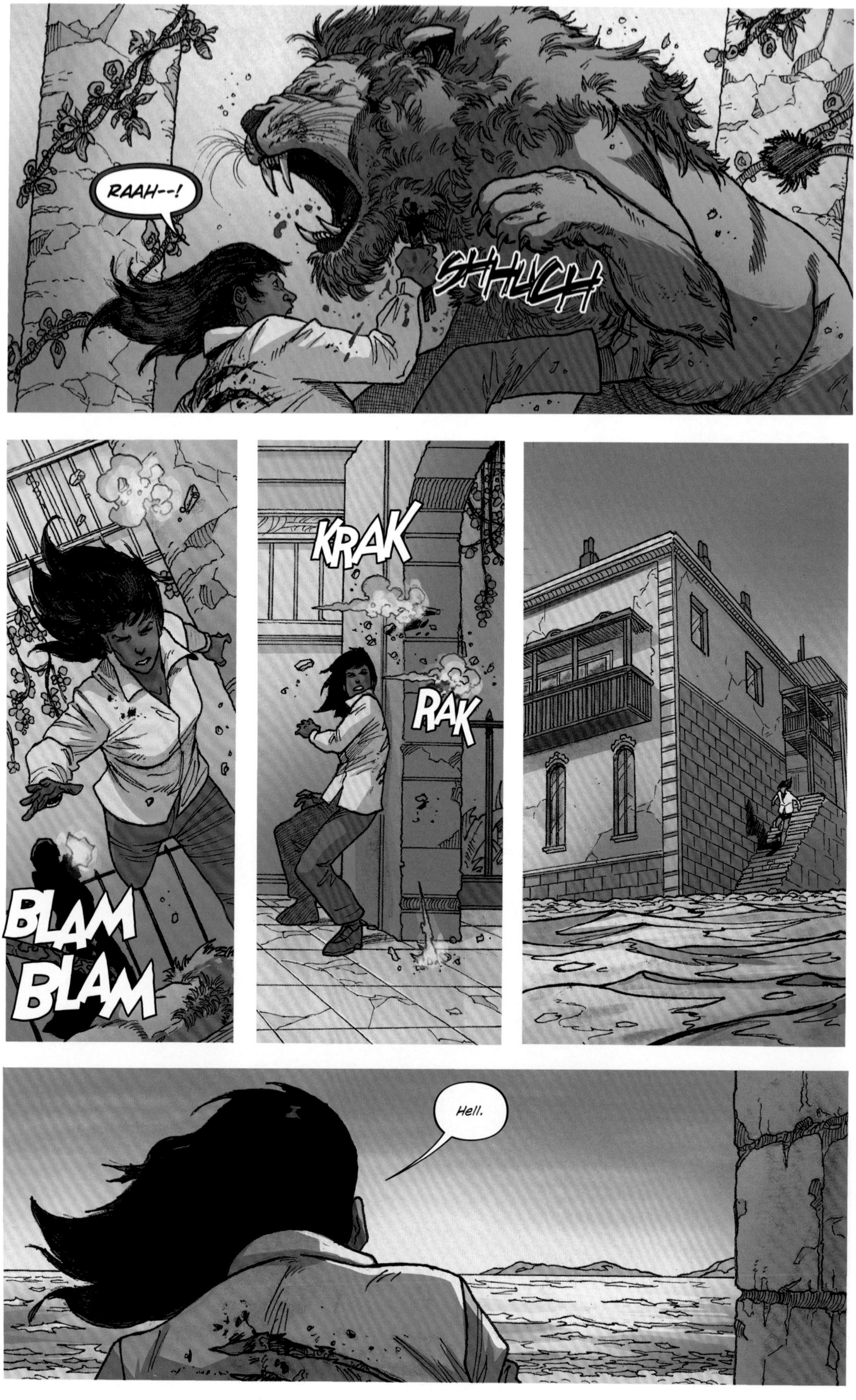
RAAH--!
SHLUCH
BLAM
BLAM
KRAK
RAK
Hell.

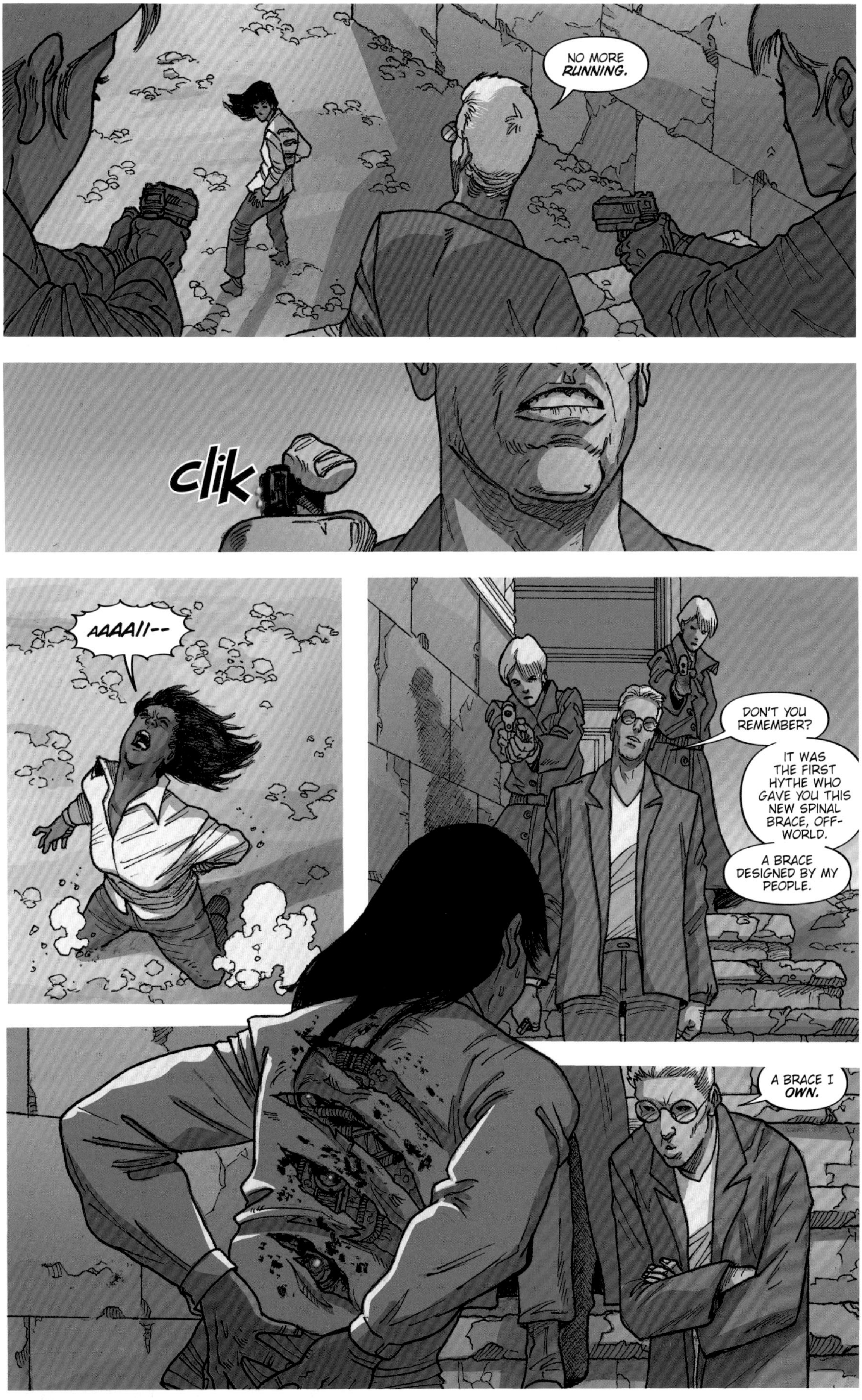
NO MORE RUNNING.
clik
AAAAII--
DON'T YOU REMEMBER?
IT WAS THE FIRST HYTHE WHO GAVE YOU THIS NEW SPINAL BRACE, OFF-WORLD.
A BRACE DESIGNED BY MY PEOPLE.
A BRACE I OWN.

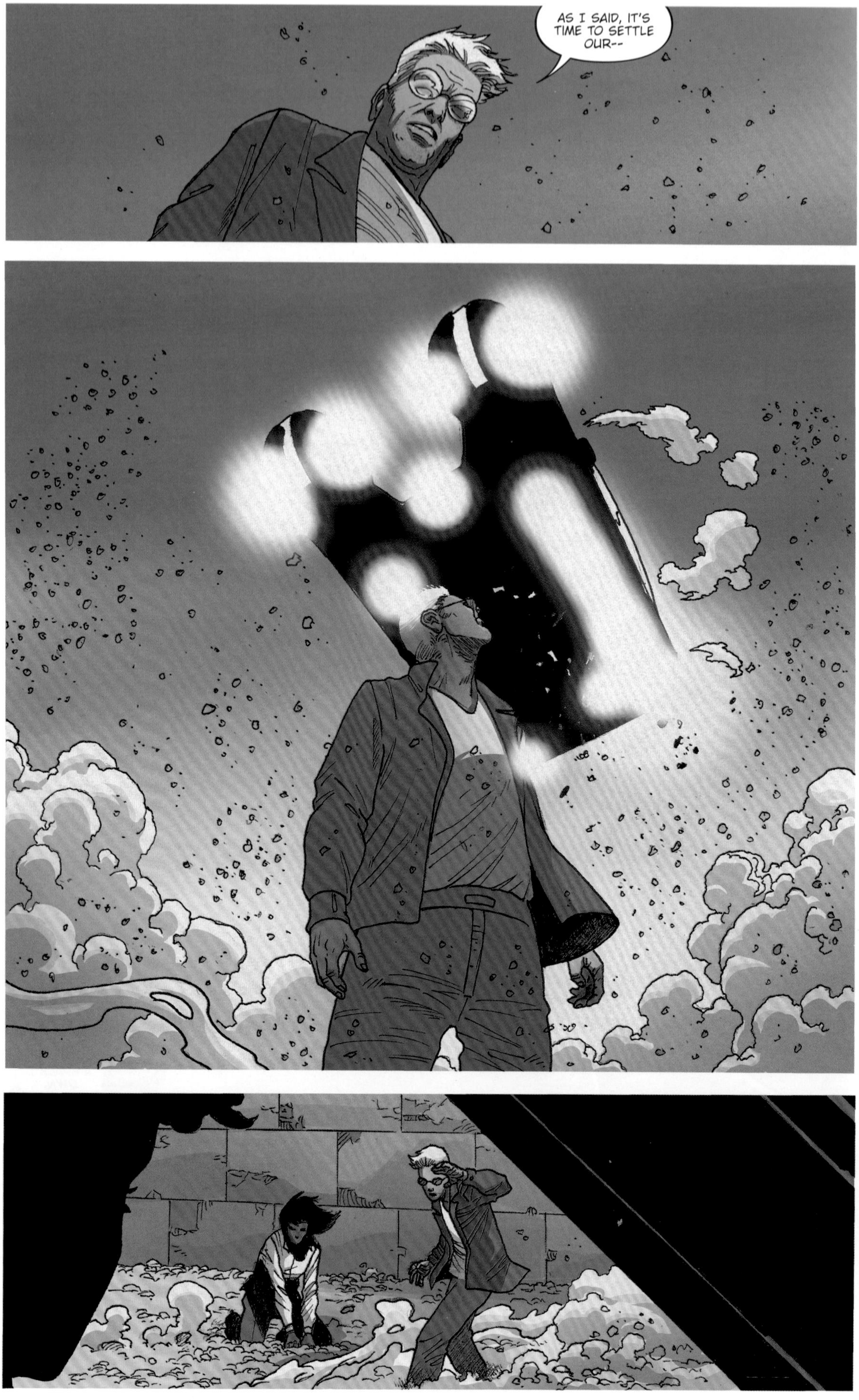
AS I SAID, IT'S TIME TO SETTLE OUR--

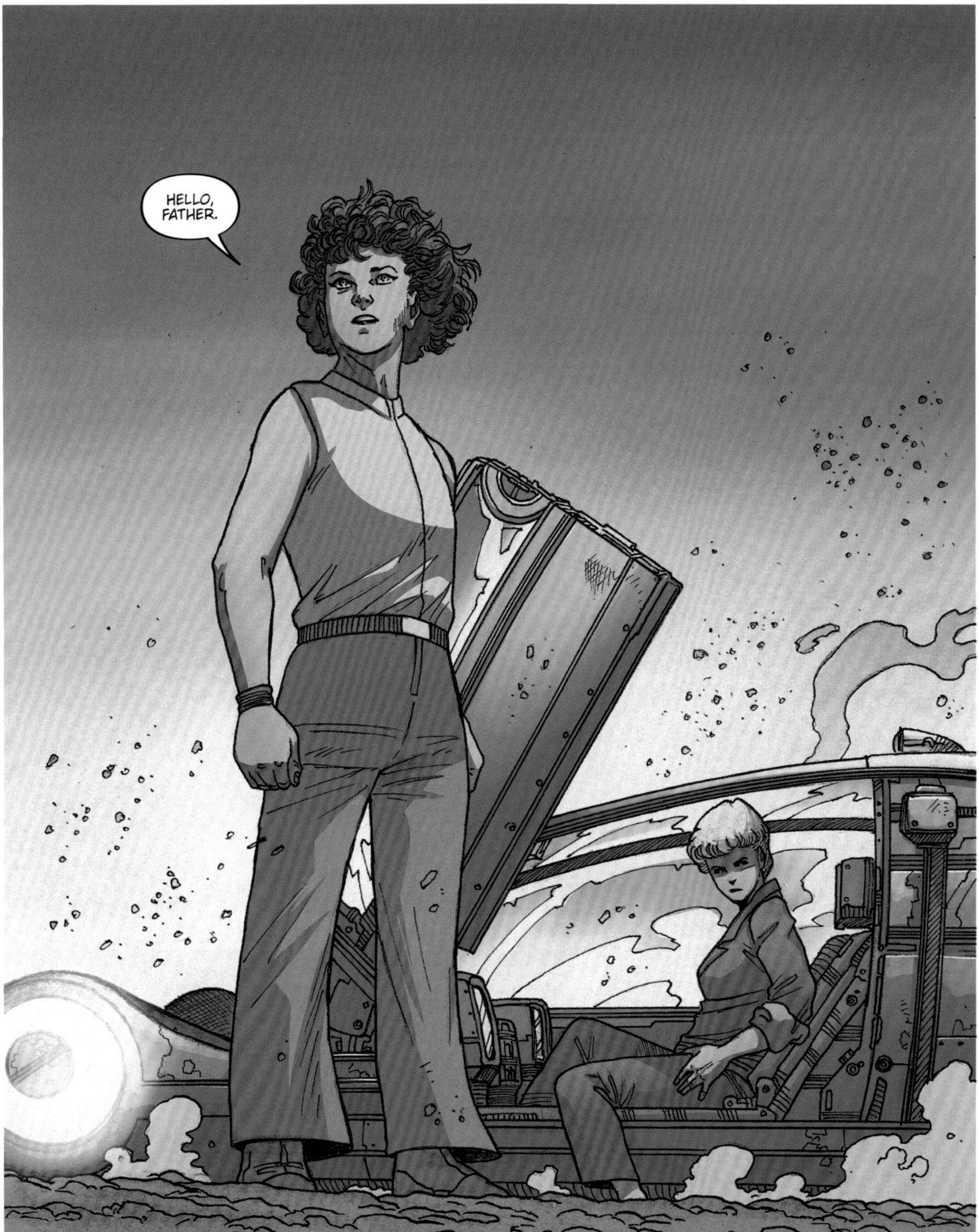
HELLO, FATHER.

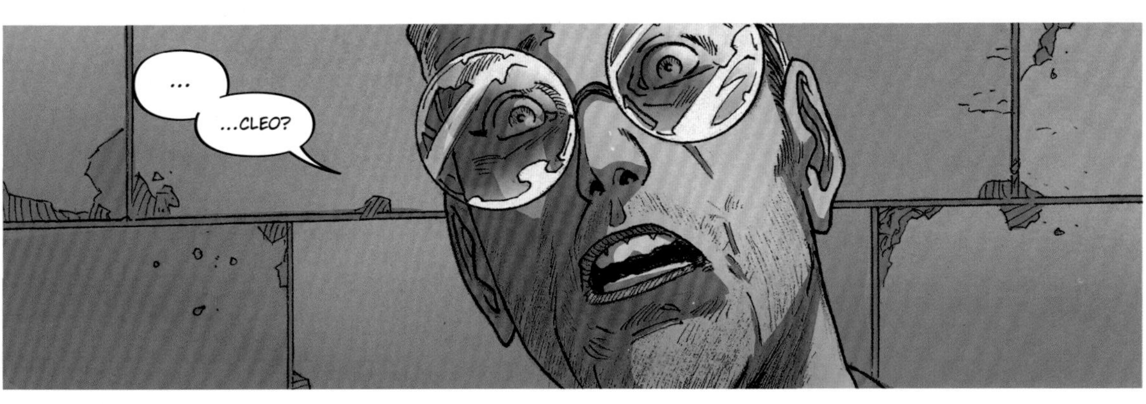
...
...CLEO?

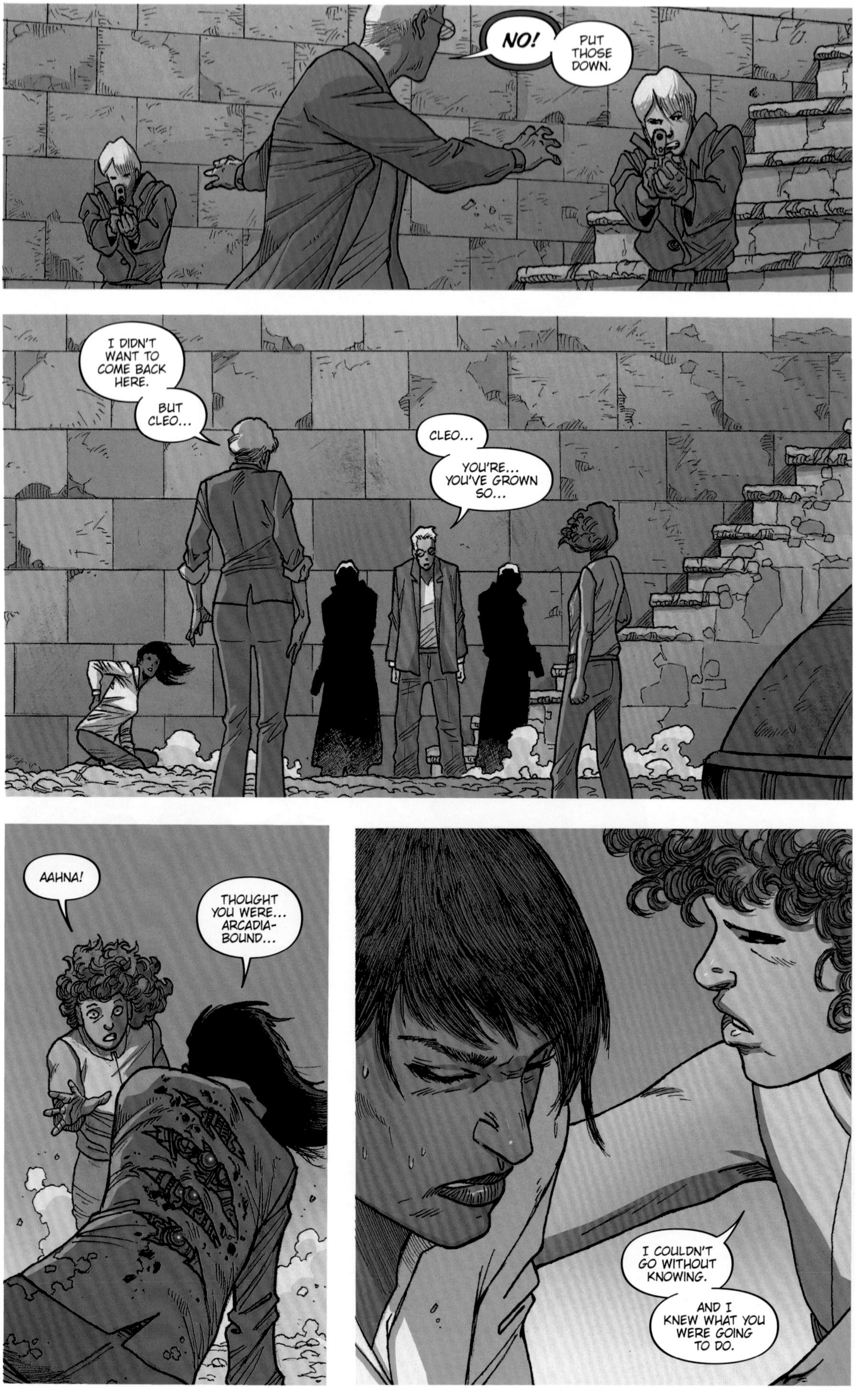
NO!
PUT THOSE DOWN.
I DIDN'T WANT TO COME BACK HERE.
BUT CLEO...
CLEO...
YOU'RE... YOU'VE GROWN SO...
AAHNA!
THOUGHT YOU WERE... ARCADIA-BOUND...
I COULDN'T GO WITHOUT KNOWING.
AND I KNEW WHAT YOU WERE GOING TO DO.

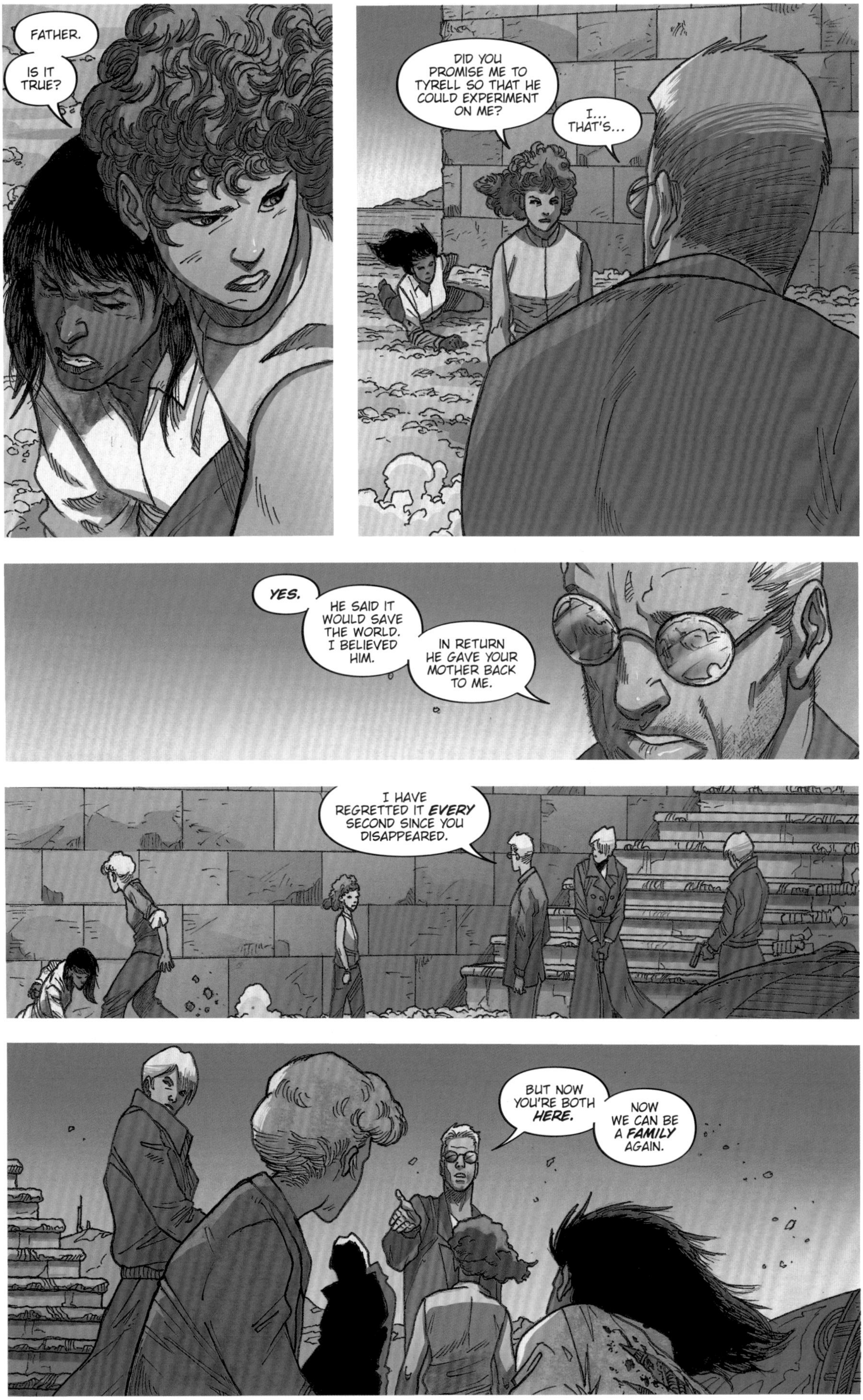

FATHER.
IS IT TRUE?
DID YOU PROMISE ME TO TYRELL SO THAT HE COULD EXPERIMENT ON ME?
I... THAT'S...
YES.
HE SAID IT WOULD SAVE THE WORLD. I BELIEVED HIM.
IN RETURN HE GAVE YOUR MOTHER BACK TO ME.
I HAVE REGRETTED IT *EVERY* SECOND SINCE YOU DISAPPEARED.
BUT NOW YOU'RE BOTH *HERE.*
NOW WE CAN BE A *FAMILY* AGAIN.

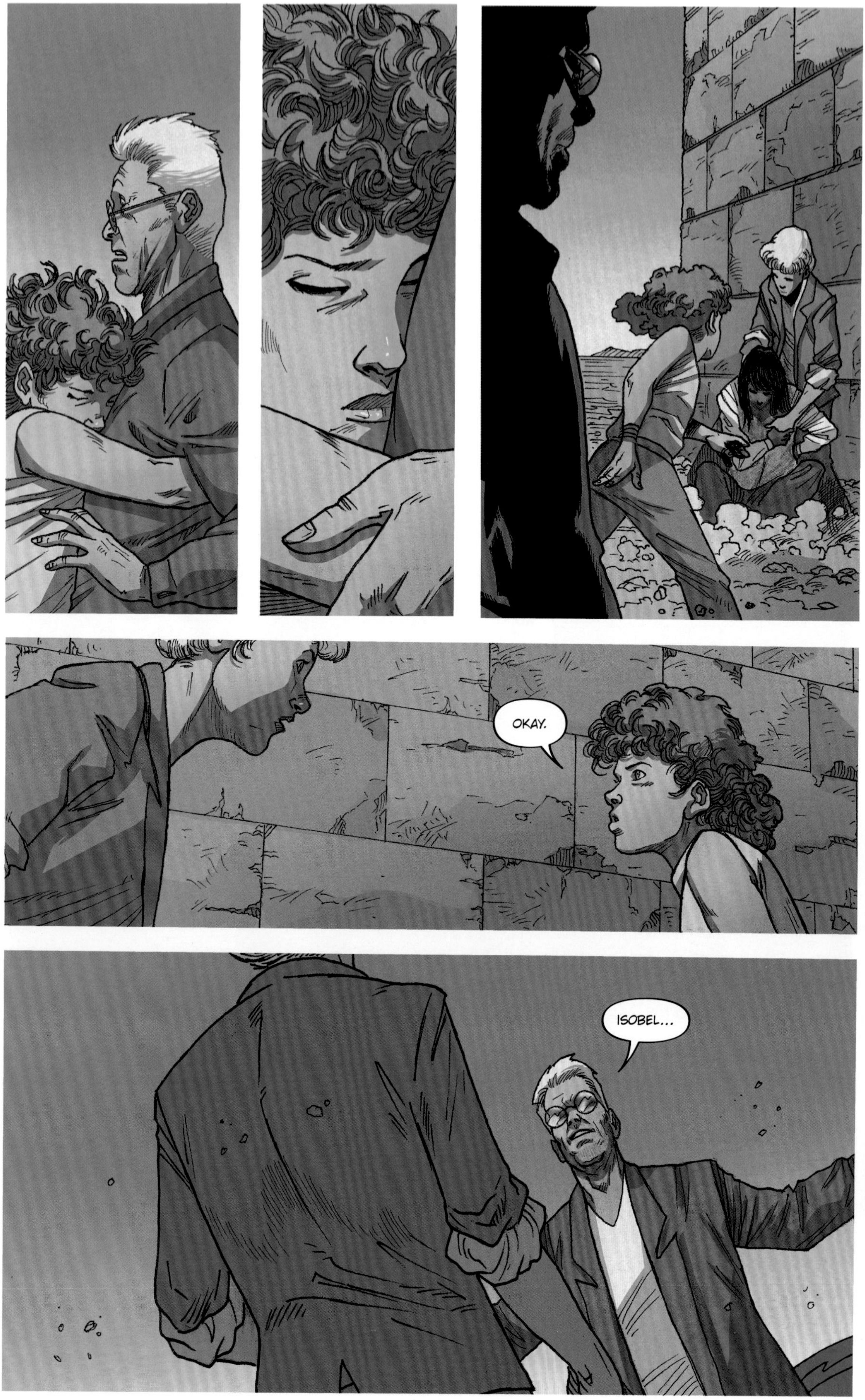
OKAY.
ISOBEL...

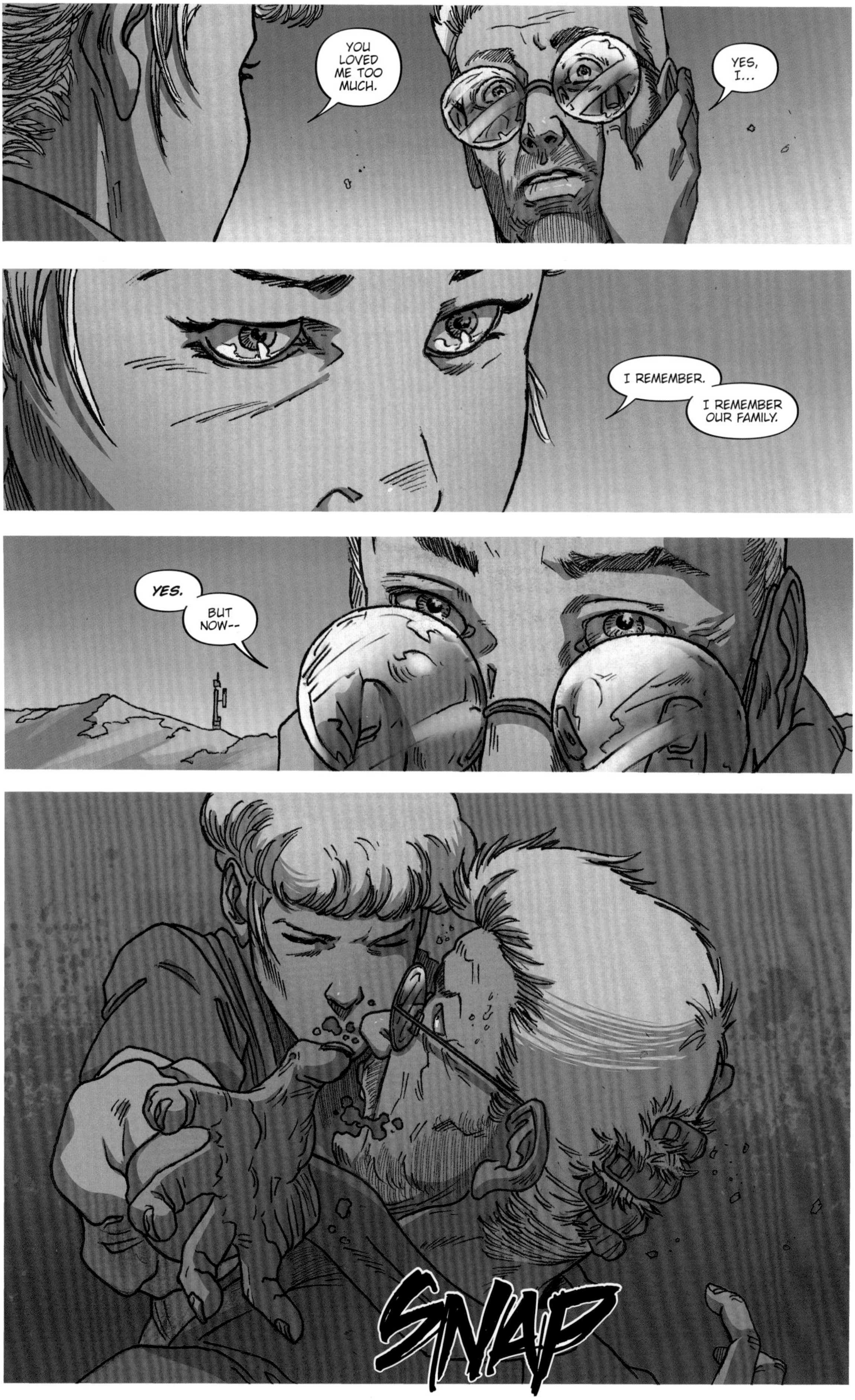
YOU LOVED ME TOO MUCH.
YES, I...
I REMEMBER.
I REMEMBER OUR FAMILY.
YES.
BUT NOW--
SNAP

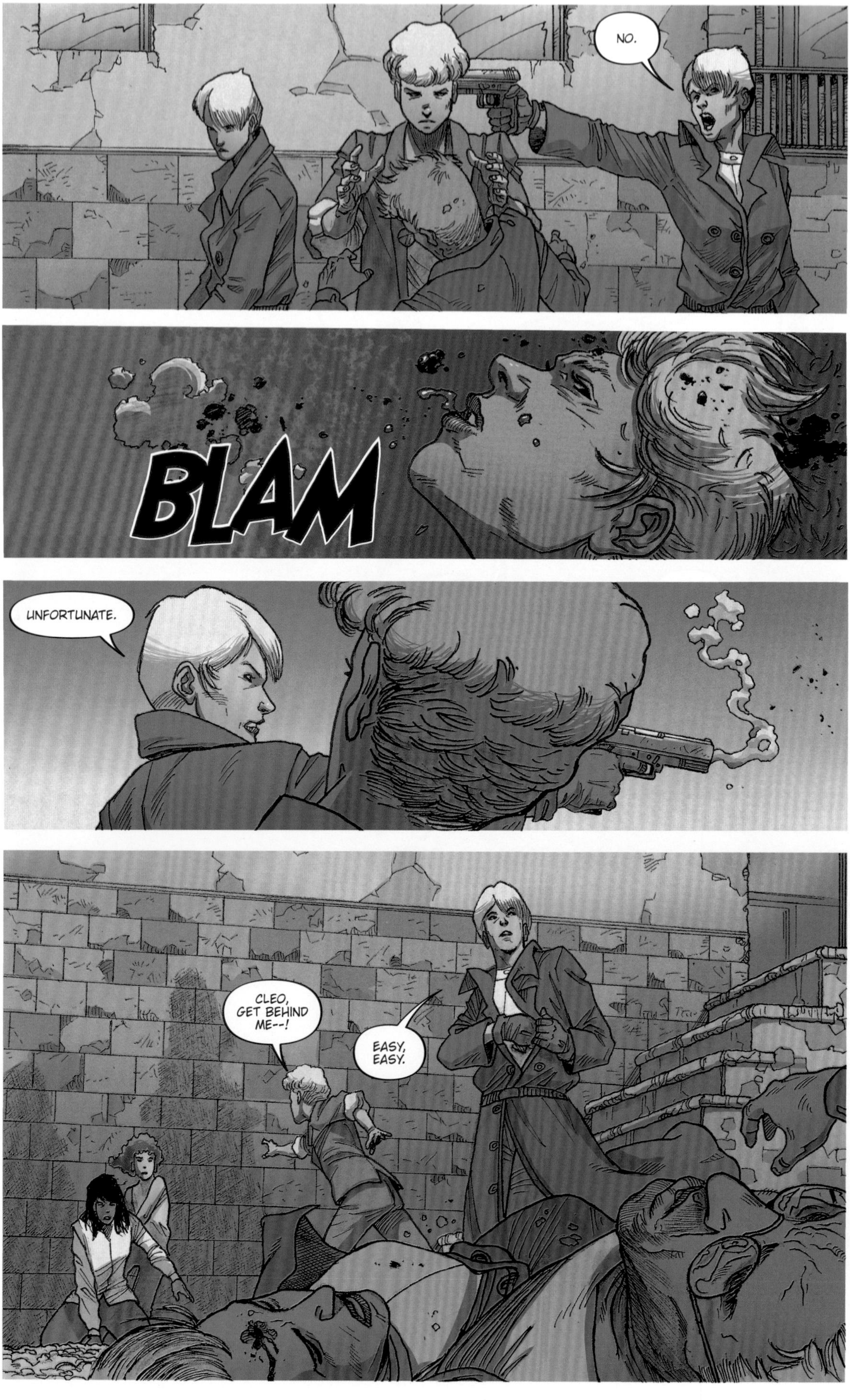
NO.
BLAM
UNFORTUNATE.
CLEO, GET BEHIND ME--!
EASY, EASY.

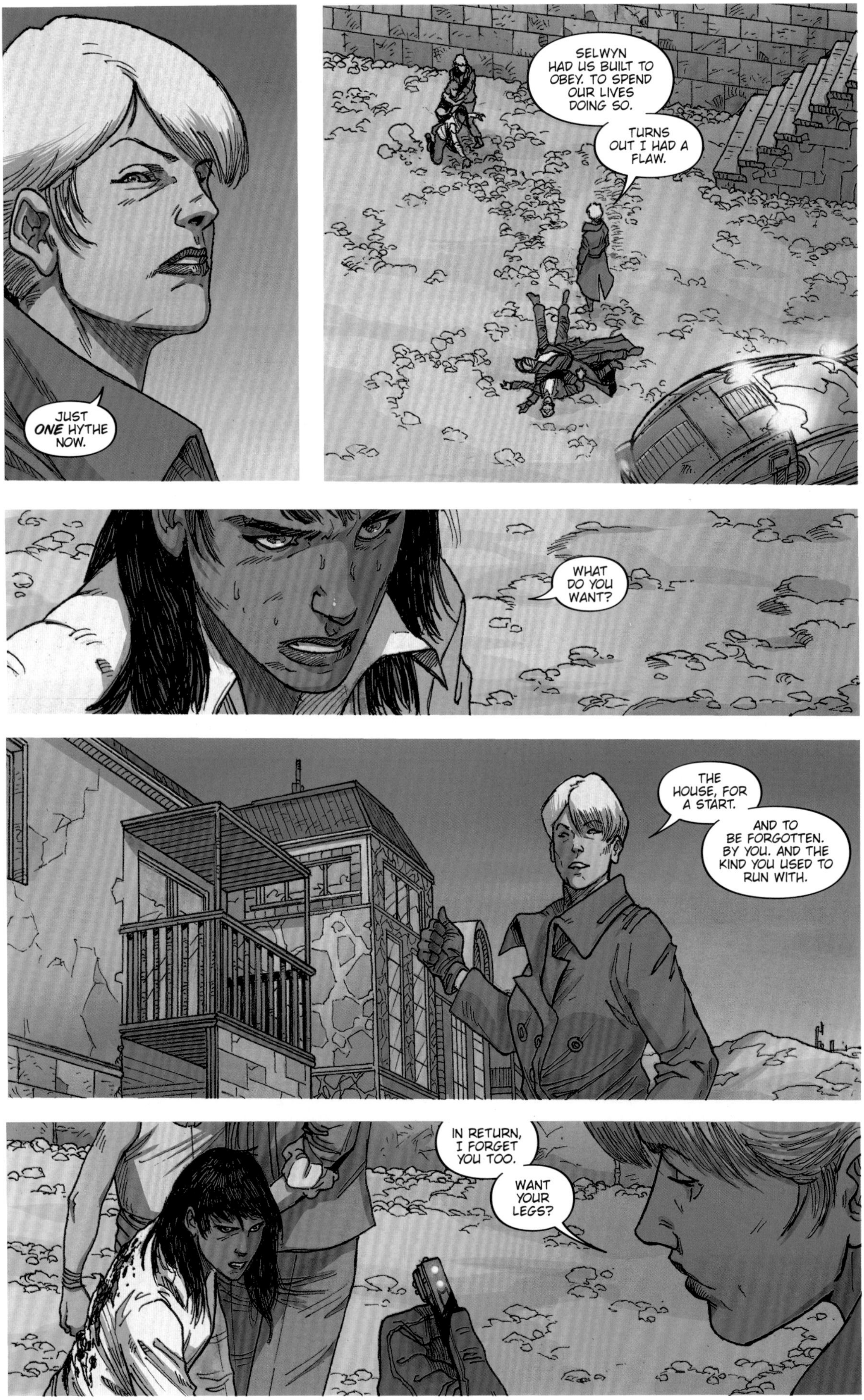
JUST **ONE** HYTHE NOW.
SELWYN HAD US BUILT TO OBEY. TO SPEND OUR LIVES DOING SO.
TURNS OUT I HAD A FLAW.
WHAT DO YOU WANT?
THE HOUSE, FOR A START.
AND TO BE FORGOTTEN. BY YOU. AND THE KIND YOU USED TO RUN WITH.
IN RETURN, I FORGET YOU TOO.
WANT YOUR LEGS?

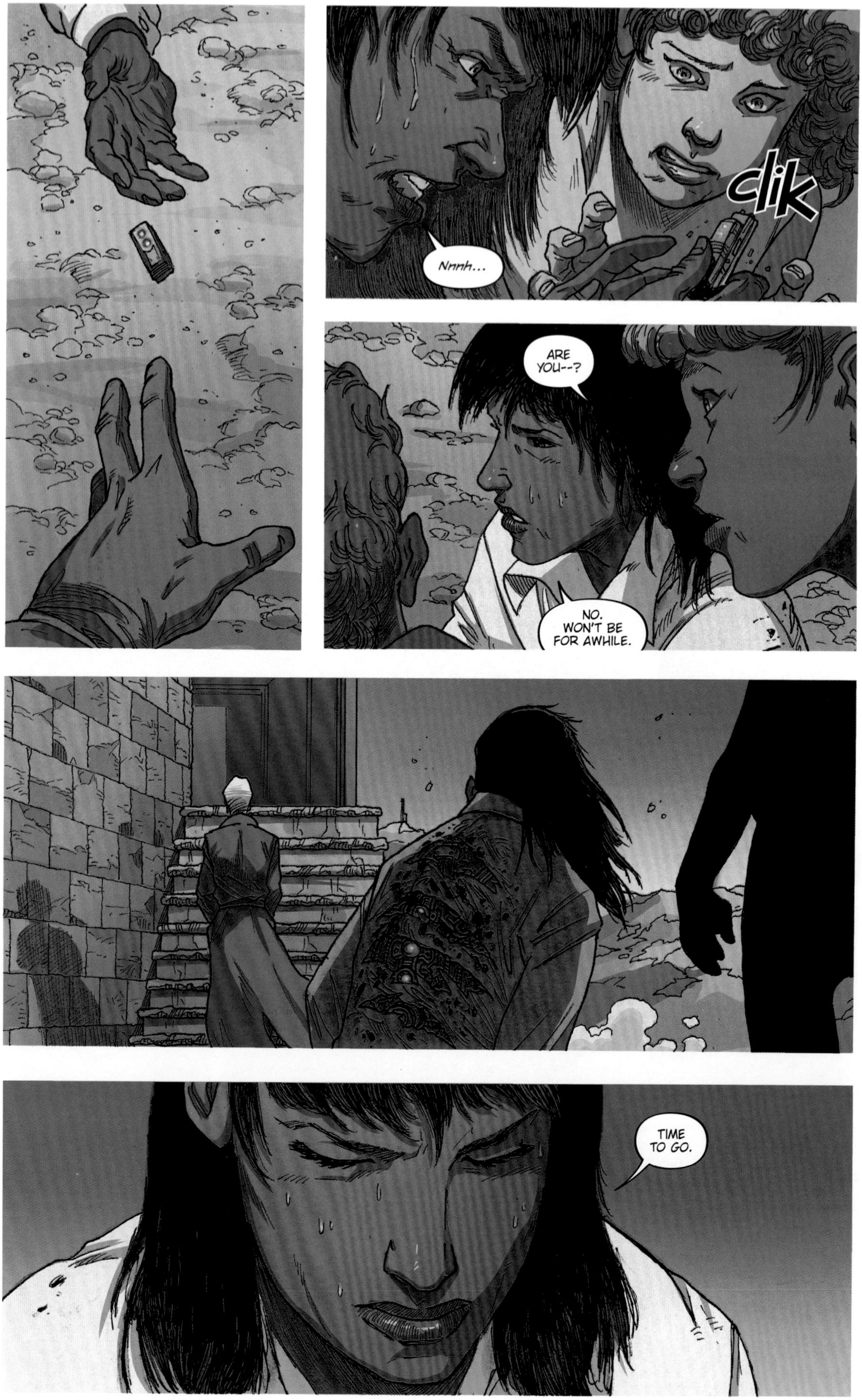
Nnnh...
CLIK
ARE YOU--?
NO. WON'T BE FOR AWHILE.
TIME TO GO.

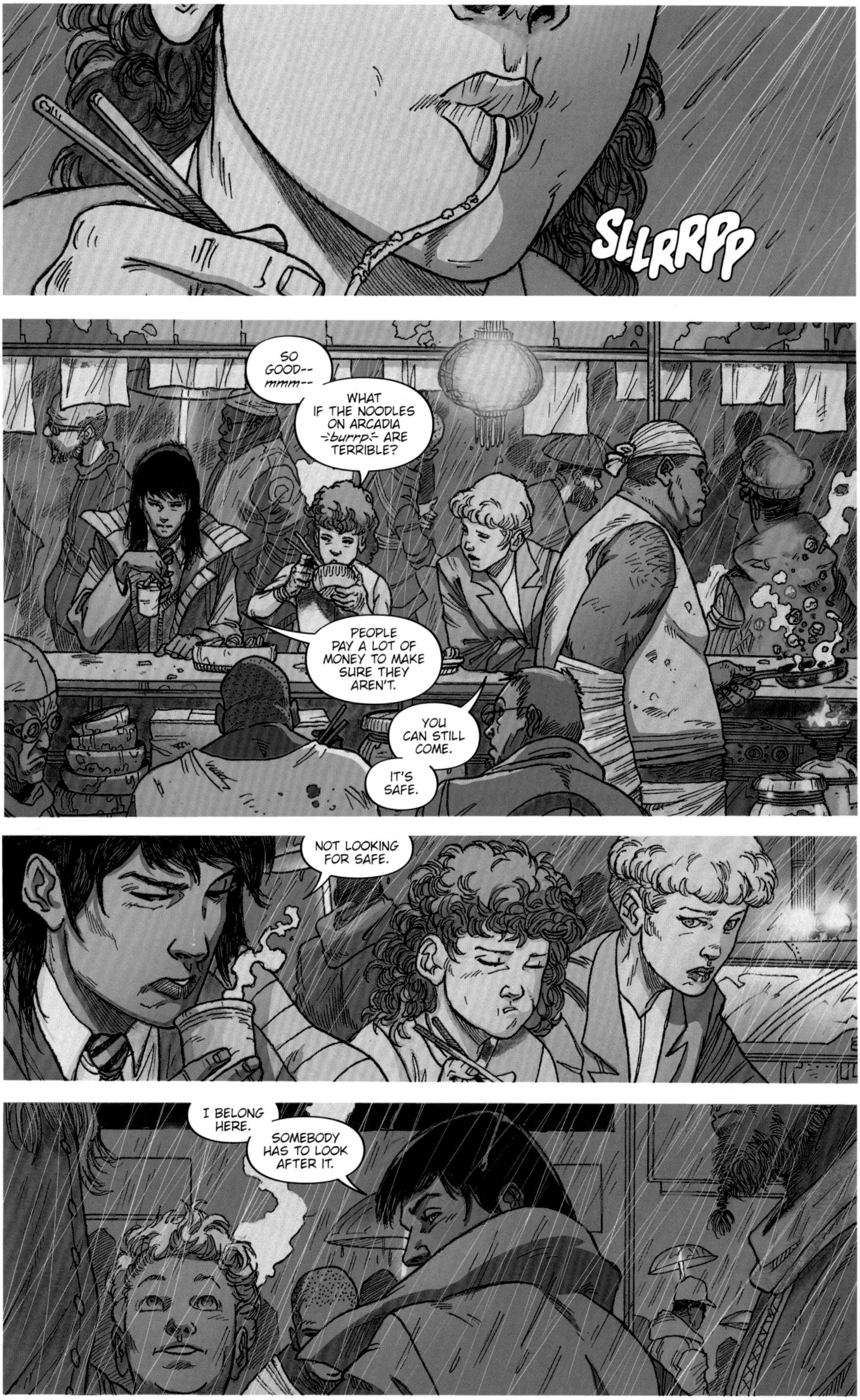
SLLRRPP
SO GOOD-- mmm--
WHAT IF THE NOODLES ON ARCADIA -burrp- ARE TERRIBLE?
PEOPLE PAY A LOT OF MONEY TO MAKE SURE THEY AREN'T.
YOU CAN STILL COME.
IT'S SAFE.
NOT LOOKING FOR SAFE.
I BELONG HERE.
SOMEBODY HAS TO LOOK AFTER IT.

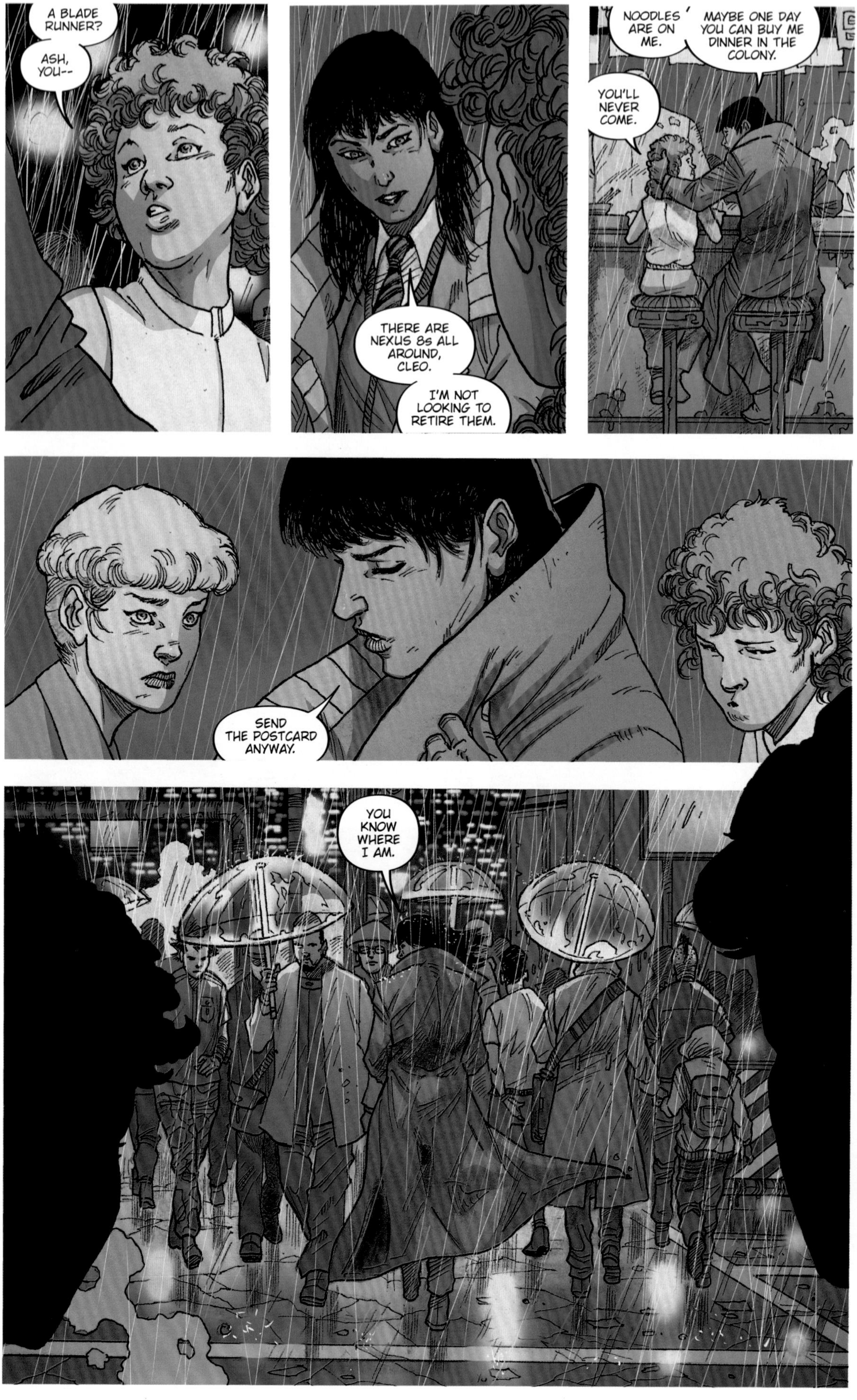
A BLADE RUNNER?
ASH, YOU--
THERE ARE NEXUS 8s ALL AROUND, CLEO.
I'M NOT LOOKING TO RETIRE THEM.
NOODLES ARE ON ME.
MAYBE ONE DAY YOU CAN BUY ME DINNER IN THE COLONY.
YOU'LL NEVER COME.
SEND THE POSTCARD ANYWAY.
YOU KNOW WHERE I AM.

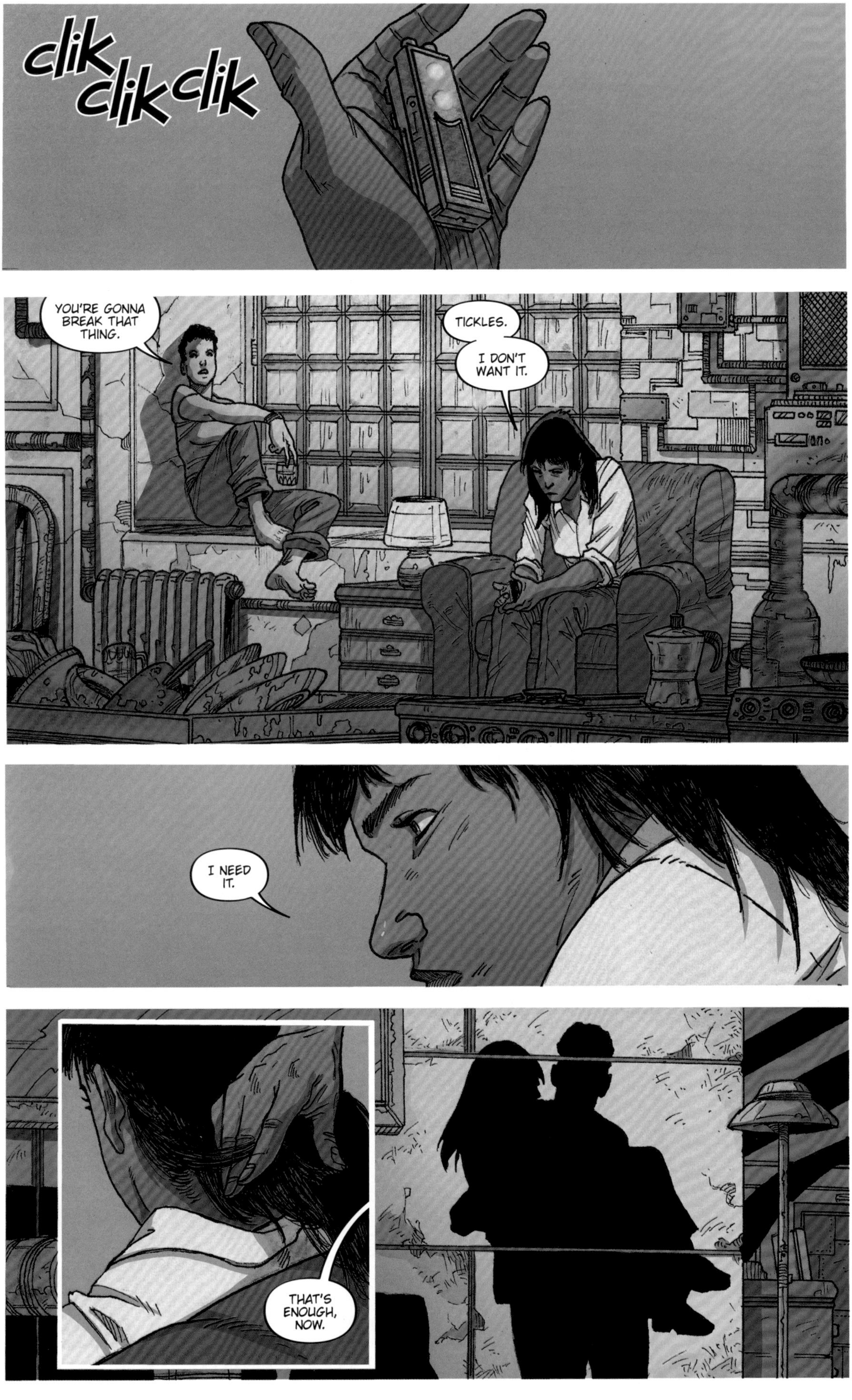
clik clik clik
YOU'RE GONNA BREAK THAT THING.
TICKLES.
I DON'T WANT IT.
I NEED IT.
THAT'S ENOUGH, NOW.

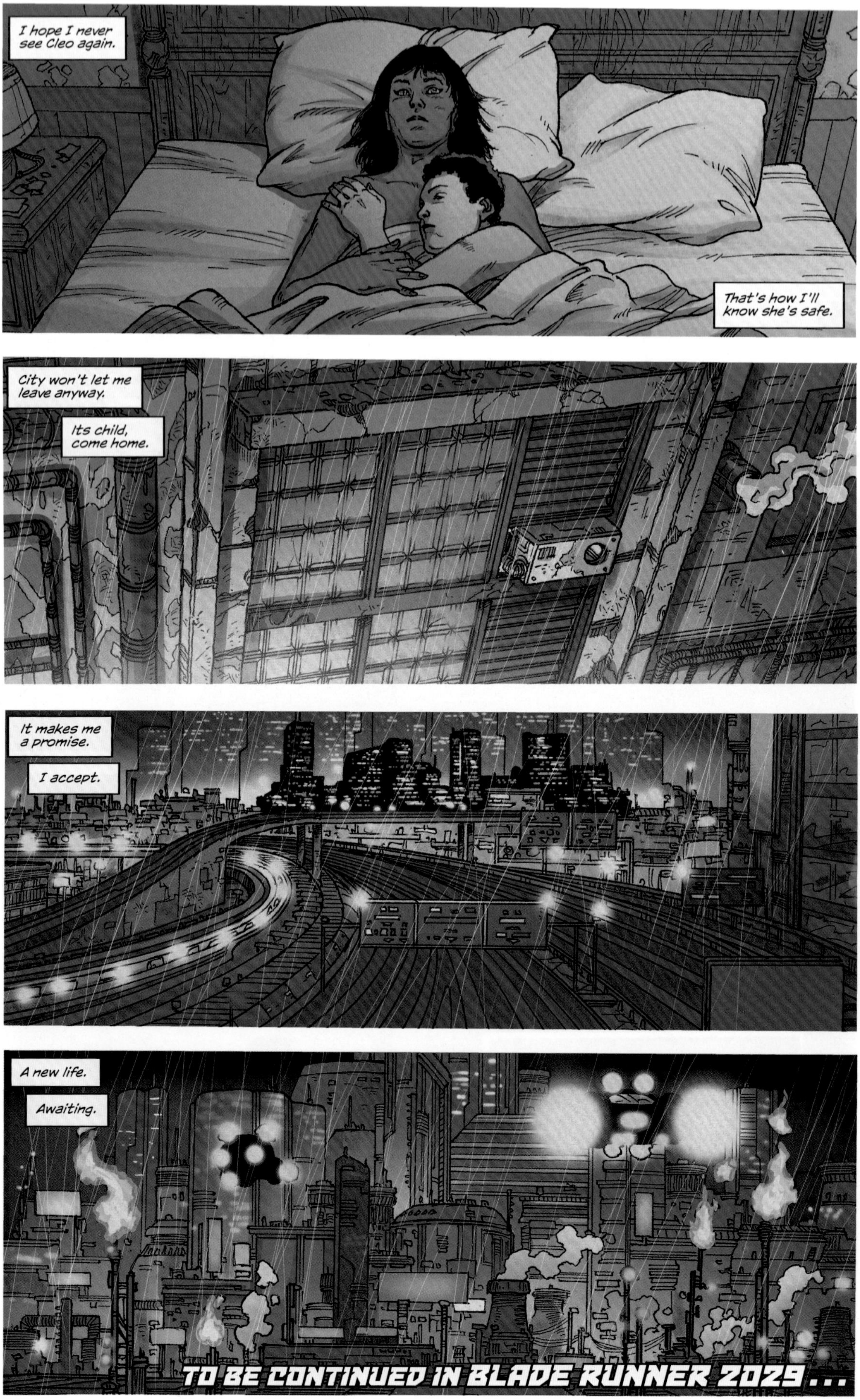
I hope I never see Cleo again.
That's how I'll know she's safe.
City won't let me leave anyway.
Its child, come home.
It makes me a promise.
I accept.
A new life.
Awaiting.
TO BE CONTINUED IN BLADE RUNNER 2029...

COVER GALLERY

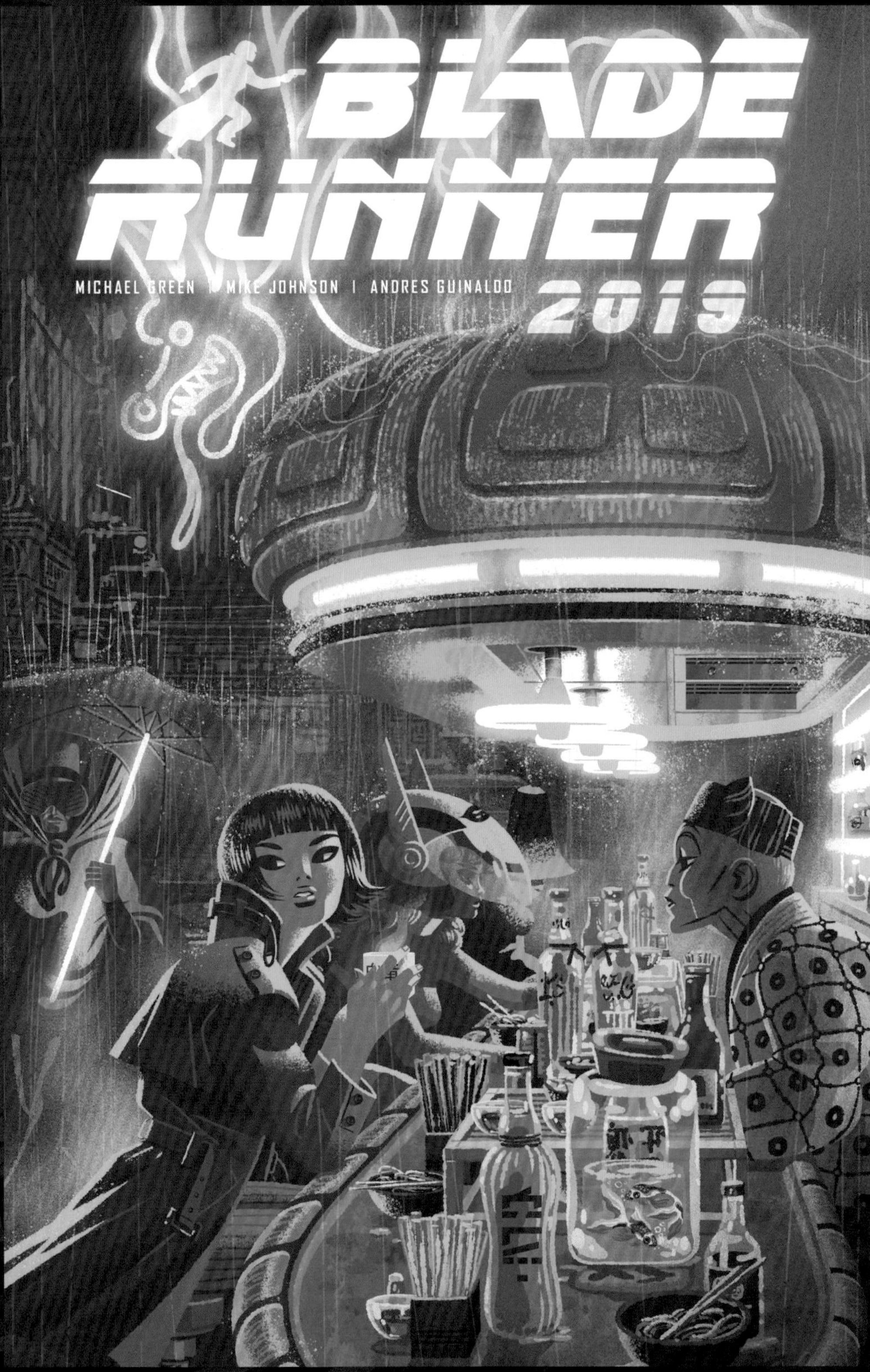
BLADE RUNNER
MICHAEL GREEN | MIKE JOHNSON | ANDRES GUINALDO
2019

COVER D
GEORGE CALTSOUDAS

BLADE RUNNER 2019 ISSUE NINE

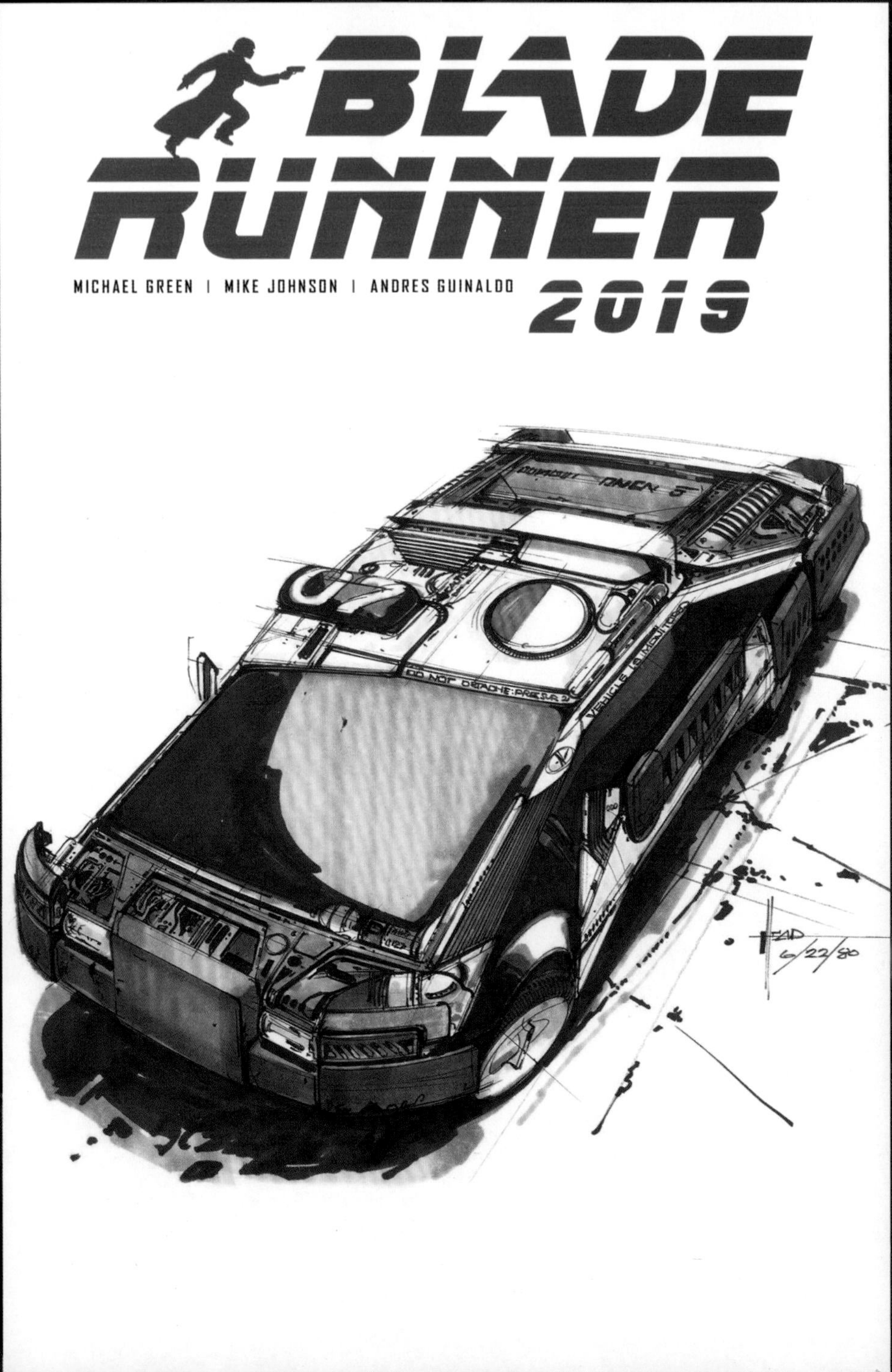
BLADE RUNNER
MICHAEL GREEN | MIKE JOHNSON | ANDRES GUINALDO
2019

ISSUE NINE / COVER B
SYD MEAD

BLADE RUNNER 2019
ISSUE TEN

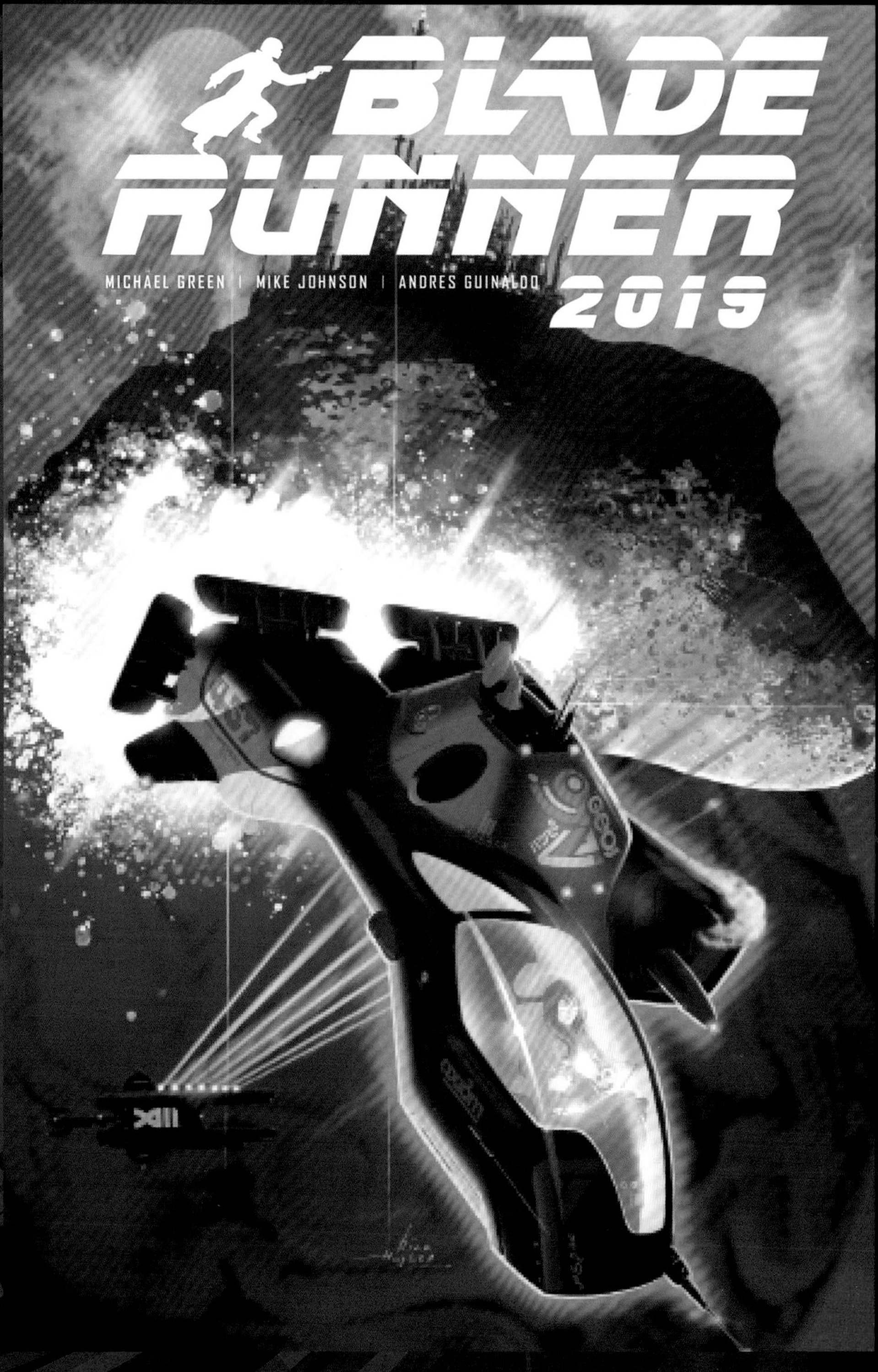
BLADE RUNNER
MICHAEL GREEN | MIKE JOHNSON | ANDRES GUINALDO
2019

COVER A
RIAN HUGHES

BLADE RUNNER
2019
MICHAEL GREEN | MIKE JOHNSON | ANDRES GUINALDO

COVER B
SYD MEAD

BLADE RUNNER
2019
MICHAEL GREEN | MIKE JOHNSON | ANDRES GUINALDO

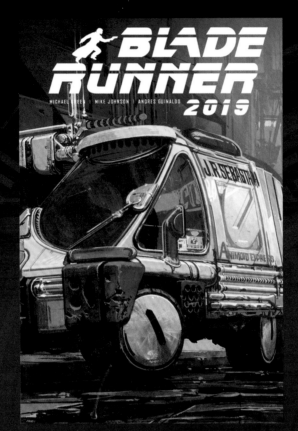

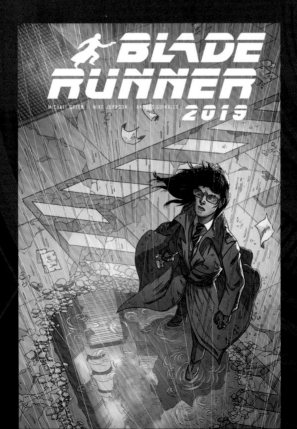

BLADE RUNNER 2019 ISSUE ELEVEN

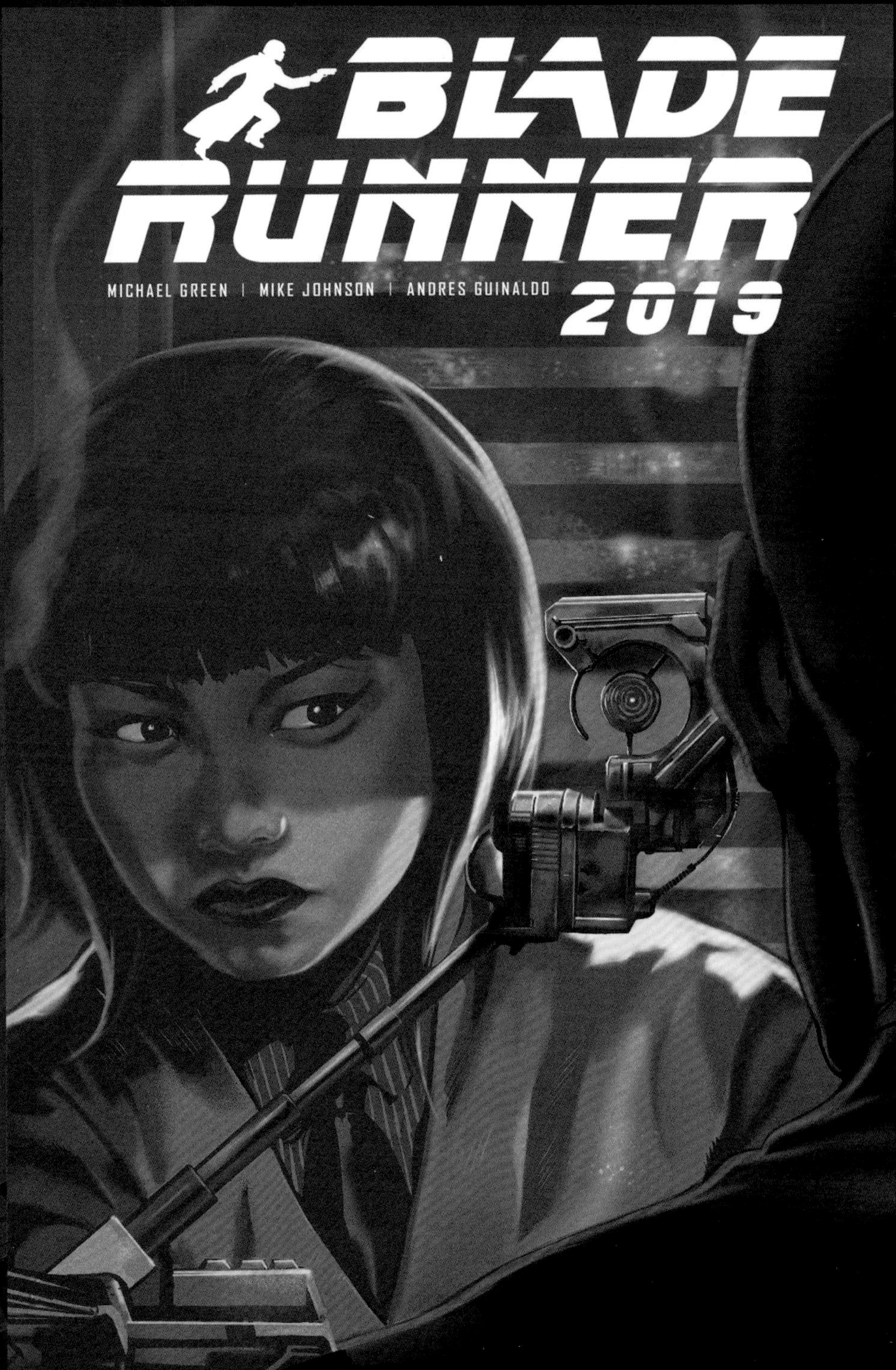
BLADE RUNNER
MICHAEL GREEN | MIKE JOHNSON | ANDRES GUINALDO
2019

COVER A
FERNANDO DAGNINO

BLADE RUNNER 2019
ISSUE ELEVEN

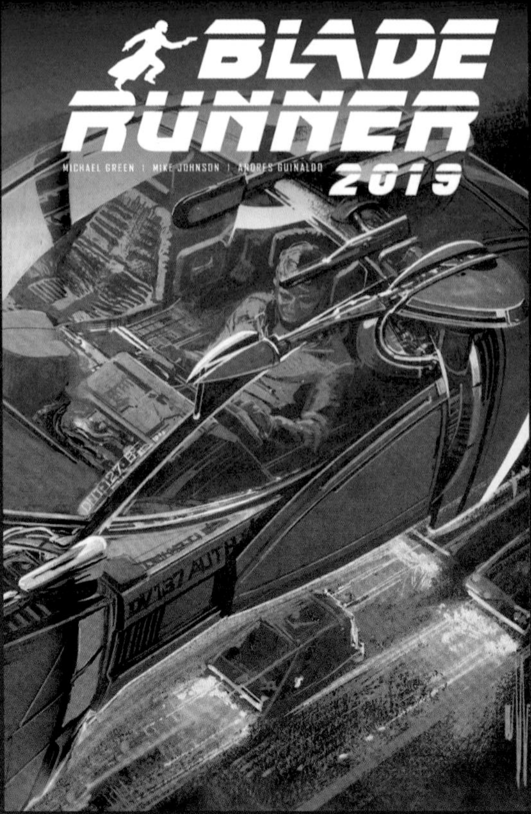
BLADE RUNNER
MICHAEL GREEN | MIKE JOHNSON | ANDRES GUINALDO
2019

COVER B
SYD MEAD

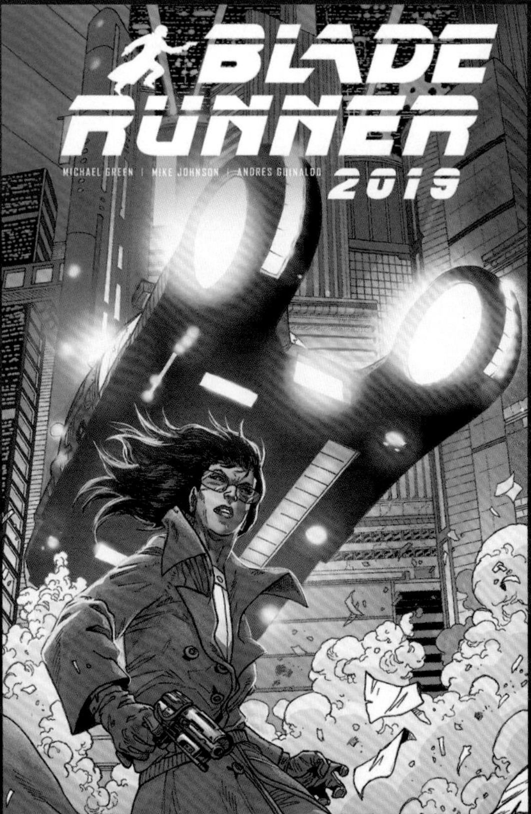
BLADE RUNNER
MICHAEL GREEN | MIKE JOHNSON | ANDRES GUINALDO
2019

COVER C
ANDRES GUINALDO

BLADE RUNNER
MICHAEL GREEN | MIKE JOHNSON | ANDRES GUINALDO
2019

COVER B
SYD MEAD

BLADE RUNNER
MICHAEL GREEN | MIKE JOHNSON | ANDRES GUINALDO
2019

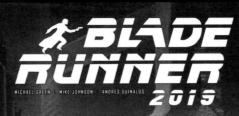

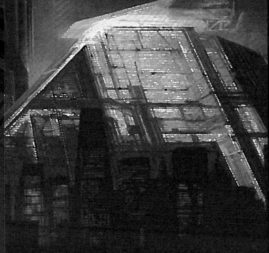

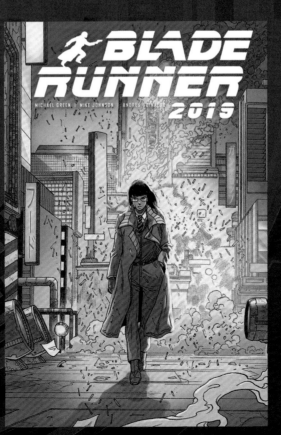

COVER C
ANDRES GUINALDO

BLADE RUNNER
– Issue #9
Written by Mike Johnson and Michael Green
Art by Andres Guinaldo. Colors by Marco Lesko

[Page 1]

PANEL 1:   Street level Los Angeles, 2027. Night. A crowd even more diverse than we saw in 2019. Among the crowd – but we don't highlight her – is WOJCIECH, Ash's captain from her LAPD days. Hair is gray now, in long dreads. Grocery bag in hand.

1. ASH CAPTION: Every face a story.

PANEL 2:   Closer on Wojciech in the crowd, looking up as a few raindrops start to fall.

2. ASH CAPTION: This story I know well.

3. WOJCIECH: Goddamn, not now…

PANEL 3:   Rain pours down as Wojiech unlocks the door of her old apartment building. Two hooded homeless huddle in the shadow of her stoop.

4. ASH CAPTION: Lydia Wojciech, Los Angeles Police
                       Department, retired.

PANEL 4:   We're inside Wojiech's apartment, dark, as she reaches for the light switch, her wet sleeve dripping.

5. ASH CAPTION: She loved making my life hell, back when.

6. ASH CAPTION: Now…

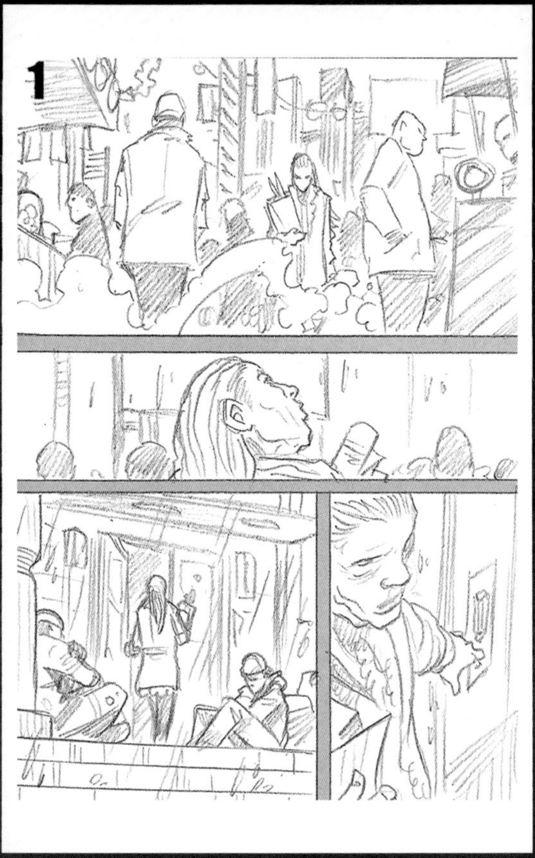
1

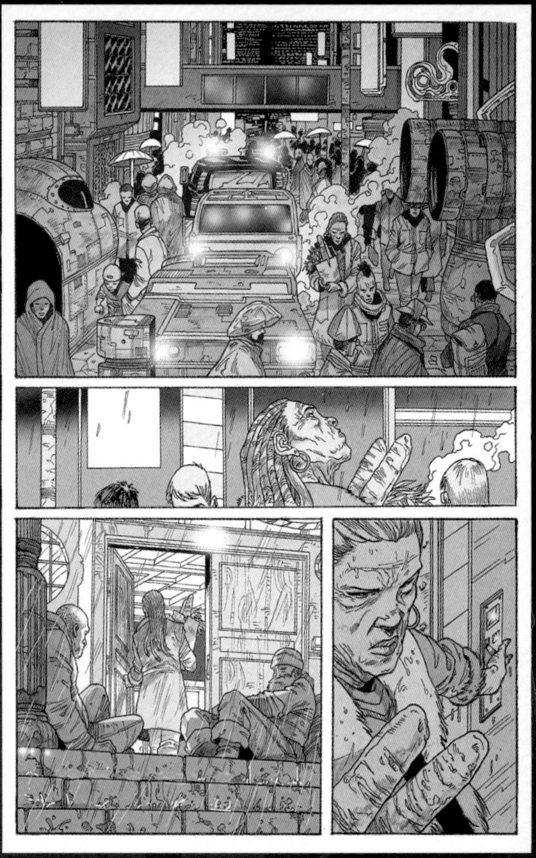

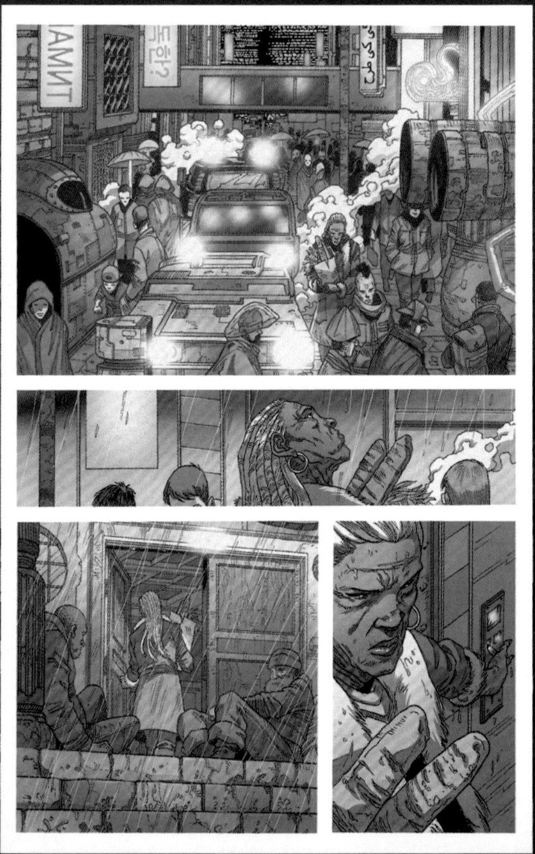

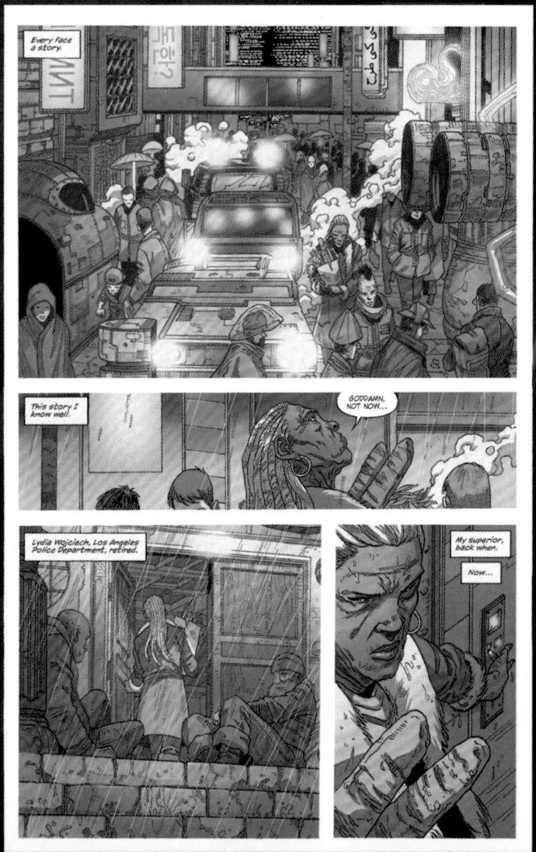
Every face a story.
This story I know well.
GODDAMN, NOT NOW...
Lydia Wojciech, Los Angeles Police Department, retired.
My superior, back when.
Now...

BLADE RUNNER
– Issue #10

Written by Mike Johnson and Michael Green
Art by Andres Guinaldo. Colors by Marco Lesko

[Page 3]

PANEL 1:   Taking up the top 2/3rds of the page.

Another angle on the ruins of the Tyrell Corporation.

Sunset paints the broken buildings red and gold.

1. ASH CAPTION:	Replicant attack shuts down Los Angeles.
2. ASH CAPTION:	Tyrell Corporation servers destroyed.
3. ASH CAPTION:	No more record of who's artificial.
4. ASH CAPTION:	With no old man Eldon, nobody around to stop a ban

on production.

5. ASH CAPTION:	And here we are.

PANEL 2:   Bottom 1/3 of the page. Close on ASH, her face lit GLOWING GREEN by an off-panel display. In her pupils we see the tiny reflections of the green Tyrell OWL LOGO.

6. ASH CAPTION:	Sifting through the ashes of the world I left behind.
7. ASH:	This'll help, Fost.

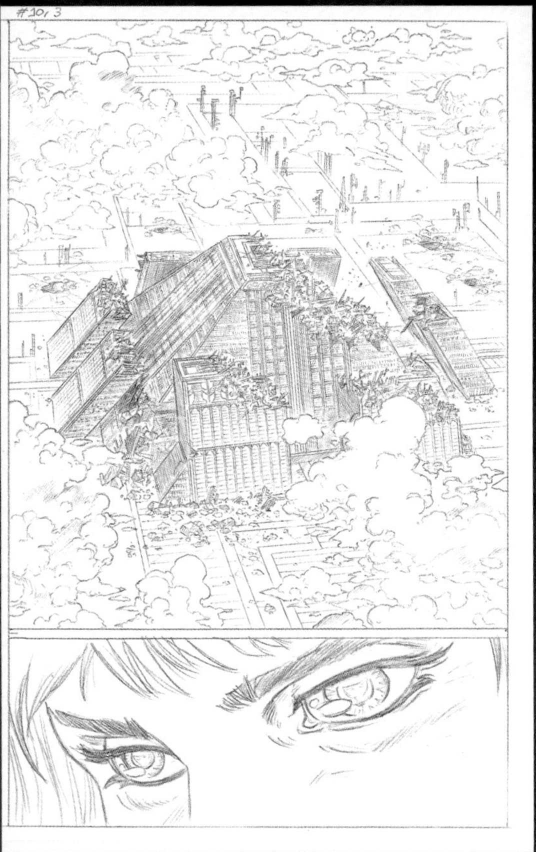
#10, 3

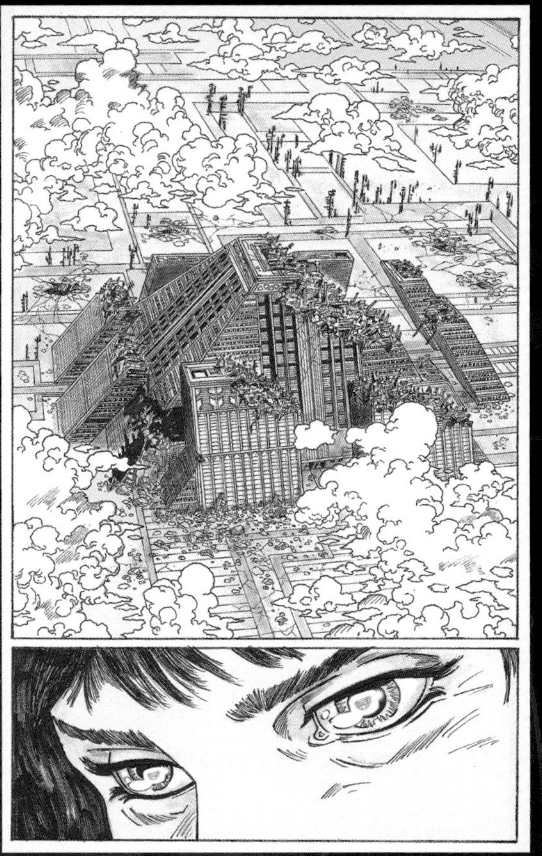

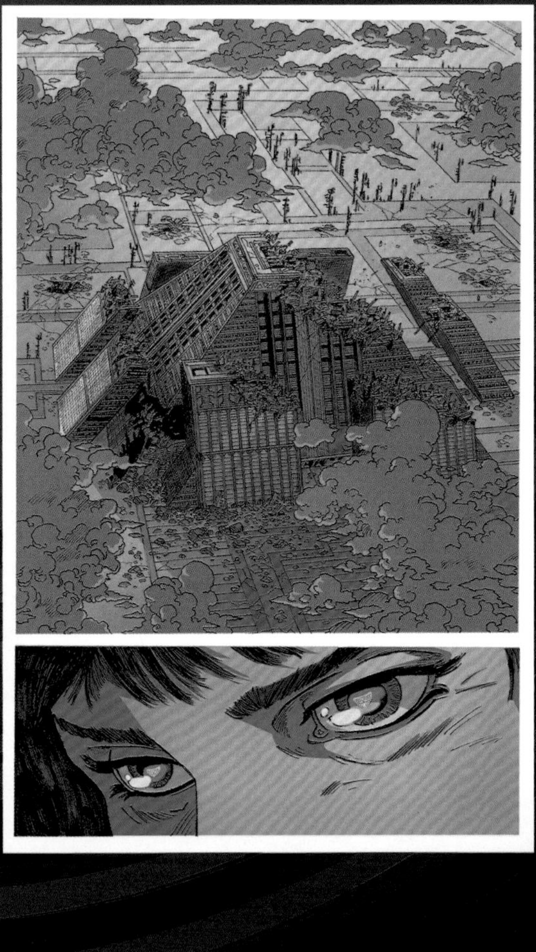

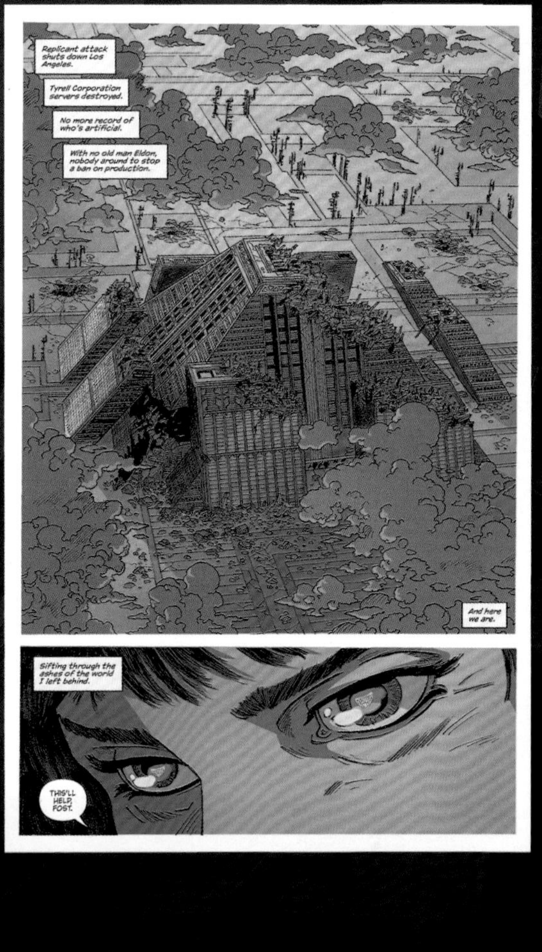
Replicant attack shuts down Los Angeles.
Tyrell Corporation servers destroyed.
No more record of who's artificial.
With no old man Eldon, nobody around to stop a ban on production.
And here we are.
Sifting through the ashes of the world I left behind.
THIS'LL HELP, FOST.

BLADE RUNNER
– Issue #11
Written by Mike Johnson and Michael Green
Art by Andres Guinaldo. Colors by Marco Lesko

[Page 1]

PANEL 1:   Close on AN EYEBALL. The GLITTERING SKYLINE of downtown Los Angeles is reflected in the pupil's black.

  1. FREYSA CAPTION: "We are everywhere."

  2. FREYSA CAPTON: "But they don't see us."

PANEL 2:   An impatient EXECUTIVE (white male, 30s) in an expensive suit checks his watch as a CHINESE CAR WASH ATTENDANT wipes down the hood of his future-slick sedan. The neon of the city reflects on the hood.

  3. FREYSA CAPTION: "We keep them clean."

PANEL 3:   A fancy restaurant. An overly-bejeweled OLDER WOMAN (Japanese, 70s) sneers as a BLACK MAN'S HAND serves a plate of beautifully arranged sushi in front of her.

  4. FREYSA CAPTION: "We keep them fed."

PANEL 4:   A rich child's bedroom. One wall is a window looking out at the glittering skyline at sunset. A HISPANIC NANNY (female, 40s) in a modest outfit sits on the bed with the CHILD (white, 6 years old), reading together from a glowing transparent tablet.

  5. FREYSA CAPTION: "We keep them safe."

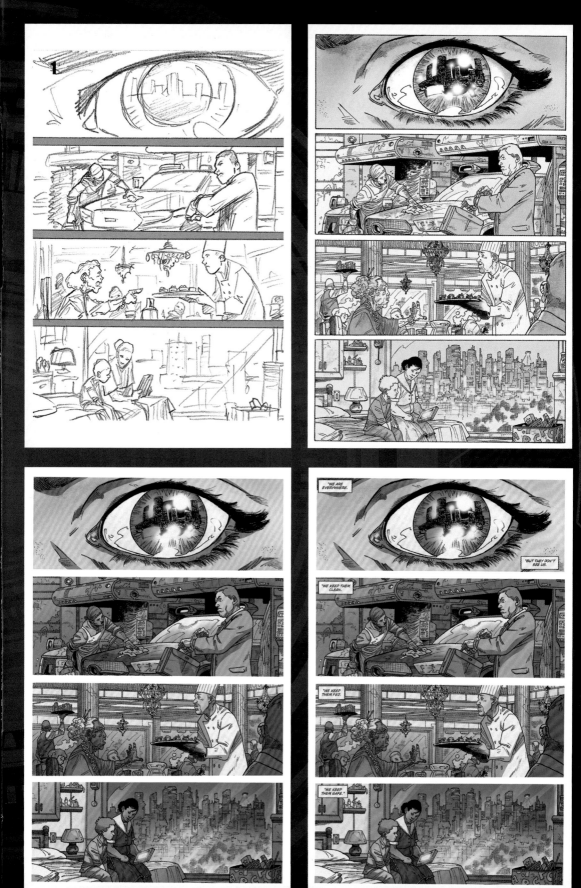

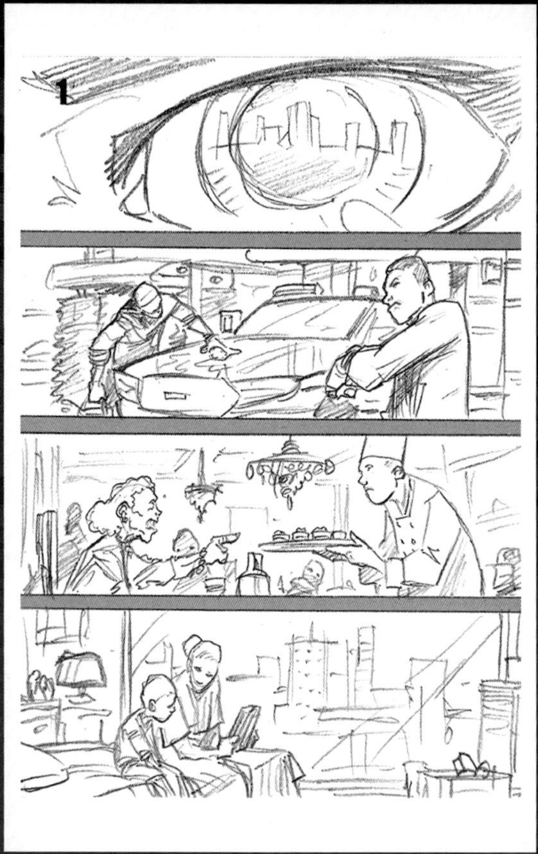
1

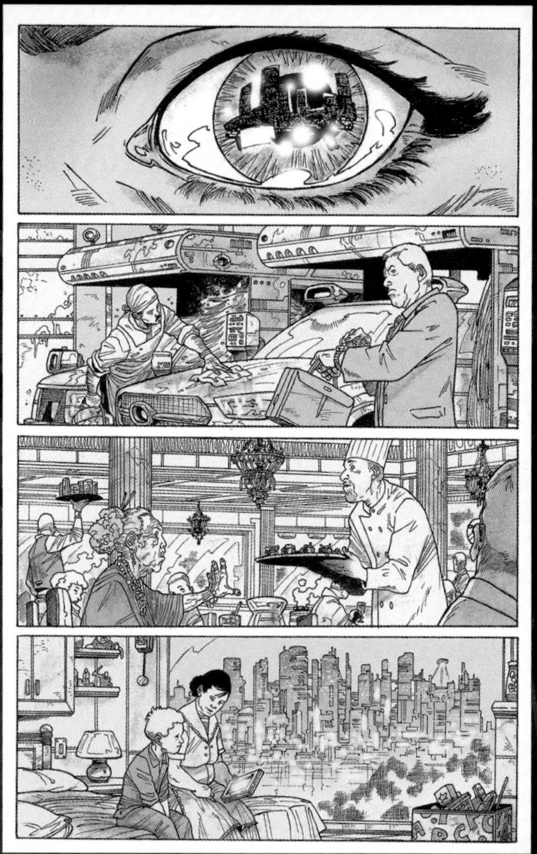

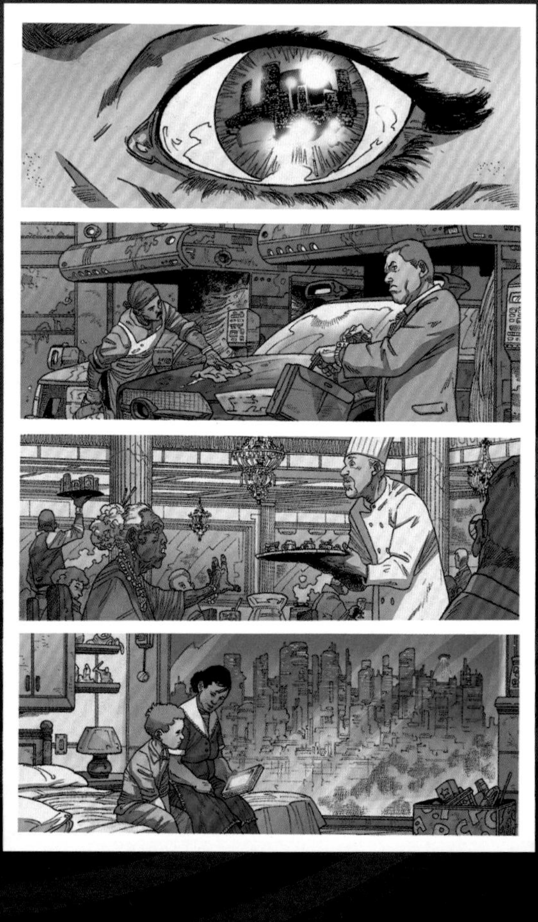

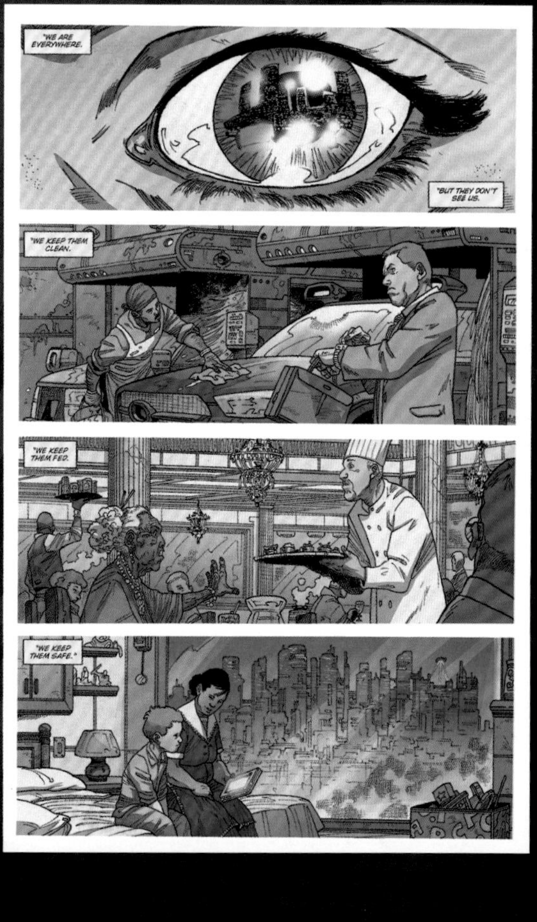
"WE ARE EVERYWHERE.
"BUT THEY DON'T SEE US.
"WE KEEP THEM CLEAN.
"WE KEEP THEM FED.
"WE KEEP THEM SAFE."

BLADE RUNNER
– Issue #11
Written by Mike Johnson and Michael Green
Art by Andres Guinaldo. Colors by Marco Lesko

[Page 19]

PANEL 1:   Side view. Freysa faces Ash.

    1. FREYSA: These aren't our kind.

    2. FREYSA: The light we have? That's gone in these new ones.

    3. FREYSA: Purely functional. Obedient. Like that one we met tonight.

    4. ASH: I don't know where he is.

PANEL 2:   Over Ash onto Freysa.

    5. FREYSA: You can start in Santa Barbara.

    6. ASH: Checked the records. He sold that place years ago. Disappeared.

PANEL 3:   On Freysa.

    7. FREYSA: Sold it to a shell corp he owns.

    8. FREYSA: Even if he's not there. A trail is.

PANEL 4:   On Ash.

    9. ASH: Possible.

    10. ASH: You stay here with the boy.

    11. ASH: This thing…

PANEL 5:   Wide view as dawn begins to break over the still-glittering city.

12. ASH DIALOGUE CAPTION: "I do on my own."

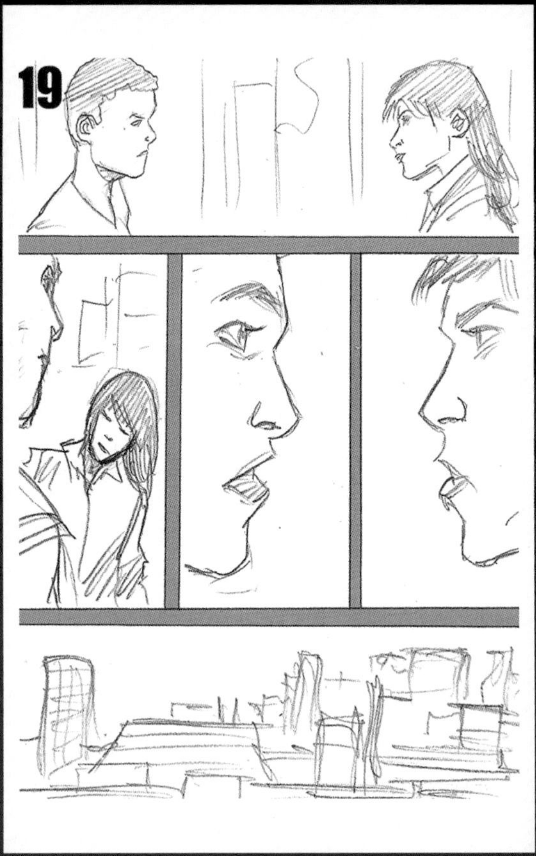
19

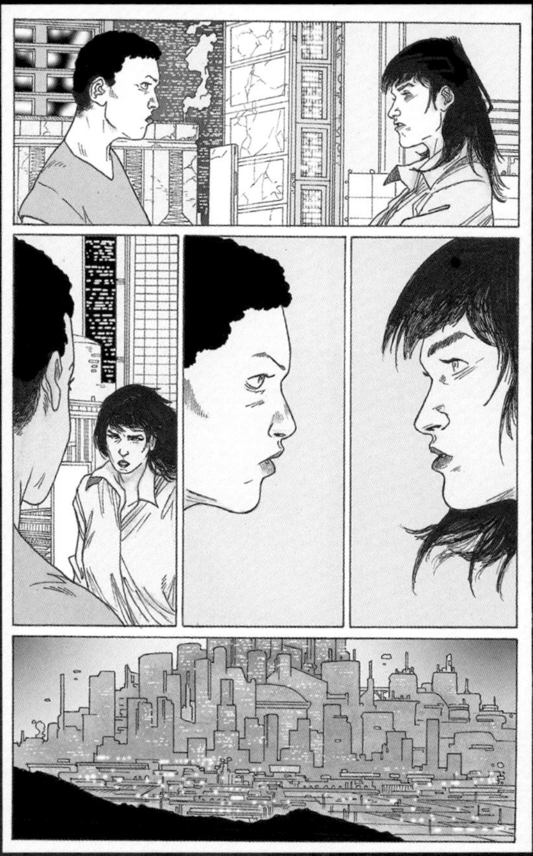

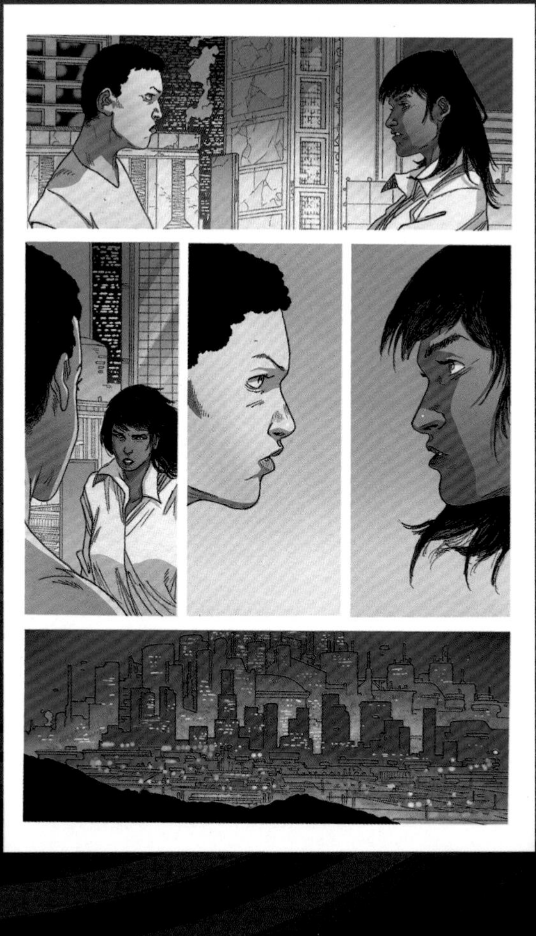

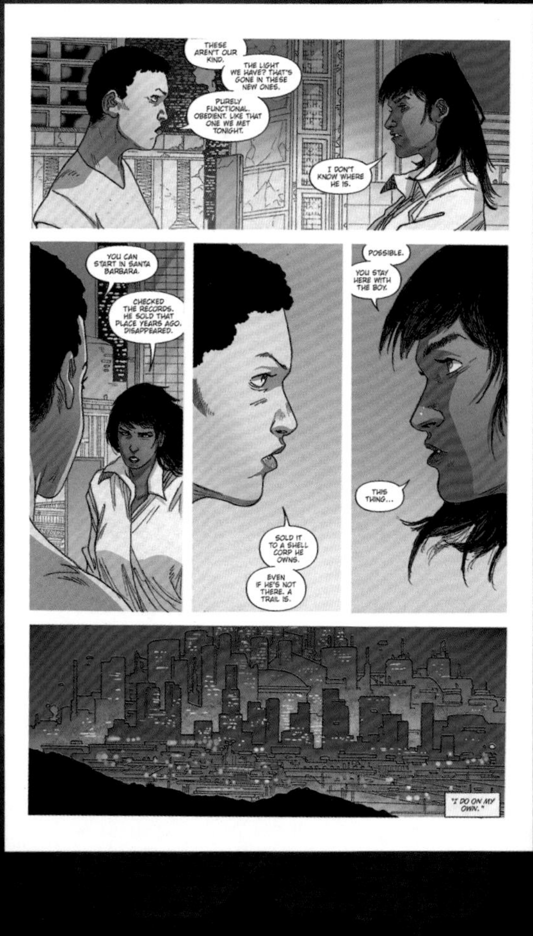
THESE AREN'T OUR KIND.
THE LIGHT WE HAVE? THAT'S GONE IN THESE NEW ONES.
PURELY FUNCTIONAL. OBEDIENT. LIKE THAT ONE WE MET TONIGHT.
I DON'T KNOW WHERE HE IS.
YOU CAN START IN SANTA BARBARA.
CHECKED THE RECORDS. HE SOLD THAT PLACE YEARS AGO. DISAPPEARED.
SOLD IT TO A SHELL CORP HE OWNS.
EVEN IF HE'S NOT THERE. A TRAIL IS.
POSSIBLE.
YOU STAY HERE WITH THE BOY.
THIS THING...
"I DO ON MY OWN."

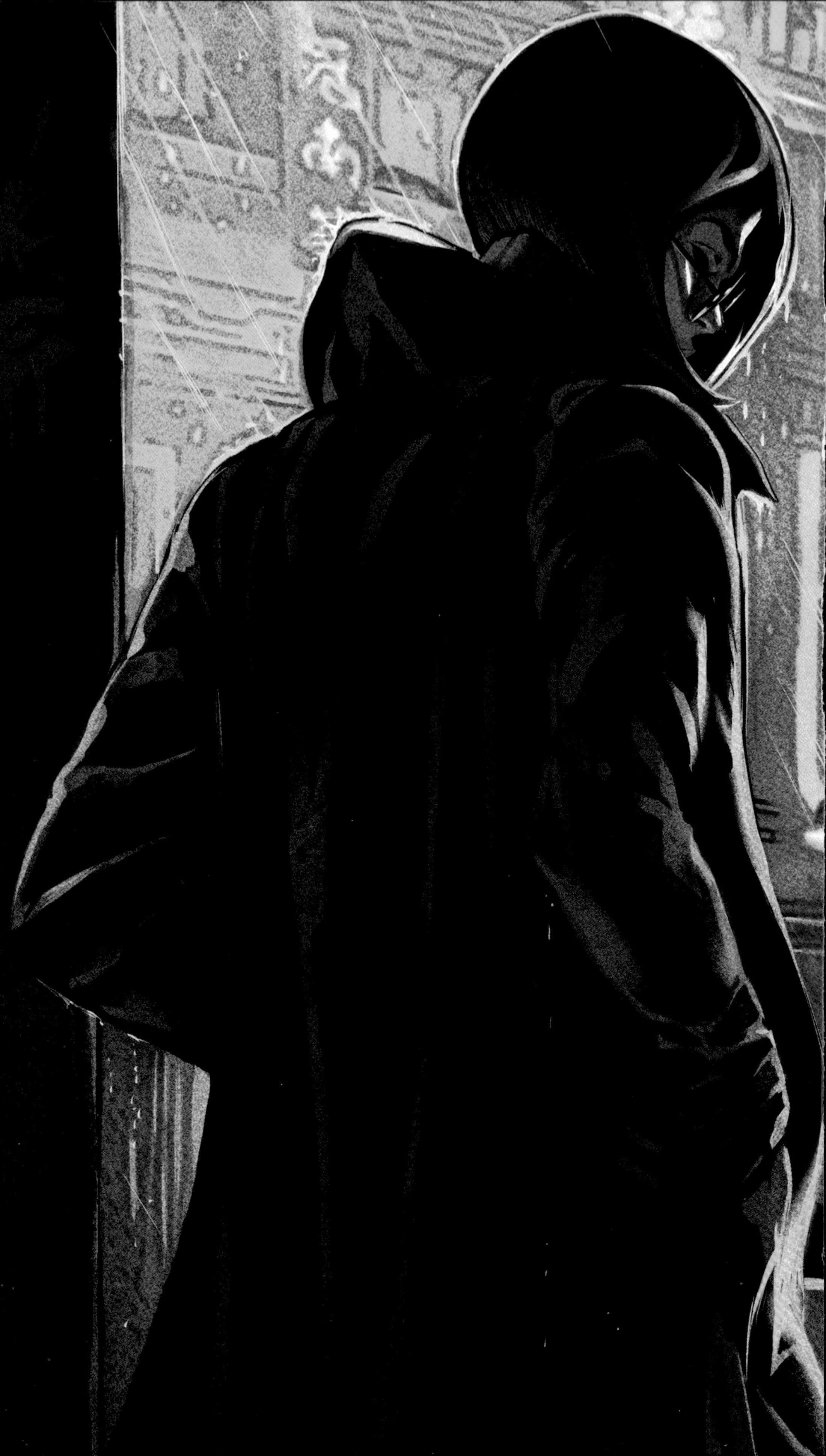

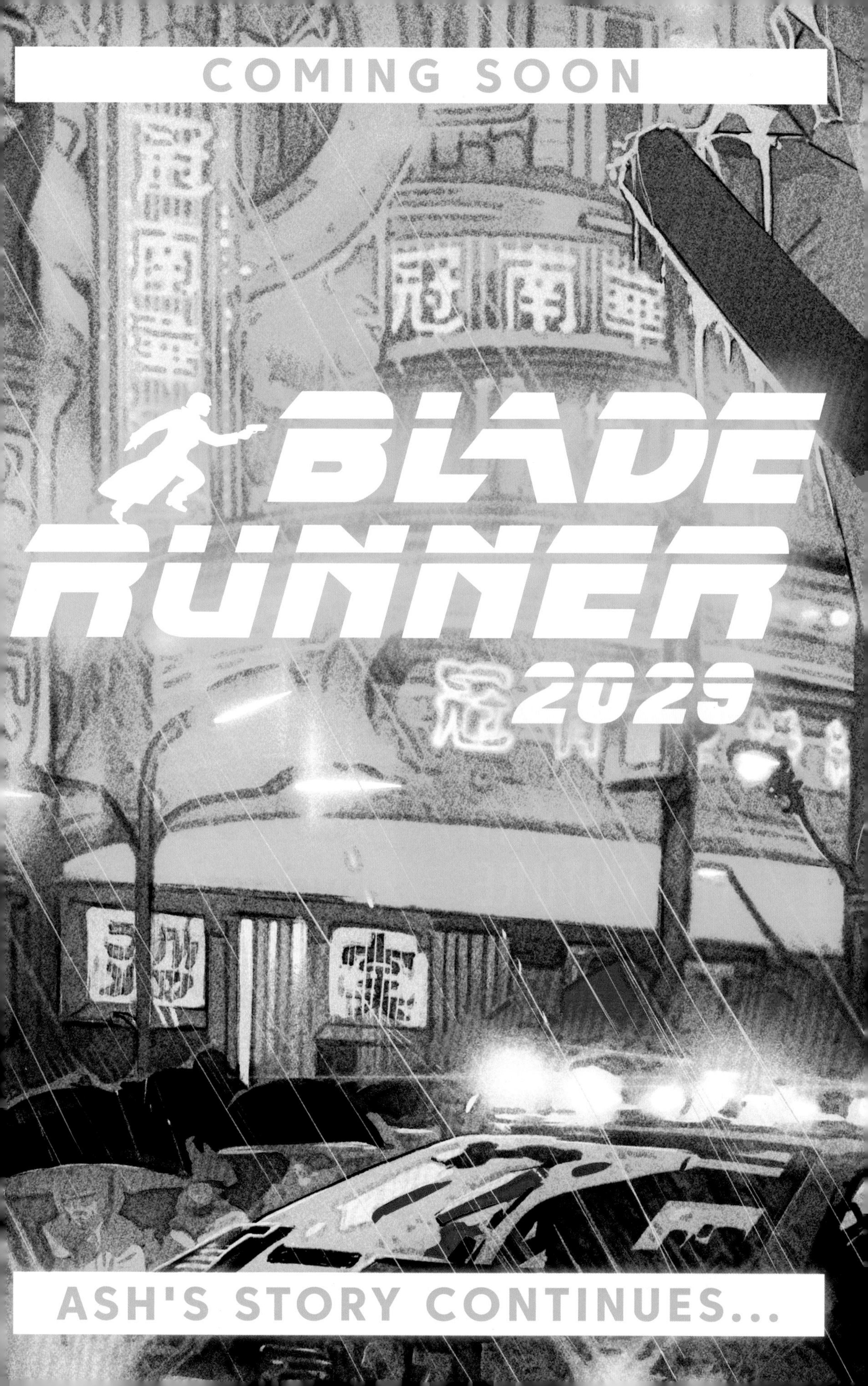
COMING SOON
BLADE RUNNER
2029
ASH'S STORY CONTINUES...

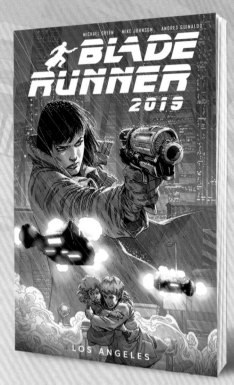

CREATOR BIOS

MICHAEL GREEN

Michael Green is a film and television writer and producer. His work includes *Blade Runner 2049*, *Logan*, *Alien: Covenant*, *Murder on the Orient Express*, and *American Gods*.

MIKE JOHNSON

Mike Johnson is a New York Times-bestselling writer of comics, animation and games. His credits include *Star Trek*, *Transformers*, *Superman/Batman*, *Supergirl*, *Fringe*, and *Ei8ht*.

ANDRES GUINALDO

Born in 1975, Andres originally studied movie making (direction) at Madrid University before making the move into comics. His first professional work was drawing Joe R. Landsdale's *The Drive-in* and *By Bizarre Hands*. He followed those with *Pistolfist: Revolutionary Warrior*, *Helios: Under the Gun*, *Purity*, and *Cartoonapalozza*. In 2010, Guinaldo started regularly penciling *Son of Hulk*, and drew issue #5 of *Dark Reign: Hawkeye*. He followed this with *Gotham City Sirens* #14-17, *Joker's Asylum: The Riddler*, *Namor: The First Mutant* #4, *Red Lanterns* #8, *Resurrection Man* #9, *Nightwing* #11-14, *Hypernaturals*, and *Justice League Dark*. In recent years he's worked on such diverse titles as *Ninjak* and *Captain America: Steve Rogers*. He currently resides in Segovia, the city of his birth.

MARCO LESKO

Hailing from Brazil, Marco Lesko has been a professional comic book colorist since 2014. His credits include *Rat Queens*, *Assassin's Creed Uprising*, *Doctor Who*, *Robotech*, *The Shadow* and many more. When he's not coloring comics, he spends endless hours studying color theory from many different areas, including: cinema, conceptual art design, Japanese anime, videogame design, and classic Disney animations.

JIM CAMPBELL

Jim Campbell is an Eisner Award nominated letterer whose work can be seen on everything from Titan's *Robotech* books to *Roy of the Rovers* graphic novels to the *Firefly* series. He lives, works, and very occasionally sleeps in darkest Nottinghamshire, UK, in a house he shares with his wife and an unfeasibly large collection of black clothes.